JEWISH CULTURE
BETWEEN
CANON AND HERESY

STANFORD STUDIES IN JEWISH HISTORY AND CULTURE
Edited by David Biale and Sarah Abrevaya Stein

JEWISH CULTURE BETWEEN CANON AND HERESY

DAVID BIALE

STANFORD UNIVERSITY PRESS
Stanford, California

Stanford University Press
Stanford, California

©2023 by David Biale. All rights reserved.

No part of this book may be reproduced or transmitted in any form or by any means, electronic or mechanical, including photocopying and recording, or in any information storage or retrieval system without the prior written permission of Stanford University Press.

Printed in the United States of America on acid-free, archival-quality paper

Library of Congress Cataloging-in-Publication Data
Names: Biale, David, 1949- author, editor.
Title: Jewish culture between Canon and Heresy / David Biale.
Other titles: Stanford studies in Jewish history and culture.
Description: Stanford, California : Stanford University Press, [2023] | Series: Stanford studies in Jewish history and culture | Includes bibliographical references.
Identifiers: LCCN 2022015717 (print) | LCCN 2022015718 (ebook) | ISBN 9781503634336 (cloth) | ISBN 9781503634343 (paperback) | ISBN 9781503634350 (ebook)
Subjects: LCSH: Jews—History. | Jews—Intellectual life. | Jewish philosophy.
Classification: LCC DS102.5 .B527 2023 (print) | LCC DS102.5 (ebook) | DDC 909/.04924—dc23/eng/20220616
LC record available at https://lccn.loc.gov/2022015717
LC ebook record available at https://lccn.loc.gov/2022015718

Typeset by Elliott Beard in Garamond Premier Pro 11/15
Cover design: Rob Ehle
Cover art: "Shindig" screen print. Peretz Wolf-Prusan

To the memory of Amos Funkenstein, with whom it all began

Contents

Preface and Acknowledgments   ix

INTRODUCTION: Between Canon and Counterhistory   1

PART ONE
Countertraditions within the Tradition

1. The God with Breasts   13
   El Shaddai in the Bible

2. Korah in the Midrash   29
   The Hairless Heretic as Hero

3. Counterhistory and Jewish Polemics against Christianity   44
   The Sefer Toldot Yeshu *and the* Sefer Zerubavel

4. "The Torah Speaks the Language of Human Beings"   59
   Abraham Ibn Ezra's Radical Interpretation of the Bible

5. Between Melancholy and a Broken Heart   74
   A Note on Rabbi Nahman of Bratslav's Depression

CONTENTS

PART TWO
Ambivalent Modernity

6 The Kabbalah in Nachman Krochmal's Philosophy of History 85

7 Masochism and Philosemitism 97
   The Strange Case of Leopold von Sacher-Masoch

8 Historical Heresies and Modern Jewish Identity 114

9 Shabbtai Zvi and the Seductions of Jewish Orientalism 129

PART THREE
Weimar Antinomians

10 Leo Strauss 153
    The Philosopher as Weimar Jew

11 Arendt in Jerusalem 163
    Hannah Arendt on the Eichmann Trial

12 Gershom Scholem's "Ten Unhistorical Aphorisms on the Kabbalah" 178
    Translation and Commentary

PART FOUR
Heretical Politics

13 The Threat of Messianism 207
    An Interview with Gershom Scholem (August 14, 1980)

14 Mysticism and Politics in Modern Israel 212
    The Messianic Ideology of Abraham Isaac Ha-Cohen Kook

15 The End of Enlightenment? 222

EPILOGUE: By the Waters of San Francisco 227
    A Partial Autobiography

Notes 241

Preface and Acknowledgments

THE ESSAYS IN THIS COLLECTION were published between 1974 and 2016. I have selected them on two criteria. The first is that they all represent, albeit in different ways, a certain method, which I call "counterhistory" and which I define in the Introduction. The second is that they do not duplicate material to be found in my published books. There are four partial exceptions to this general principle. The first is that the argument in chapter 1, "The God with Breasts," appeared in very compressed form in the first chapter of my book *Eros and the Jews*. The second relates to chapter 12, my translation and commentary on Gershom Scholem's *Zehn unhistorische Sätze über die Kabbala*. I excerpted and commented on the first of these aphorisms in my book *Gershom Scholem: Kabbalah and Counter-history* (1979). Third, chapter 6, on Nachman Krochmal, is greatly abbreviated in my Scholem book. Finally, in my recent biography, *Gershom Scholem: Master of the Kabbalah* (2018), I noted Scholem's position on the Israeli settlement movement articulated in the interview in the *New York Review of Books*, reprinted here.

These essays reflect the development of my own scholarship over the years. The first was published while I was still a graduate student, in 1974, the last only a few years ago. I have preserved their language and arguments. Although I have added annotations to some works that have appeared subsequently, I have deliberately not updated the content of the essays to reflect later scholarship. I have also edited the essays to avoid duplications (especially between chapters 7, 8, and 9).

I thank Rachel Biale, Naomi Seidman, Sarah Stein, and Noam Zion for comments on parts of the manuscript. Peter Gordon offered some valuable corrections to the translation of Scholem's aphorisms in chapter 12. Special thanks to my *hevruta*, Ron Reissberg, who helped me transcribe the essays that were written in the dark ages before computers and who worked with me to fix the footnotes.

The essays in this book were originally published in the following venues, and I thank their publishers for permission to republish them:

"The God with Breasts: El Shaddai in the Bible," *History of Religions* 21 (February 1982): 240–56.

"Korah in the Midrash: The Hairless Heretic as Hero," in "Approaching Shared Heroes: Cultural Transfer and Transnational Jewish History," ed. Micha J. Perry and Rebekka Voss, special issue, *Jewish History* 30 (2016): 15–28.

"Counter-history in Jewish Anti-Christian Polemics: The *Sefer Toldot Yeshu* and the *Sefer Zerubavel*," *Jewish Social Studies* 6, no. 1 (Fall 1999): 130–45.

"Philosophy and Exegesis in the Writings of Abraham Ibn Ezra," *Comitatus* (UCLA Medieval and Renaissance Center) 5 (Fall 1974): 43–62.

"Between Melancholy and a Broken Heart: A Note on Rabbi Nahman of Bratslav's Depression," *Graven Images* 3 (1996):107–11.

"The Kabbala in Nachman Krochmal's Philosophy of History," *Journal of Jewish Studies* 32 (Spring 1981): 85–97.

"Masochism and Philosemitism: The Strange Case of Leopold von Sacher-Masoch," *Journal of Contemporary History* 17 (Spring 1982): 305–24.

"Historical Heresies and Modern Jewish Identity," *Jewish Social Studies* 8, nos. 2/3 (2002): 112–32.

"Shabbtai Zvi and the Seductions of Jewish Orientalism," in *The Sabbatian Movement and Its Aftermath: Messianism, Sabbatianism and Frankism*, ed. Rachel Elior, Jerusalem Studies in Jewish Thought (Jerusalem: Hebrew University Institute for Jewish Studies, 2001), 2:85*–110*.

"Leo Strauss: The Philosopher as Weimar Jew," in *Leo Strauss's Thought: To-*

wards a Critical Engagement, ed. Alan Udoff (Boulder, CO: L. Rienner, 1991).

"Arendt in Jerusalem: Hannah Arendt on the Eichmann Trial," *Response* 40 (Summer 1980): 33–44.

"Gershom Scholem's 'Zehn unhistorische Saetze ueber die Kabbala': Text and Commentary," *Modern Judaism* 4 (February 1985): 67–93. Suhrkamp Verlag granted me permission to publish a translation of Scholem's text within this essay.

"The Threat of Messianism: An Interview with Gershom Scholem," *New York Review of Books*, August 14, 1980.

"Mysticism and Politics in Modern Israel: The Messianic Ideology of Abraham Isaac Ha-Cohen Kook," in *Religion and Politics in the Modern World*, ed. Peter Merkl and Ninian Smart (New York: New York University Press, 1983), 191–202.

"The End of Enlightenment?" *Jewish Social Studies*, n.s., 22, no. 3 (Spring-Summer 2017): 141–45.

"By the Waters of San Francisco: A Partial Autobiography" [in Hebrew], in *Kavim le-Demuteinu*, ed. Avner Ben-Amos and Ofer Shiff (Beersheva, Israel: Ben-Gurion Institute and Yediot Aharonot, 2020), 79–98.

JEWISH CULTURE
BETWEEN
CANON AND HERESY

INTRODUCTION

Between Canon and Counterhistory

IN A FAMOUS 1944 ESSAY on the history of Jewish studies, the great twentieth-century historian, Gershom Scholem, described how his study of Jewish mysticism aimed at overturning the rationalism of his nineteenth-century predecessors.[1] He quoted a wonderful verse from Psalm 122: "The stone the builders despised has become the capstone." This was Scholem's method, which I have described as "counterhistory,"[2] that is, the discovery of vital forces precisely in what others have considered marginal, disreputable, and irrational, those that occupy, in his words, "the fine line between religion and nihilism."[3]

The principal underpinning of counterhistory is the insight that the Jewish tradition is not defined by an "essence" (the word that appears in the title of a book by the liberal German rabbi Leo Baeck, *The Essence of Judaism*).[4] To be sure, the tradition is made up of a body of canonical texts, starting with the Bible. But these texts are all multivocal, full of contradictions. As one famous rabbinic text puts it about the disagreements between the School of Hillel and the School of Shammai: "These and these are the words of the living God."[5] Beyond rabbinic literature, the thousands of volumes in the Jewish library down to today cannot be reduced to a single formula or catechism.

And neither can that library be reduced to what we today call "religion," arguably an invention of modernity.[6] Jewish culture—as opposed to just religion—is a big tent that includes the writings of a rabbinic elite and the customs of the folk; law, and legend; the abstract formulations of philosophers and the symbolic language of the mystics; the practices of men and the practices of women and children; and dogmatic authority versus heretical rebellions against it.[7] In the modern period, that tent spread even further. Peter Berger has suggested that in modernity we are all heretics, in the sense meant by the Greek origins of the word *haeresis*, namely "to choose."[8] All Jews since the Enlightenment, including the most Orthodox, are "Jews by choice" in that they must choose how they define their Judaism rather than accept an unchanging, fixed tradition. In reality, of course, even though most Jews before the modern period felt themselves bound by that tradition, it was never either unchanging or fixed.

While medieval philosophers like Moses Maimonides tried to distill Judaism to a set of thirteen principles (or three, or even one), the search for an "essence of Judaism" became one of the dominant characteristics of modern Jewish thought.[9] This search often identified some religious principle, such as monotheism or biblical ethics, as the defining characteristic of Judaism. But Judaism—a term that itself became preeminent only in the modern era—could never be shoehorned into such narrow boxes. Against thinkers like Moses Mendelssohn, Moritz Lazarus, and Hermann Cohen, secular Jews have sought a more dynamic definition of Jewish identity that could encompass conflictual strands within it. This secular Jewish tradition, beginning with Baruch Spinoza, but with roots in even older writers, animates my own understanding of the history that I have spent half a century trying to unravel.[10]

My own work has drawn inspiration from Scholem's radical philosophy of Jewish history. Although the subjects to which I have devoted my attention are highly diverse, they are united by the way Jewish culture contains not only canonical texts but also countercanonical and even heretical voices that test its own boundaries. This oeuvre spans the whole three thousand years of Jewish history, a result of the "catholic" (in the original meaning of the term as "all-inclusive") training I underwent with my teacher Amos Funkenstein. He taught his students to embrace all of Jewish history as their own and to dare to write about broad subjects. For me, these subjects have included power, sexuality, blood, and secular Jewish thought.[11]

I would define these studies in two ways: they are constructive and genealogical. By *constructive*, I mean that they are often driven by contemporary questions and therefore construct the past in order to answer those questions. I would distinguish this method from "presentism" (the bane of all historians!), which uses the past for contemporary purposes, often political. For my method, the present dictates the questions but not the answers. Constructive historians must be faithful to their sources, even as they ask questions of those sources that both those sources' authors and earlier historians may not have asked. We must understand such sources not as modern but as rooted in their own historical contexts. To take an example from my study of the history of sexuality in the Jewish tradition, the rabbinic discourses on sexuality must be grounded in their Greco-Roman and Babylonian settings. They are at once familiar and alien, and if, to quote a favorite phrase of Gershom Scholem, "Nothing Jewish is alien to me," it is their very alienness that arouses the deepest affinity.

I call the second method that I have employed "genealogical," that is, the tracing of concepts—sexuality, blood, power—from their earliest origins to their most recent manifestations. Early in my career, I took inspiration from a provocative book by Karl Löwith, *Meaning in History*. There he writes, "An adequate approach to history and its interpretations is necessarily regressive for the very reason that history is moving forward, leaving behind the historical foundations of the more recent and contemporary elaborations. The historical consciousness cannot but start with itself, though its aim is to know the thought of other times and of other men, different from our times and ourselves. . . . We understand—and misunderstand—ancient authors, but always in the light of contemporary thought, reading the book of history backward from the last to the first page."[12] If our present culture throws up certain new questions, then one is driven to the historical representations that lie behind this contemporary culture, to see where they have come from and how they have been transformed.

Indeed, each of the three books I have mentioned actually started with wondering where certain modern phenomena came from. Take, for example, my book *Power and Powerlessness in Jewish History*. I started with a contemporary question—the relationship of Jews today to the problem of political power—and then sought to discover its roots in the past. The myth that the

Jews were politically powerless until regaining statehood in 1948 itself has deep historical roots. My work was twofold: an examination of the history of the myth of Jewish powerlessness and an investigation into the actual, historical relationship of the Jews to power. The work was driven counterchronologically, from the problems of the State of Israel and the contemporary Diaspora Jewish communities to the recent and, finally, more distant past. What started as a modern study eventually reached back to the Bible.

The synoptic historian,[13] who seeks to encompass a whole history, holds that where we stand now can never be fully understood without its context in the past, even the distant past, just as no construction of the past can proceed except from where we stand today. To be sure, this involves assuming a totalizing vantage point from outside the history, a kind of critical observation post from which one can construct a past based on questions thrown up by the present. Indeed, such a position is unavoidable for any historian. As Martin Jay has noted, "There is no 'view from nowhere' for even the most scrupulously 'detached' observer."[14]

This relationship between present and past effectively attacks much of the periodization that conventional historians hold dear. In all of my work, I have been preoccupied with the circuitous transition from the "traditional" to the "modern." Modern Jewish history never represents a total break with the past. Instead, the modern period evolved and still exists in dialectical relationship to its predecessors, and modern Jews define themselves in constant, if often only partly conscious, tension with their tradition. This was an argument that I made in *Not in the Heavens: The Tradition of Jewish Secular Thought*, where I tried to demonstrate how secular Jewish thinkers developed their thought in constant dialogue with the earlier religious tradition.[15] To do justice to "modern" questions requires extensive treatment of the tradition as a whole, from its very points of origin. Every attempt to discover the point of transition between "tradition" and "modernity" demands a search further back in history, and, ultimately, these terms themselves dissolve and become increasingly uncertain.

At the same time, I do not contend that Jewish history, or any other history for that matter, is a seamless whole, devoid of ruptures. One might expect such a view from a defender of religious orthodoxy, but hardly from a secularist. Modernity is, indeed, a radical rupture in the fabric of tradition, but Jewish history as a whole was never monolithic and always consisted of ruptures and conflicts. The "break" between tradition and modernity is just a very extreme version of what can be found in other forms in earlier periods. Here, too, the study of remote ages can illuminate the very conflicts that we sometimes regard as uniquely modern.

The essays you will read here were all written with this sense of the entangled relationship between tradition and modernity. They are all counterhistorical, or, to use Walter Benjamin's felicitous phrase, they "brush history against the grain."[16] Some of them feature inversions of convention or hidden traditions that challenge the canon. In others, I read authors against their commonly understood or self-proclaimed positions. The best way to illustrate what I mean is to examine the contents of this book.

I start the first section of the book, "Countertraditions within the Tradition," by considering one of the Bible's names of God, El Shaddai. Against the canonical idea that God either is male or has no gender and that ancient Israelite religion rejected the fertility rituals of the Canaanites, Shaddai appears to have been a name of God associated with fertility blessings. One very early biblical text even makes a wordplay between Shaddai and *shadayim* (breasts). The God of ancient Israel may therefore have been understood to be both male and female. This leads to the conclusion that monotheism was much more "gender-bending" than has been traditionally assumed. Thus, what I unearth here is a countertradition within the Bible itself: where late books of the Bible (especially the book of Job) understood Shaddai as the powerful or "Almighty" God, an earlier tradition seems to associate this name of God with a nursing mother.

A biblical figure I consider in a second essay is a mere human, and a deeply flawed one at that: the Levite leader Korah, who challenges Moses by claiming that all of Israel should have equal access to God. The rebel Korah is one of the Bible's villains, but in later rabbinic midrashim Korah appears in a different guise, as a trickster who subverts the law by taking it to absurd extremes. One might say that Korah was resurrected as a rebellious rabbi. In the Hasidic movement of the eighteenth and nineteenth centuries, Korah became a foil for how the leaders of the movement understood their own leadership. As opposed to the Bible, where Korah and his followers are swallowed up by the earth, these later texts bring him back to life in surprising new forms. Here, as in many other places, the midrashic tradition often works against—or, at least, dramatically expands—the biblical text.

In roughly the sixth or seventh century, two strange texts provide excellent examples of counterhistories, inversions of Christianity in the service of Jewish polemics. The first is the *Toldot Yeshu*, which inverts the biography of Jesus: the founder of Christianity is the son of a menstruant Jewish woman and a Roman soldier who steals the name of God, only to be brought down to earth by the story's hero, Judas Iscariot. The second is the apocalyptic *Sefer Zerubavel*, which turns Jesus and the Byzantine emperor into the Antichrist, who will be defeated by two Jewish messiahs. In evident response to the cult of the Virgin Mary, the mother of one of the messiahs plays a role for the first time in Jewish literature. But the two texts are actually quite different counterhistories, which allow us to more sharply define this concept.

The twelfth century witnessed a kind of medieval Enlightenment in which there arose radical interpretations of the Bible, of the sort we associate more with Baruch Spinoza and later secular biblical criticism. A leading figure in this movement was Abraham Ibn Ezra, whose Bible commentary is regarded as canonical by Orthodox Jews. But Ibn Ezra advanced daring, even incipiently heretical, arguments that some passages in Torah could not have been written by Moses and, even more strikingly, that the Bible does not contain all knowledge. A full understanding of how he could reconcile such a radical position with tradition takes us into the larger question of the relationship between philosophy and exegesis in this thinker, whose own metaphysics came close to pantheism. Hardly modern, Ibn Ezra nevertheless startlingly prefigures modern ways of reading the Bible.

Moving now to eighteenth-century Hasidism, I examine some of the teachings of the iconoclastic Hasidic master Nahman of Bratslav. Seen by many as the most "modern" of the Hasidic masters, Nahman reveled in paradox and gave theological meaning to his own inner existential struggles. Evidently suffering from profound depression, Nahman developed a taxonomy of depressive states, which he correlated with his role as a religious leader. Here is an example of a figure embedded in the religious tradition who nevertheless evinced a subjective sensibility that we typically associate with modernity.

The next section of the book, entitled "Ambivalent Modernity," has as its focus the way nineteenth- and twentieth-century Jewish writers interpreted in new and surprising ways motifs and figures from Jewish history. At a time when most modernizing thinkers saw the Kabbalah as medieval superstition, Nachman Krochmal, a leading figure in the eastern European Jewish Enlightenment, developed an Idealist philosophy of history that allowed mysticism a positive role in Jewish history, one that anticipated Gershom Scholem's later work.

A much stranger figure, who lived roughly in the same place and time as Krochmal, was the Christian writer Leopold von Sacher-Masoch. Sacher-Masoch was both a pornographer (the word *masochism* comes from his name) and a philosemite, two identities that equally challenged boundaries in European society. How these two seemingly unrelated vocations come together makes for a strange story in the history of Jewish integration in the nineteenth century. Sacher-Masoch inverted many of the stereotypes of Jews and especially Jewish women. This study of Sacher-Masoch was an early foray of mine into the new field of gender in Jewish studies.

One of the most striking philosemitic novels of Sacher-Masoch was a biography of the seventeenth-century messiah Shabbtai Zvi. Two essays examine the way nineteenth- and twentieth-century writers turned Shabbtai, as well as other heretics from Jewish history—Jesus, the rabbinic figure Elisha ben Abuya, and Spinoza—from heretics into heroes. Even those who took highly defensive or apologetic positions often attempted to incorporate these heretics back into the tradition, a move that recapitulated similar transformations of heretics (like Korah) in earlier rabbinic literature. Here are striking examples of the way modern Jewish culture remains inextricably entangled with its past.

This fascination with historical heretics continued into the Weimar period of German Jewish history. The philosophers Leo Strauss and Hannah Arendt, each in their own way, offered idiosyncratic and subversive understandings of historical traditions that were informed by a particular Jewish sensibility. Strauss offered esoteric readings of Jewish philosophers, especially Maimonides. But while Strauss believed that he came to timeless philosophical conclusions, I argue that he must be read, not as "he read himself" (one of his favorite phrases), but as a Weimar Jew, concerned with the same questions of esotericism, secularism, and tradition with which other Jewish intellectuals of his time struggled.

Arendt's most controversial book was her *Eichmann in Jerusalem*. As a result of this controversy, Arendt suffered a similar fate to that of heretics in a less secular age. In this essay, I argue against this unofficial *herem*. The most radical aspect of Arendt's book was not in the oft-quoted phrase the "banality of evil" but in the legal theory she developed, which argued for a kind of multiculturalism *avant la lettre*. This theory takes the Jewish experience as emblematic of human diversity, a startling conclusion in light of attacks on Arendt for lack of sympathy with her people. I therefore read Arendt's Eichmann book through this lens in the context of her other writings against the more widespread understanding of her work.

It is in this intellectual milieu that we must situate Gershom Scholem, whose work brought together fascination with heresy with an antinomian sensibility of his own. Scholem's "Ten Unhistorical Aphorisms on the Kabbalah," written in conscious imitation of Walter Benjamin's "Theses on the Philosophy of History," has never been translated into English and is published here for the first time. An elucidation of this difficult text reveals Scholem's profundity as a modernist thinker (and not only as a historian) who identified paradoxes and heresies in the Kabbalah with extraordinarily contemporary resonance.

Scholem provides the bridge between these Weimar intellectuals and Jewish politics, particularly related to Zionism. Scholem's path to Zionism led through anarchistic rejection of German nationalism, a rejection that later informed his critique of what he considered reactionary and apocalyptic forms of Jewish nationalism. Although his years of political activity in favor of what today is called "liberal Zionism" ended in 1933, he retained much of his suspicion of militant Jewish nationalism. In an interview that I did with him in 1980, he connected his views of Sabbatianism as a spiritual catastrophe with a critique of the religious Zionist settler movement as "latter-day Sabbatians," who threatened an even worse catastrophe for his own Zionist ideals. Although forty years old, this warning about the dangers of Jewish messianism remains entirely relevant today.

In the decade after this interview, I studied the intellectual underpinnings of the messianic Zionism that Scholem criticized, seeking to elaborate his claim that this movement draws from the heretical wellsprings that he had elucidated. I focused in particular on the messianic ideology of

Abraham Isaac Ha-Cohen Kook, chief rabbi of Palestine from 1921 to 1935. Kook's dialectical philosophy of Jewish messianism made it possible for this ultra-Orthodox leader to ascribe positive meaning to secular Zionism. But the heretical implications of his position, which bear startling resemblance to Sabbatian motifs, also laid the groundwork for the apocalyptic Zionism articulated by his son, Zvi Yehudah Kook, and his son's students after the Six-Day War. It is these ideas that continue to bedevil Israeli politics today.

A final essay, written shortly after the election of Donald Trump in 2016, offers my own broad reflections on the current condition of the Jewish people in historical perspective. The forces—Jewish, European, and American—seeking to dismantle the Enlightenment in favor of ethnonationalism and illiberalism have only grown stronger in the subsequent five years. Indeed, the rather gloomy prognosis that I suggest about the fate of the Enlightenment in the early twenty-first century finds tragic confirmation as I write these lines with the news of Russia's invasion of Ukraine.

As an epilogue, I have included an autobiographical essay that has only appeared in Hebrew in a volume of scholars writing about the connection between their personal histories and their professional work. This autobiography provides a personal perspective on the essays in the present collection and the rest of my work as well. The overarching question I ask, which has been at the forefront of my work since my first book on Gershom Scholem, is: What is the relationship of a secular historian to his or her religious tradition? The various essays in the present book are all attempts, in different forms, to answer that question.

In his celebrated little book *Zakhor*, Yosef Hayim Yerushalmi argued that historians sever us from tradition and thus provide little basis for a Jewish identity in the modern world.[17] Yet it seems to me that historians can play a different role: they can expose our myths about the past, or, in Walter Benjamin's pregnant phrase, "wrest tradition away from a conformism that is about to overpower it."[18] Such historians can present us with a new past we may not have yet considered. If the very phrase "new past" appears to be an oxymoron, it is the task of historians, in their constructive creativity, to give it legitimacy and life.

PART ONE

COUNTERTRADITIONS WITHIN THE TRADITION

CHAPTER 1

The God with Breasts
El Shaddai in the Bible

WITH THE EXCEPTION OF THE tetragrammaton YHWH, no divine name has generated so much controversy as El Shaddai or Shaddai. The Greek and Latin translators of the Bible agreed that Shaddai must be understood to mean "omnipotent" (Vulgate: *omnipotens*), while the rabbis' midrashic exegesis suggested self-sufficiency (*she-dai*). On the basis of this tradition, the King James translation rendered the name as "the Almighty God," an interpretation, as we shall see, that is not far from the way one biblical tradition understood the name. Modern scholarship, however, has searched in another direction.[1] Since Friedrich Delitzsch (1883) and particularly William F. Albright in 1935, the scholarly consensus is that the name must be a derivative of the Akkadian *shadu*, meaning "mountain."[2] Following E. P. Dhorme,[3] Albright argued that the original meaning of *shadu* was probably "breast" (*shadwi* in Old Akkadian, *tud* in Ugaritic and Arabic, and *shad* in Hebrew), which, by a psychological association evident to the author of the *Enuma Elish* in ancient times and to Freud in our own, came to mean "mountain." The particular form *shaddai* (double "d" and the "ai" suffix) derives not directly from *shadu* (mountain) but from *saddau* or *shaddu'a*, meaning "mountaineer." Hence, this god was originally conceived as "the one of the mountains." Albright speculates that this god of the mountains was an Amorite god brought to Syria, where he became the Canaanite Baal-Hadad, the storm god who was a mountain deity. The patriarchs, themselves probably of Amorite origin, worshiped Shaddai in conjunction with the Canaanite El, but this worship later gave way to the worship of Yahweh. Albright argues that Yahweh, although repeatedly associated with mountains (Sinai, Horeb, Zion, Moriah, etc.), was not essentially a mountain god and that this attribute was assimilated into Yahwism from the Amorite-Canaanite Shaddai.

Albright's thesis has been generally adopted by more recent scholars, though they have added various refinements. F. M. Cross strengthened Albright's philological arguments, while Lloyd Bailey, Sean Ouellette, and E. L. Abel suggested quite persuasively the possibility that El Shaddai derives from the Amorite lunar god Sin il Amurru or Bel Shade, who was at once a storm and war god and also a god of the mountains.[4] It was therefore natural for the wandering Amorite patriarchs to identify this god with the Canaanite El and later to transfer the epithet to Yahweh. These scholars believe that the name El Shaddai is extremely ancient and may indeed have been one of the authentic pre-Canaanite epithets for the "god of the fathers" brought along by the patriarchs from their Mesopotamian homeland.[5]

A strong counterargument was proposed in 1961 by Manfred Weippert,[6] who argued that El Shaddai should rather be understood as El Sade, the god of the plain. Weippert believed that a Canaanite provenance of El Shaddai was much more convincing than the Akkadian. He quoted a Ugaritic royal poem that features "Astarte of the plain" (*'ttrt shʻd*), as well as the late Bronze Canaanite word for "plain," namely, *shadä*, from which the Hebrew derives its word for "plain" by altering the Canaanite sibilant. As a result of these controversies, E. A. Speiser, in his commentary on Genesis in 1964, was forced to conclude that, while the weight of opinion still lies on the side of "god of the mountain," the jury is still out on the original meaning of El Shaddai.[7]

I do not propose in the following remarks to settle the continuing debate over the Near Eastern origins of the name El Shaddai. The painstaking hunt for Near Eastern cognates of intractable Hebrew expressions occasionally begins to look like a wild goose chase when critics lose sight of the biblical context in which the expressions are used. It is a methodological mistake to assume that the biblical authors knew as much about Near Eastern cultures and languages as do modern philologians. They inherited a language composed of words that had lost their original meanings, and their own writing was often an attempt to impose meanings on such words as a result of their own contemporary concerns. The understanding of a biblical expression must therefore begin by adopting the point of view of the biblical authors, a method pioneered by Baruch Spinoza but also anticipated, as I show in chapter 4, by Abraham Ibn Ezra. Such a method asks: What did the biblical authors mean when they used a certain word or phrase? Only then can the search for cognates bear fruit.

As Weippert observes, the original meaning of El Shaddai may well have vanished into the mists of ancient history by the time the compositions incorporating the name were put together. We should not forget that the patriarchal events took place at the latest near the beginning of the second millennium, while the various documents (J, E, P, etc.) adduced by modern scholarship cannot be dated earlier than the tenth century BCE, and some would argue for a much later date for at least some of them. It is interesting that the author of the Genesis texts using the name El Shaddai (usually associated with the Priestly tradition) makes no attempt to decipher its etymology by either a philological gloss or an etiological tale. Moreover, if El Shaddai were originally a lunar god associated with a cosmic mountain—as the Albright school maintains—why is he not attached to any specific mountainous sanctuary in the biblical texts?

If, on the other hand, Weippert is correct that the name means "god of the plain," the biblical authors seem similarly unaware of any plain in which he dwells. Some have suggested that the utter lack of location characteristic of El Shaddai is simply a result of the Priestly theology, in which God is universal (see the Creation account of Gen. 1).[8] But surely this argument is self-serving. At the very least, we can conclude that the author of the Genesis texts had no knowledge of a specific dwelling place for El Shaddai, a fact that may have suited his or her theological purposes but does not prove conscious suppression. The evidence in Genesis, and in all the other passages using this name, suggests that the biblical authors were entirely ignorant of the presumed Amorite or Canaanite origins of El Shaddai. While authentic traces of the old patriarchal god can perhaps be detected in the texts that have come down to us (and we shall follow some of these traces), there is not sufficient proof that the biblical writers ever consciously used the name El Shaddai in its original context, whatever that might have been.

Our task, therefore, is to try to reconstruct the possible meanings that the old god El Shaddai may have had for the authors of the various passages in which he appears.[9] The problem is made more difficult but also more interesting by the fact that the name has a very peculiar frequency of occurrence, which points to its popularity in certain periods but relative unpopularity in others. It appears six times in Genesis and once in Exodus 6:3, where the author announces that whereas the patriarchs knew God as El Shaddai, henceforth he will be known as YHWH. Within the Pentateuch, it appears only twice more—in the Balaam oracles of Numbers 24—and it also appears in several theophoric names in the Priestly lists in Numbers. It is completely absent from the historical books but appears twice in Psalms (68:15 and 91: l), in identical passages in Isaiah 13:6 and Joel 1:15, twice in Ezekiel (1:24 and 10:5), twice in Ruth (1:20, 21), and thirty-one times in Job. Without prejudicing the question of the date of the Priestly document from Genesis and Exodus, to which we shall return, we can say quite safely that the name Shaddai or El Shaddai is certainly an early name in Israelite literature, since it occurs in three early poems: the Testament of Jacob (Gen. 49:25), the Balaam oracles, and Psalm 68—all of which date from the tenth century BCE at the latest.[10] In addition, its appearance in the lists of names in Numbers also suggests, though it does not establish, its antiquity, since the names there seem very old.[11] At the same time, we can say with certainty that the name Shaddai achieved great popularity in the late literature, since Ezekiel, Ruth, and Job (where it appears in total disproportion to all its other occurrences) are all books from the sixth century at the earliest.[12] It is very likely, as a preliminary hypothesis, that Shaddai was an ancient divine name that was more or less abandoned, but not entirely forgotten, after the literary activity of the early monarchy, only to become popular once again in late texts with definite archaizing tendencies.

Complicating the problem is the fact that the name sometimes occurs in its compound form, El Shaddai (meaning probably either "the god of Shaddai," "the god Shaddai," or "El who is also known as Shaddai"), and sometimes simply as Shaddai. The Genesis texts and their Exodus postscript all have El Shaddai, as does Ezekiel 10. But every other occurrence uses Shaddai alone. What sense can we make of this distribution? Albright argued that Shaddai must have been the original name, since it appears as such in the early poetry. However, this argument is by no means definitive, since Genesis 49 has El Shaddai, according to the best textual traditions,[13] and the Balaam oracles use Shaddai in parallelism with El. Only Psalm 68, of all the manifestly early material, has Shaddai by itself. Moreover, if the contention that our divine name originated with the Amorite il Amurru is correct, we would not be surprised if El Shaddai were the original biblical usage and that later occurrences without the preceding El were either ignorant archaisms or a shorthand form presuming El.[14] While these speculations by no means settle the question, it will be important to our argument that the occurrence of El Shaddai does *not* prove a late text and may, in fact, point to an early one.

We now turn to the pressing question of whether any pattern of meaning or meanings can be detected from the various occurrences of El Shaddai and Shaddai. As I have suggested, very few scholars have taken up this question. However, in his book *Canaanite Myth and Hebrew Epic*, Frank Moore Cross points out a number of similarities between some of the exilic texts.[15] Isaiah 13 is a prophecy against the Babylonians and therefore stems from the author of Deutero-Isaiah. Verse 6, which appears in similar form in Joel 1:15, reads: "Cry out because the day of Yahweh is close, because destruction [*keshod*] will come from Shaddai." The military imagery from the chapter as a whole suggests Yahweh as a warrior god, from whom destruction and death will come. Now, the author's wordplay between *shod* and Shaddai should not be taken as a serious etymology, for it is tailored to fit neatly into the military context of the poem. But the fact that Shaddai in Isaiah should be a warrior god assumes significance in relation to other texts. Cross points out that Ezekiel speaks of a "noise like the voice of Shaddai," suggesting to him a reminiscence of the Amorite storm and war god, il Amurru. These associations are strengthened by the frequent occurrence of Shaddai in Job, where storm and even warlike descriptions of the deity are common. Cross therefore concludes from this evidence that "in the sixth century, Ezekiel, Job and Deutero-Isaiah resurrected the ancient symbols and mythic forms of the storm theophany in descriptions of Yahweh's appearances and in war songs describing his universal victory in the new age. It may be that Shaddai received the traits of the storm god from Shaddai's assimilation to Yahweh."[16]

I am in agreement with Cross's argument that the meaning given to Shaddai in the sixth century was of a storm and war god and that this meaning was part and parcel of the image of Yahweh in the exilic and postexilic period. To be sure, not all the late texts support the interpretation of Shaddai as a warrior god, but if we generalize this image, we find that the understanding of Shaddai does correspond closely to Israelite theology in this period. In books like Job, Ecclesiastes, Ezekiel, and Deutero-Isaiah, God often appears as a remote, mysterious, and even destructive deity. All of the contexts in which Shaddai is attested suggest such an incomprehensible and transcendent God.

The most important late work in which Shaddai appears frequently is the book of Job. The first systematic analysis of the use of Shaddai in Job was undertaken recently by Klaus Koch.[17] He concludes that Shaddai represents the personal aspect of the deity, to whom Job appeals for comfort. This argument is tenable only if the relevant verses are stretched beyond their plain sense. The image of God in Job is of a remote, incomprehensible deity with whom man has no contact. As in Ruth's lament,[18] this God is inexplicably malevolent: "For Shaddai's barbs pierce me" (Job 6:4). The author of Job uses different names for God (most commonly El, Eloah, and Shaddai; less frequently Elohim and Yahweh) but—as opposed to Koch's interpretation—does not seem to associate different meanings with these different names. The names are used interchangeably, and their main function seems to be to impart an archaic, patriarchal flavor to the book.

Hence, in the late texts, Shaddai—used as a substitute for Yahweh—has the associations common to late Israelite theology: awe and veneration at best, fear and hostility at worst. In the context of all this material, it is no surprise that in his description of the terrible day of Yahweh to come, Deutero-Isaiah should pun that "destruction comes from Shaddai." It is equally understandable that the Septuagint and the Vulgate should render Shaddai as the "Almighty."

Was the tradition understanding Shaddai as the Almighty God invented in the sixth century or borrowed from earlier sources? The authors of the late tradition might have drawn on the Balaam oracles of Numbers 24, but it is not clear whether Balaam intended to praise the Hebrew God as a warrior or, as seems more probable, to glorify the military and political might of the Israelites themselves. A better source might be Psalm 68, which is a military poem based, as Albright has shown, on Ugaritic sources. Shaddai appears as he who "scatters kings." In both the Balaam oracles and Psalm 68, Shaddai appears together with other divine names—El, Elyon, and Yahweh. Hence, if Shaddai was associated with an early tradition of warrior god, it was not the only divine name in this tradition. The tradition of Shaddai as a remote, powerful warrior god may therefore have its roots in early Israelite poetry influenced by the Canaanites, but it is primarily a late tradition.

The tradition of Shaddai as "the Almighty God" is not the only interpretation of Shaddai in the Bible. As Koch has pointed out, all of the passages using El Shaddai in Genesis, with one exception, are fertility blessings.[19] An examination of these texts demonstrates that a tradition, which I believe to have been early, understood El Shaddai as a fertility god, an understanding that has startling consequences. El Shaddai occurs six times in Genesis and once in Exodus. Five of the Genesis occurrences and the passage in Exodus are usually attributed to the Priestly author, while the sixth Genesis text—in the Testament of Jacob (Gen. 49)—stands outside the accepted typologies. The Exodus text may be dismissed from the discussion because it is most probably a late editorial note explaining the change in God's name from El Shaddai to Yahweh. Of the five passages presumed written by P, four are fertility blessings using the "Be fruitful and multiply" formula of Genesis 1 and 9 or varying it slightly. In Genesis 17, God introduces himself to Abram as El Shaddai and promises to "increase" (*ve-arbeh*) and "fructify" (*ve-hifreti*) Abram's progeny. In Genesis 28:3, Isaac invokes El Shaddai in blessing Jacob when he sends him to Paddan-aram to acquire a wife and thus become fertile: "And El Shaddai will bless you and fructify and increase you and you will become a community of nations." In Genesis 35:9–12, God appears to Jacob in a passage that seems to refer to his successful escape from Laban. Like Abraham, Jacob receives a new name, and God says (verse 11): "I am El Shaddai, be fruitful and increase [*preh u-reveh*]." Finally, when Jacob blesses Ephraim and Manasseh in Genesis 48:3–4, he says: "El Shaddai appeared to me at Luz in the Land of Canaan and he blessed me. And he said to me: 'Behold, I am fructifying you and I have increased you.'"

Only in the Joseph story (Gen. 43:14) is El Shaddai invoked in a blessing of protection rather than fertility, but here too we might suggest that the author senses the association between *rahamim* (mercy) and *rehem* (womb). Moreover, the verse is implicitly connected with fertility, for it is uttered by Jacob when he sends Benjamin to Joseph, and the last phrase ("For if I must suffer bereavement, I will suffer it") suggests that if El Shaddai does not protect Benjamin, then, given Joseph's presumed death, Rachel's line will vanish.

There is only one other occurrence of El Shaddai in Genesis, and it is the crucial one, for it suggests how the fertility tradition of El Shaddai understood the name. This occurrence is in the Joseph blessing of the Testament of Jacob, a text that is not associated with any of the main documents and that is usually dated to the very early monarchy, although probably based on poems from the period of the Judges. The relevant passage is Genesis 49:25: "And El Shaddai will bless you with the blessings of the heavens above, blessings of the deep lying below, blessings of breasts [*shadayim*] and womb [*rahem*]." Here we have not only a fertility blessing similar to the others noted above but also a wordplay suggesting a meaning for the name El Shaddai. The author associates Shaddai with *shadayim* (breasts). As with the wordplay between *shod* (destruction) and Shaddai in Isaiah and Joel, we cannot assume that the author of this text actually believed that *shadayim* was the correct etymology of Shaddai: a poetic association is not a scientific etymology. But given the persistent fertility traditions in which El Shaddai appears in Genesis, the association is contextually and phonetically reasonable, if not scientifically persuasive.

I am trying to suggest that the author or authors of the various fertility blessings in Genesis may well have understood El Shaddai in the same way as the author of the Joseph blessing, regardless of the original meaning of the name. These traditions, which I will try to prove date from the early monarchy, may or may not have received the divine epithet from patriarchal provenance, but they interpreted it in their own way. Albright points out that its grammatical form resembles that of many early Hebrew personal names with a gentilic-adjectival ending.[20] In this case, the author might have understood the name to mean "El with breasts" or "the breasted El." But it may even have been interpreted as "El with *two* breasts," following Ezekiel 13:18, in which the same form means "two hands."[21]

It is at this point that the search for ancient cognates might prove helpful. Albright argued in 1935 that the "primitive" meaning of the Akkadian *shadu* is "breast."[22] The root then came to mean "mountain." Now, there is no apparent reason for assuming that one meaning of *shadu* is primitive and the other "secondary." They could certainly have coexisted.[23] In fact, it appears that the biblical author may well have associated breasts with mountains, for the "blessings of breasts and womb" of Genesis 49 are immediately followed by "blessings of ancient mountains; bounty of everlasting hills" (verse 26). It is, however, unimportant whether or not this refers to some unidentified cosmic mountain, as Cross thinks,[24] for the association with breasts is the critical one here, since it fits into the fertility context. In any event, if the name Shaddai has an Akkadian provenance, breasts would not contradict its original context. But perhaps a better place to search for a cognate would not be in Akkadian but in Egyptian, where *shdi* is a verb meaning "to suckle."[25] Here it is not even necessary to tinker with the suffix, since it is identical to the Hebrew. In this case, El Shaddai might be better rendered as "El who suckles" or "the suckling El."

Whether derived from Akkadian or Egyptian, the God with breasts is a natural interpretation of the fertility deity in Genesis. Yet the argument has a certain weakness. The mainstream of biblical criticism still agrees with Karl Heinrich Graf and Julius Wellhausen that the Priestly document is postexilic.[26] If the Priestly blessings are late, it would be hard to argue that the early meaning of El Shaddai was "the god of fertility," later to be supplanted by "the Almighty God." Moreover, I have presumed that the Priestly tradition was aware of the poetic association between Shaddai and breasts, which we identified in Genesis 49. It is therefore necessary (1) to establish the connection between the Testament of Jacob and the Priestly fertility blessings in Genesis and (2) to show that the date of the "God with breasts" tradition is early. Several internal considerations would argue for a date during the monarchy for all the Genesis blessings. First, I suggested above that the compound form of the name is more likely the early form, with Shaddai by itself an inaccurate, late archaism. Second, two of the fertility blessings (Gen. 17:6 and 35:11) promise the patriarchs that the consequence of their fertility will be the issue of kings, suggesting that they originated in monarchic circles. It can readily be demonstrated that the two uncontested early uses of El Shaddai (the Testament of Jacob and the Balaam oracles) were both compiled in their present form in the period of David and Solomon. The Balaam oracles are replete with monarchical allusions and references to David's conquest of Moab and Edom. The Testament of Jacob, although probably composed of tribal poems from the time of the Judges, strongly suggests the ascendancy of the tribe of Judah over its brothers (verses 8–11), the situation characteristic of the period of David and Solomon. The "scepter" (*shevet*) and "mace" (*mehokek*) that Judah holds, though probably relics of the tribal system, suggest the monarchy in their present context. In particular, the "mace between his legs" appears to be a metaphorical rather than a literal staff, representing the sexual organ of Judah and promising the continuation of the royal line. The blessing is therefore in part a fertility blessing reflecting the special covenant that the royal theology believed existed between God and David's progeny.

There is an additional similarity between the Priestly blessings and the Testament of Jacob that has hitherto not been noticed. The blessing Jacob gives to Ephraim and Manasseh contains one of the El Shaddai fertility blessings and is explicitly tied to the rest of the El Shaddai tradition.[27] Hence, it is possible to speculate that the author of this tradition may have had a special affection for the northern Joseph tribes. The Testament of Jacob bears a similar bias. The blessing accorded to Joseph that contains the El Shaddai reference is by far the longest and most positive of all the blessings in the Testament, suggesting Joseph's superiority over his brothers as a *nazir*.

In contrast, Judah's blessing contains evidence of the author's reluctance to give full support to that tribe. The royal scepter will remain in Judah's hands, but the verse ends with what appears to be a qualification: *ad ki yavo shiloh*. This phrase, the classic sticky wicket of Genesis criticism, can best be interpreted without mutilating the Masoretic text as "until it [the mace] comes to Shiloh."[28] I therefore understand the text to mean that Judah will remain the dominant tribe controlling the monarchy until the "staff" or "mace" of monarchy is transferred to the cultic site of Shiloh in the province of Ephraim. If this interpretation is correct, then we may conclude that the compiler of the Testament of Jacob was an Ephraimite who supported the principle of monarchy but preferred a king from his own tribe. He probably wrote before the secession of the northern tribes following the death of Solomon, for by then Ephraim did indeed acquire its own king. Or, alternatively, the key phrase analyzed above may have been composed as a prophecy *ex eventu* shortly after the secession of the north.

The Priestly El Shaddai blessings elsewhere in Genesis seem to follow in the same tradition: we find a bias for Ephraim and an intimate connection with the idea of monarchy. While we cannot reach a conclusion as to when these blessings were written down in their present form, the evidence does point to their close affinity with the Testament of Jacob, and we might thus reasonably suppose that the tradition understanding El Shaddai as a fertility god—a god with breasts—began in the early monarchy in a circle of Ephraimite authors.

It is interesting that the author or authors of the fertility blessings in Genesis should restrict the use of the name El Shaddai to the stories of the patriarchs. The author of Exodus 6 insists that God was known to the patriarchs as El Shaddai but shall henceforth be known as Yahweh, and he is also careful to use the name Elohim in the prepatriarchal stories he writes, some of which contain identical fertility blessings (Gen. 1 and 9). It may well be that this author possessed an authentic tradition according to which the patriarchs worshipped a god named El Shaddai, whom he wished to associate with Yahweh. But more importantly, his use of a special divine name in conjunction with fertility blessings for the patriarchs is a result of his view of the patriarchal legends, a view seemingly shared by the other literary schools. The repeated emphasis in Genesis on the miraculous birth of sons and the unnatural preference for the younger son (Isaac over Ishmael, Jacob over Esau, Joseph and Benjamin over their brothers, and Ephraim over Manasseh) suggests the necessity of God's intervention in the process of reproduction to guarantee the future of the Israelite nation. Nowhere else in the Bible is fertility such a persistent focus of concern; nowhere is it so central to the theological and historical message of the text. The purpose of the Genesis stories, for P as well as perhaps for the other authors, is to demonstrate that the covenant between God and his people is the consequence of the deity's active intervention in the family affairs of the patriarchs. Given his well-known interest in genealogies, it makes sense that the Priestly author might use a special divine fertility name in the patriarchal stories.[29]

This concern with fertility illuminates the association in Genesis 49 between the "God of your father" and El Shaddai. The cult of the god of the fathers, which Alt has shown to have been central to the patriarchal religion, was intrinsically preoccupied with the biological future of the clan. Whether or not the patriarchs actually worshiped El Shaddai as a fertility god, it is no surprise that a later author would see the connection between the cult of the god of the fathers and the divine name he associated with fertility.

It is additionally no surprise that when the Priestly author introduces God by the name El Shaddai in Genesis 17, Abraham is promised many progeny (symbolized by his name change) and is commanded to circumcise his sons. This passage is striking evidence of the connection between fertility and the rite of circumcision, which may be understood as a symbolic sacrifice in gratitude for God's blessing of fertility.[30] For P, circumcision is both an act of thanksgiving for sons in each generation and also a remembrance of God's primal act of fertility intervention in the days of the patriarchs. According to this view, circumcision is both a personal gesture and a sign of a national covenant.

The conception of the Hebrew God as a fertility god in general and as represented by breasts in specific has support in both biblical and extrabiblical sources. God's role as a partner in fertility is attested in virtually all the patriarchal stories, as well as in stories of the births of Samson and Samuel.[31] God is portrayed as giving birth in Deuteronomy 32:18 and in Isaiah 49:15 and 66:7–9.[32] Deutero-Isaiah says that the Israelites will be forced to "suck milk from the nations and nurse from the breast of kings" (60:16), implying that this experience will teach Israel to return to the "breast" of the true God. Similarly, Hosea curses the Israelites: "What shall you give them, Yahweh? Give them a womb which miscarries and dried-up breasts" (9:14). By implication, when God favors Israel, he will give them the blessing contrary to this curse, namely, the "blessing of breasts and womb." It is just possible that Hosea, a prophet from Ephraim, might have derived his fertility images from the El Shaddai tradition of earlier Ephraimite writers.

There is remarkable evidence that these fertility traditions may have derived from Canaanite sources. As Raphael Patai has admirably demonstrated in *The Hebrew Goddess*, the worship of the Canaanite fertility goddess Asherah was widespread and persistent from the period of the Judges to the seventh century, when it was finally stamped out by the Deuteronomic reforms.[33] Unlike Baal, who aroused the wrath of the orthodox Yahwists quite early in the period of the divided monarchy, Asherah was a much more legitimate part of popular Israelite worship and was even represented by a statue in the Jerusalem temple. When Elijah persecuted the prophets of Baal, he did not take similar action against the prophets of Asherah mentioned in the text. The archaeological evidence from Tel Beit Mirsim (the biblical Devir) suggests that the worship of Anat during the Canaanite period was replaced by the worship of Asherah figurines during the subsequent Israelite period.[34] A seventh-century Hebrew incantation text found in Arslan Tash invokes the help of Asherah in childbirth, which some believe may throw light on Leah's naming of Asher (Gen. 30:13).[35] Finally, and most significantly for our purposes, the inscriptions found at Kuntillet 'Ajrud in the Sinai record blessings to "YHWH . . . and to his Asherah."[36] Later monotheism notwithstanding, this ninth- or eighth-century text seems to suggest that the Hebrew God had a Canaanite consort.

As is well known, Asherah was typically depicted as a goddess with prominent breasts, which represent her powers of fertility. She and Anat are together referred to as "the wet nurses of the gods" (*mshnqt ilm*).[37] The Ugaritic record contains numerous references to "the nipples of Asherah's breasts" and "the divine breasts, the breasts of Asherah and Raham."[38] The latter reference looks suspiciously like the biblical "blessings of breasts and womb," and indeed, as Cross notes, Genesis 49 seems to betray knowledge of the epithet of El's consort Rahmay, as well as of other Canaanite mythological characters such as the *tehom*.[39] In addition, the "Astarte of the plain" (*'ttrt shd*) may have been understood by the Israelites as "Astarte of the breast," although such a reading would have been laughed out of court by a native speaker of Ugaritic, for whom breast was *td* rather than *shd*. Hence, there is abundant evidence that the fertility tradition of El Shaddai may have originated with the Israelite interest in the figure of Asherah, the fertility goddess represented by breasts.

The Priestly school represents a significant stage in the development of Israelite monotheism. As the text of Exodus 6 demonstrates, the Priestly author was concerned to assimilate all of the patriarchal gods, including the Canaanite El, to Yahweh. It would make sense that he would have wanted to give Yahweh the fertility functions of El's consort, Asherah, who was so venerated by the Israelites. Hence, it is possible that, just as El was assimilated to Yahweh, so Asherah was adopted into Priestly Yahwism by a surreptitious sex change: the Canaanite "wet nurse of the gods" was reincarnated as El Shaddai, the God with breasts. Such a view of Yahweh as both male and female would symbolize neatly the miraculous fertility relationship between the deity and the patriarchs. In fact, this "androgynous monotheism" can already be discerned in the first chapter of Genesis, where we learn that "God created Adam in the image of himself, in the image of God he created him, male and female he created them." If the first man was androgynous—as the midrash thought[40]—so must be the God who created "him."

The Canaanite background to the fertility tradition of El Shaddai may help us to understand why the fertility interpretation was suppressed and replaced by the "Almighty God" of the sixth century. We know that the seventh century witnessed a radical attack on all vestiges of Canaanite religion. The fertility cult, which had evidently found a place in Israelite religion, was mercilessly stamped out by Josiah, especially in his slaughter of the ritual prostitutes and the destruction of the Asherahs. The psychological associations between El Shaddai and Asherah must have become embarrassing and even dangerous. Yet the old divine name could not be utterly suppressed. Instead, it was given a new meaning, perhaps based on the old Psalm 68. This new meaning, in which Shaddai came to represent Yahweh variously as remote, mysterious, and destructive, was not entirely arbitrary. It is possible that it was adopted precisely because it so thoroughly contradicted the fertility interpretation.

It is even possible that, although the evidence remains sketchy, the attack on the fertility traditions that one school associated with El Shaddai may have reflected hostility to the role of women in cultic matters. A number of sixth-century texts refer in unflattering terms to women as the purveyors of alien worship. Jeremiah 44 seems to blame primarily women for the worship of the "Queen of heaven," an epithet of Astarte or Anat. In 2 Kings 23:7 there is a description of how Josiah destroyed the house in the Temple "where the women wove clothes for Asherah." It would not be surprising if women were particularly interested in fertility rites and if they were therefore one of the targets of the Deuteronomic reforms. If women were blamed for these rituals, we can better understand Ezra's uncompromising attack in the fifth century on marrying foreign women, a Deuteronomic ban unknown earlier in the First Temple period.

The transformation of the "God of breasts" into the "Almighty God of war" may have received an additional impetus from the Canaanite sources themselves. The chief enemy of the Yahwists was Baal, and the Yahwists must have been aware of Baal's sister and consort, the goddess Anat, although the Bible scarcely mentions her. Anat shared many of Asherah's fertility characteristics, notably the prominence of breasts in the iconography. Indeed, the Ugaritic literature, and other Near Eastern sources as well, often confuse the two. But Anat was a much more complex goddess than the relatively benign Asherah. She was not only a goddess of fertility but also a goddess of war and destruction. The epic poems about her are replete with unspeakable and bloody deeds that she commits in defeating Mot, the enemy of Baal. Anat was therefore a thoroughly ambiguous figure: at once the giver of life and purveyor of death, a mediator between fertility and mortality. One of the poems dedicated to her begins with a totally enigmatic introduction that seems to suggest this ambiguity: "He arose, took portions and gave him to eat / He cut up a breast before him / With a suckling sword, a nipple of a fatling."[41] Here the laceration and eating of the breast and the peculiar image of the "suckling sword" seem to symbolize the combination of fertility and destruction in Anat. Is it possible that in suppressing the fertility cult, the Yahwists of the seventh century, confusing Anat with Asherah, exploited the destructive side of her personality as a source for their interpretation of Shaddai? The inversion of the meaning attributed to Shaddai would therefore have a historical as well as psychological rationale through the mediation of the paradoxical figure of Anat.

The transformation of El Shaddai from a fertility god with feminine characteristics to a seemingly male god of war makes great theological and even psychological sense, for what better way to suppress one interpretation of a god than by substituting its opposite? But it is startling that one of the two traditions of El Shaddai should have remained forgotten to the present day; only recently have we become aware of the feminine characteristics that the Israelites sometimes allowed their God to possess. It is well known that postbiblical monotheism contains numerous fertility notions connected to the image of an androgynous God. The Christian Gnostics in the second century frequently conceived of God as a composite of male and female, and even the orthodox Clement of Alexandria wrote that "to those infants who seek the Word, the Father's loving breasts supply milk."[42] In the Middle Ages, Jewish mysticism portrayed the emanations of God (*sefirot*) as a dynamic interaction between male and female principles.[43] None of these traditions derives explicitly from the suppressed biblical God with breasts. Yet the possibility that God reflects the whole human condition—and not just its masculine aspect—was already evident to some biblical authors. From its very beginnings to the present day, monotheism has persistently, if not always successfully, resisted a purely masculine interpretation.

CHAPTER 2

Korah in the Midrash

The Hairless Heretic as Hero

HEROES COME IN MANY FLAVORS and colors. There are tragic heroes and epic heroes. And there are comic heroes, of which the trickster is a well-known type, especially in folklore. As opposed to the straightforward hero, the trickster often appears to subvert the norms of a culture while at the same time reinforcing them.[1] At the extreme end of the spectrum lies the villain, whose role may resemble the trickster's but who lacks the trickster's amusing charm. How a villain can be transmuted alchemically into a species of hero is the subject of this essay.

KORAH, THE VILLAIN

Perhaps the least likely hero among biblical characters is Korah, the villain of Numbers chapter 16.[2] If one dissects that text, then Korah is the leader of not one but four rebellions that an editor wove together into a compendium of Levitical and non-Levitical challenges to the leadership of Moses and Aaron. These revolts may have been retrojections into the desert period of later struggles within the priesthood between Aaronide and Levitical priests as well as other groups. But whatever may have been the true historical background of Numbers 16, it is Korah whom later tradition regarded as the arch-rebel and heretic.

Yet even within the biblical text, Korah's challenge to Moses and Aaron may not be entirely groundless. He and his followers proclaim: "You [i.e., Moses and Aaron] have gone too far. For all the community are holy, all of them, and the Lord is in their midst" (Num. 16:3). We need only read a few verses earlier, at the end of Numbers 15, where God commands the Israelites to wear fringes on their garments as a reminder of all the commandments. Those who are so reminded and observe the commandments are said "to be holy to your God" (Num. 15:40). Or, if we return to the revelation at Mount Sinai, we read even more pointedly: "Now, then, if you will obey me faithfully and keep my covenant, you shall be my treasured possession among all the peoples. Indeed, all the earth is mine, but you shall be to me a kingdom of priests and a holy nation" (Exod. 19:6). Thus, the demand of Korah, a Levite who the genealogies tell us was Moses's first cousin, to be recognized as a priest and to be accorded holiness equal to that of his close relatives certainly had legs on which to stand. If Korah was making a narrow claim for equality with Aaron and Moses, his rebellion certainly had a broader democratizing basis in scripture itself.[3]

Moreover—and surprisingly—the sons or descendants of Korah appear in the superscripts of a number of the psalms either as the authors of these psalms or as those to whom they were dedicated.[4] How we should understand these attributions is a problem of biblical criticism that I do not intend to solve. In any case, these psalms demonstrate that, whenever they were composed, the Korahites had an honored place in Israelite worship, hardly what one would expect from reading Numbers 16. On the other hand, as David Mitchell has argued, the Korahite psalms have in common the hope for redemption from Sheol, the underworld to which Korah and his followers were consigned.[5] If this theory is correct, then perhaps the author (or authors) of those psalms was able to harmonize the holy sons of Korah with their evil forefather.

The rabbis could not ignore this seeming contradiction between Korah the rebel and the persistence of the *benei korah* in later scripture. Their solution was a simple one and one that reflects Mitchell's thesis: the sons of Korah did not suffer their father's fate, which, according to the midrash, was to be both burned and swallowed up by the earth.[6] They repented in time and either survived or were given a special place in hell where they perched on a special column as custodians of the remains of the Temple.[7] In one version, Jonah is given a Dantesque tour of hell by the great fish who has swallowed him and comes upon the *even ha-shtiyah*, the foundation stone of the Temple, at whose base the sons of Korah recite prayers.[8] As we shall see, this midrash was to recur in a somewhat different form in Muslim sources.

In the midrash, Korah is said to have had prophetic gifts, which already hints that he was not so different from Moses. However, his ability to prophesy led to his downfall. He foresaw that Samuel would be one of his descendants, which led him to believe that he could survive God's wrath.[9] He failed to intuit, however, that his three sons would survive, so that his lineage would continue but he himself would not. It would be Hannah, Samuel's mother, who would pray on behalf of the Korahites and mitigate their eternal punishment.

The midrash also exhibits a certain historical-critical understanding when it proposes that the core of the biblical story is really a dispute between priests and nonpriests (either Levites or Israelites). Korah's sin lies in violating boundaries or mixing things that must be kept separate. He starts by violating the distinction between night and day, which will then lead to violating the distinctions between priests and Levites (or Aaron and all the rest of the Israelites) and ultimately between Israel and the nations. Korah's desire to make all his followers priests would be akin to idolatry, since the idolaters have many temples and therefore many priests, while "we have only one God and one temple."[10] The biblical prohibitions on mixing are linked to monotheism: keeping things separate affirms divine unity.

KORAH, A REBELLIOUS RABBI

This last midrash tries to turn Korah into the close cousin of an idolater. But other midrashim, in the process of understanding and explaining Korah's heresy, "rabbinize" him, that is, turn him into a rabbi who violates the boundaries of rabbinic discourse. But he does so in the terms of that discourse. As such, he becomes a hero in spite of himself. The rabbis' treatment of Korah bears some relation to how they treat the greatest heretic of their own circles, Elisha ben Abuya, also known as Aher.[11] Without entering into a detailed analysis of the Elisha texts, it is possible to conclude that this second-century rabbi, who became some kind of Epicurean (his heresy is not entirely clear), remained a rabbi even when he was banned. His student, Rabbi Meir, says that one should ignore his deeds and remember his Torah, by which he means that Elisha's teachings were still valid even after he had sinned. The Talmud's description of the relationship between Rabbi Meir and Elisha suggests further that the teacher always remains a teacher and the student always a student, no matter how far either has strayed.

Indeed, the rabbis frame the dispute between Moses and Aaron, on the one hand, and Korah and his company, on the other, as a dispute between teacher and student: "Rabbi Hama bar Hanina said: 'Anyone who creates a conflict with his teacher is as if he creates a conflict with the *shekhinah* [that is, with God himself]. . . . Anyone who challenges [*mitra'em*] his teacher, is as if he challenged the *shekhinah*, and everyone who doubts his teacher [*meharher*] is as if he doubted the *shekhinah*."[12] Korah is like the bad student who rails against his *rebbe*. A bad student, perhaps, but one whose proper place is still in the *bet midrash*. In fact, the rabbis use Korah as a limit case for rabbinic dissension. It is a firm rabbinic principle that minority opinions must be preserved, either as precedents to overturn a majority opinion in a later generation or, more minimally, to indicate to a later generation what was considered and dismissed by the majority.[13] But are all minority opinions legitimate? In the famous Oven of Akhnai story,[14] Rabbi Eliezer is in a minority of one, but despite his mobilization of miracles and a heavenly voice on his side, the rabbis reject his opinion and go so far as to ban him. The story, brilliantly analyzed by Jeffrey Rubinstein, concludes with a critique of the majority for shaming Rabbi Eliezer.[15] His dissent is therefore legitimate even if he does not win the halakhic dispute.

Korah, on the other hand, is the type of dissenter whose dissent does not enjoy protection under the rabbinic canopy. As the Pirkei Avot says: "When an argument is for the sake of heaven, the argument will lead to an established result. When an argument is not for the sake of heaven, it will not lead to any established result. What is an argument for the sake of heaven? That of Hillel and Shammai. What is an argument not for the sake of heaven? That of Korah and his group."[16] The distinction that the rabbis make is between one who dissents and then accepts majority rule and one who persists in dissension (*mahzik ba-mahloket*). The latter is a violation of a negative commandment. But the very terms on which the rabbis place Korah outside the tent are rabbinic: his heresy is of the type that one might expect of an obstreperous student.

In another midrash, to which I shall return, On, a minor character in the Korah story who takes on a major role in the midrash, is said by his wife to be at once a student (*talmida* in Aramaic) of Moses and of Korah. She refers to the latter two as *rav*, that is, in rabbinical parlance, as rabbis. Of course, it is no surprise to find Moses turned into a rabbi, since the rabbis always refer to him as *Moshe Rabbenu*, Moses our Rabbi. But Korah? In this version, Korah is not so much a student as the rabbi of a school that competes against the school of Moses.

Turning Korah into a miscreant rabbi finds a parallel in patristic literature when Cyprian comments on Numbers 16: "People who obey the precepts of the Lord and fear God ought to separate themselves from a sinful leader and should not take part in the sacrifices of a sacrilegious bishop, especially since they themselves have the power either of electing worthy bishops or of refusing the unworthy."[17] Korah becomes the exemplar of a heretical bishop whom the Christians have the power to boycott and ban, a sign of a church still very much in the process of formation.

As befits a rebellious rabbi, the midrashic Korah uses classically rabbinic argumentation. His first challenge is to the commandment of *tzitzit*, the blue fringes that are the subject of the biblical chapter immediately preceding his rebellion. Korah wants to know whether a garment wholly dyed the correct shade of blue does not qualify as fulfilling the commandment, even without the special fringes. He asks: "A cloak that is entirely composed of blue cannot free itself from the obligation, yet the four blue threads do free it?"[18] To this challenge he adds another: Does a house containing a Torah scroll need to have a *mezuzah* on the door? The *mezuzah* contains certain biblical verses, but a Torah scroll would obviously have those verses in addition to all the others. When Moses tells him that the house is still under the obligation of *mezuzah*, he responds: "The whole Torah, which contains 275 sections, cannot exempt the house, yet the one section in the *mezuzah* exempts it?"[19] Korah's principle seems to be that if the whole (blue cloth) contains the part (the *tzitzit*), then the whole suffices to discharge the commandment, an argument quite close to one of the rabbinic principles of exegesis. This principle is also the functional equivalent of Korah's argument that if the whole nation is holy, then there is no need for a separate priesthood. The Torah's laws appear to Korah as thoroughly irrational, and he concludes that they must be the inventions of Moses. Implicit in these challenges is that divine law must pass an elementary test of rationality and that anything that falls short of this test must be of human provenance.

These challenges are the kinds of limit cases, so beloved of the rabbis, that test the scope and meaning of the law. Can a *sukkah* be built on the side of an elephant?[20] How small a quantity of milk can fall into a pot of meat without rendering it unkosher?[21] The list goes on and is virtually as long as the Talmud itself. Korah's questions, clearly intended to subvert the law rather than to truly test its limits, nevertheless use the same logic as rabbinic dialectic. One might even say that his questions are a satire of rabbinic discourse, an example of what can happen to this argumentation when taken to an extreme. The midrash therefore uses Korah to set the limits of legitimate discourse by staking out a position that uses the quintessential midrashic method but goes too far.

In a variant on this hyper-rational attack on the law, Korah is said to construct a Judaism based on the Ten Commandments, a kind of ancient version of Reform Judaism: "When we were given the Ten Commandments, every one of us nursed [*yonek*] from Mount Sinai. We were given only the Ten Commandments, and we were not given *hallah, terumah, ma'aserot*, or *tzitzit*, but rather you [Moses] made them up yourself to give yourself power and to give honor to Aaron your brother."[22] Korah's reading of the revelation at Sinai is much more literal than the rabbinic tradition, which holds that all of the Torah, and not just the Ten Commandments, was revealed at Sinai. Moses responds to Korah by showing that the Levites prosper under the law more than priests, thus turning the question into a debate between priests and Levites but not ultimately addressing the core of Korah's challenge.

While Korah's goal in these midrashim, as in the Bible, is to challenge the authority of Moses, he does so by clever sophistry rather than brute force. Indeed, the midrash calls Korah "a great *hakham*."[23] This could be translated in one of three ways: "Korah was shrewd or clever"; "Korah was a sage" (since a rabbi is called a *talmid hakham*); or, with the meaning it might acquire if translated into Yiddish, "Korah was a *hokhem*," that is, a wiseass, a trickster who used his knowledge of the text to cause trouble. All three seem to be true.

In another midrash, Korah mounts a different kind of attack on Moses and Aaron, by posing as a defender of social justice against the strictures of the law.[24] He attempts to make fun of the rabbis and seduce the masses by telling them a tale of a widow and her two orphaned daughters trying to eke out a living from a small plot of land. No matter what she does—plow with an ox and an ass, or sow with diverse seeds—Moses blocks her by quoting the law against her. When she finally succeeds in harvesting wheat or raising sheep, Aaron comes along and confiscates his priestly share, leaving her once again bereft. Korah concludes: "Is such a thing right? Oh, the ruined woman.... Moses and Aaron have done all these things to her, but blame the Holy One, blessed be He."

What is fascinating about this text is that it gives voice to what one could imagine to be actual grievances against the law. To be sure, the heretic receives his comeuppance, but his accusation remains unanswered. Where is the justice promised by the law if the political and religious establishment look out only for themselves? Korah is no atheist: he certainly believes in a just God. But by displacing the burden of the law onto Moses and Aaron, he suggests that the injustice he discerns in the law is due to its human origins. Taken together, all these midrashim demonstrate that rebellion against the law goes hand in hand with doubting revelation: the *epikoros* Korah claims to be more of a believer than Moses, but he doubts the divine source of Moses's law.

THE ROLE OF WOMEN AND HAIR

The midrash's use of a widow introduces another fascinating theme in a number of the Korah midrashim: the role of women both as abettors of rebellion and as defenders of the law. One tradition holds that the jealousy people directed at Moses caused them to suspect that he was having an affair with a married woman and therefore every man warned his wife to stay away from him. As a result, Moses pitched his tent outside the camp so that he would not be suspected of adultery.[25] This rumor would seem to be related to the midrash that claims that Moses took a vow of celibacy, which led his sister Miriam to complain against him "on behalf of the Cushite woman," that is, Moses's wife.[26] Another midrash claims that it was Korah's wife who encouraged him to rebel against Moses and that it was she who argued that there was a logical fallacy in the law of *tzitzit*.[27]

If Korah's wife is the instigator of rebellion, the wife of On becomes the heroine.[28] On is mentioned as one of Korah's lieutenants, but the midrash turns him, like Korah's sons, into a conspirator who repents and returns to the fold. And his wife gets the credit for his repentance. Since On has taken a vow to follow Korah, he cannot renounce his vow. As mentioned earlier, he is like a student with respect to Korah, his teacher (or master), but he is equally a student with respect to Moses. On cannot choose sides. His wife solves his problem by getting him drunk in their tent (an allusion to the drunkenness of Noah?) and then sitting at the entrance to the tent with her hair undone. She says that when Korah's company come to enlist On in their rebellion, they will not dare enter the tent, since "all the people are holy." Her loosened hair turns her into a sexually provocative woman, but because the people are holy, they will retreat rather than attempt to enter the tent. This is an ironic adoption of Korah's own claim that all the people are holy and therefore should share equal access to God with Moses and Aaron. The drunken On remains comatose within his tent, while his wife creates a cunning diversion by activating the holiness of the people with a sexual provocation. Her hair as a sexual symbol has the paradoxical power to protect On from committing evil.

This episode introduces the importance of hair to the Korah story.[29] The midrash puns on Korah's name, saying that he created a bald spot (*kare'ah* means "bald") in Israel because the earth swallowed him and his followers. But Korah's baldness is also linked to his status as a Levite. In Numbers 8:7, Moses consecrates the Levites by shaving off all of their hair. As part of her incitement to rebellion, Korah's wife says that Moses did this because he was jealous of Korah's good looks and therefore, in the colorful language of one version of this story, "he had you shave off your hair and he rolls you around like excrement [as if] he had set his eye on your hair."[30] Korah's hair is seductive, and even Moses feels its erotic power. Here is another version, also with sexual overtones:

> When Korah came to seduce [*le-hazer*] the Israelites [to follow him], they did not recognize him and said, "Who did this to you?" He said: "Moses did it to me. Nay, more, he laid hold of me by my hands and feet, waved me, and told me: "Behold, you are clean." And [Moses] brought Aaron his brother and dressed him up like a bride and sat down in the tent of the meeting. Immediately, those who hated Moses began to provoke him in front of Israel, saying, "Moses is king, and Aaron his brother is high priest, and his sons are deputy priests."[31]

While Korah's "seduction" of the Israelites falls short because he lacks hair and, in fact, is humiliated by his hairlessness, Aaron, dressed like a bride, becomes the object of male desire in place of the bald and hairless Korah. But unlike Aaron, Korah is not feminized. His baldness does not emasculate him and perhaps even gives him the virility to rebel against Moses.

In the version of this midrash that blames it all on Korah's wife, Korah objects to his wife's explanation for why Moses commanded the Levites to shave off their hair. After all, he says, Moses himself, as a Levite, agreed to shave off his own hair. Korah's wife replies: "Since all of them [recognized] his greatness, he [Moses] said: 'Let me die with the Philistines,'" that is, Moses is willing to endure the same humiliation of appearing hairless as the Levites. By quoting this verse, Moses sets up an implicit opposition between himself as Samson and the Levites in the role of the uncircumcised Philistines. The verse also harks back to Delilah's shaving of Samson's hair, an emasculation of the Nazirite by removing the symbol of his dedication to God. Paradoxically, the hairlessness of the Levites is just as much a symbol of dedication to God as the unshorn hair of the Nazirite. Thus, in a variety of ways, hair—and its absence—becomes a powerful synecdoche for power, sexuality, and gender in the Korah story. And the fact that both Korah and Moses are shorn of all their hair suggests that they are really each other's *doppelgänger*.

KORAH'S WEALTH IN JEWISH, CHRISTIAN, AND MUSLIM TRADITION

A seemingly unrelated midrashic tradition sees Korah as fabulously wealthy. He had so many treasure houses that the keys alone, even though made of leather (obviously a tongue-in-cheek detail), weighed so much together as to required three hundred white mules to carry them.[32] The origin of Korah's wealth was treasure hidden by Joseph. According to one tradition, Korah was the controller of Pharoah's treasury. In the Talmud's version, Joseph had buried three treasures: one was revealed to Korah, one was revealed to Emperor Antoninus, and one would be revealed to the righteous in messianic times (*le'atid lavo*). This wealth thus had both positive and negative effects depending on those to whom it was revealed. While Korah's wealth was "to his detriment" (*le'ra'ato*), would it be too speculative to point out that just as the Messiah is supposed to ride on a donkey (*hamor*), so Korah's wealth has a messianic resonance, since its keys had to be carried on white mules? Or perhaps the white mules—that is, emasculated donkeys—signify that Korah's wealth, as opposed to that of the messianic righteous, has no productive use? Parenthetically, the tradition that the Messiah will ride on a white donkey appears to be neither Jewish nor Christian but rather Muslim in an inverted sense: the *dajjal* or Antichrist will arrive on a white donkey before the advent of the *Mahdi*, the true Messiah.[33]

The rabbis were not ascetics with respect to wealth. But as the Korah story suggests, there is salutary wealth and harmful wealth. In several midrashim, Korah's wealth is paired with Haman's: "R. Phinehas said: There were two rich men in the world, one in Israel and one among the idolaters, whose money proved their ruination. In Israel there was Korah, who found the treasures of gold and silver that Joseph had hidden. Among the idolaters there was Haman, who seized the treasures of the kings of Judah."[34] Just as Haman ended up on the gallows, so Korah ended up swallowed by the earth and burned by fire.[35] On the other hand, the biblical king Jehoshaphat is an example of someone wealthy who called out to God and received an answer to his prayer.[36] It would appear that Korah was corrupted by money and that this corruption led to his revolt against Moses. The midrash grounds this interpretation in the biblical statement that all the possessions of the Korahites—down to every last needle—descended with them into the pit.[37]

Here we find the diametric opposite of the midrashic Korah's defense of the poor widow.

It is this tradition of Korah's wealth that seems to have found the greatest resonance in early Christian and Muslim sources. The patristic treatment of Korah lacks much of the inventiveness of the Jewish and Muslim. Korah represents a kind of materialism: his punishment—being swallowed up by the earth—is fitting because he was too invested in earthly things.[38] In this sense, for the church fathers, he represents Israel of the flesh, a striking counterhistory in which the archvillain of the Bible now comes to stand for the Jews *tout court*.

The Muslim traditions are much richer and less pejorative. Following the midrash, the Qur'an groups Korah (known in the Muslim sources as Qarun) with Haman and also with Pharoah.[39] In another, more extensive treatment of Korah, the Qur'an demonstrates very detailed knowledge of the midrash about Korah's wealth: "Now Korah was of the people of Moses; he became insolent to them, for We had given him treasures such that the very keys of them were too heavy a burden for a company of men endowed with strength. . . . He [Korah] said: 'What I have been given is only because of a knowledge that is in me.'" Korah links his wealth to some kind of esoteric knowledge. But the Qur'an responds with a different kind of knowledge, that of the true believers: "Woe upon you! The reward of God is better for him who believes and works righteousness."[40] The knowledge that allows one to gain wealth must give way before divine knowledge that leads to righteous deeds. As in the patristic sources, Muslim scripture uses Korah as an example of a man who incurs God's wrath for pursuing earthly riches.

In post-Qur'anic sources, Korah is not only wealthy but also handsome and possessed of a beautiful voice when he recites the Torah (the Muslim sources here seem to imagine him like a Muslim reciting the Qur'an). He is therefore given the name the Enlightened (*al-munawwar*).[41] While the context here seems to be his ability to recite the Torah, his nickname suggests qualities similar to those of a rabbi. One wonders if midrashic traditions found an echo here as well.

One Islamic source connects Korah's wealth to his rebellion: he plans to get rid of Moses when he hears that the latter is about to impose an alms tax.

In a narrative reminiscent of the rabbinic tradition, Korah pays a woman to accuse Moses of adultery, but the woman retracts the accusation and implicates Korah. Moses then orders the earth to swallow him up. Every day, he sinks by the height of a man and will continue sinking at this rate until the time of the resurrection of the dead. Echoing the midrash cited earlier from the Pirke de-Rabbi Eliezer (which was composed in the very early years of Islam), Korah hears Jonah's voice in the belly of the great fish and says that he is sorry about the deaths of Moses and Aaron. God then pardons Korah so that he will be resurrected in the end of days. The question of Korah's own resurrection is in fact discussed in the Talmud, with some rabbis contending that he will be resurrected while others say he will not.

A final Muslim tradition holds that Korah was a goldsmith and also a master of alchemy, which may be related both to his wealth and to his secret knowledge. Some traditions claim that he knew how to change lead and copper into gold and silver. He is said to have learned this art from his wife, who turns out to be Moses's sister. Once again, women play an important role in the Korah stories, although here it isn't clear whether alchemy has a positive or negative valence. But the close familial relationship by marriage between Moses and Korah—the Muslim tradition may not know that they were cousins via their fathers—once more suggests that these two figures were not so much diametric opposites as linked heroes.

MODERN INTERPRETATIONS OF KORAH AS VILLAIN AND HERO

I have devoted this essay to a discussion of Korah in late antique sources, and it would no doubt prove fruitful to pursue the refraction of these stories in medieval exegesis, a subject that lies beyond my scope. But it may be worth concluding with several examples of Korah in modern sources. In the eighteenth century, Jews began to rebel against both the rabbis and rabbinic tradition. On the high intellectual level, this process received the name of *haskalah*, or enlightenment. But, as Shmuel Feiner has convincingly shown, this rebellion had deep roots in other social classes.[42] The opponents of these early gestures of secularization, who were often our first sources for the phenomenon, referred to the rebels by a number of names, such as Karaites (referring here to the early medieval opponents of rabbinic law). But they also deployed the biblical Korah by calling the secularizers the "Congregation of Korah."[43] As we have seen, Korah might be accused of many things, but secularism certainly misses the mark. On the other hand, as a symbol of rebellion against the rabbis, Korah has a venerable place in the Jewish tradition. It is perhaps not surprising that those seeking to defend the tradition had little choice but to reach for an archetype from within the tradition to label those trying to divorce themselves from it.

These eighteenth-century attacks on the "Congregation of Korah" scarcely reflect the ambiguous portrait of Korah as a kind of heroic antihero in the midrash as well as in Muslim sources. Here Korah is a villain pure and simple, usable as a brush to tar other rebels against the rabbis. At times, however, those tarred with this brush might embrace the brush and turn Korah into a hero. Thus, the Reform theologian W. Gunther Plaut described the midrashic attack on Korah as a thinly veiled attempt to counter opposition to the rabbis, which might also be read as an allegory of modern Reform versus Orthodoxy.[44] Similarly, two lay authors writing in the *Journal of Reform Judaism* entitled a short essay on the biblical story "Korach's Question Still Deserves an Answer."[45]

An unusual variation on these themes can be found in the Hasidic movement, which originated in the eighteenth century. Naturally, these traditionalists had to condemn Korah as a would-be usurper of Moses's leadership. Yet Korah became a useful figure for examining the proper qualities of leadership, a subject of great import to the Hasidim, who invented a social structure consisting of a charismatic leader (*tsaddik* or *rebbe*) and his followers (*hasidim*). Consider, for example, Meshulam Feibush Heller (1740–95), a disciple of Dov Baer, the Maggid of Mezeritch, and other first-generation Hasidic masters. In his *Yosher Divrei Emet*, he argues that Korah's conflict with Moses arose because Moses, who was the humblest of men, had to conduct himself as a leader and therefore had no choice but to elevate himself (*gavahut*).[46] Korah, whom Heller calls "possessed of intelligence and the holy spirit," misunderstood Moses's elevation and thought it was opposed to truth. Heller clearly wants to carve out a certain grandiosity for the Hasidic leader, in the spirit of Moses, that is nonetheless grounded in humility. Korah, for all his virtues, failed to understand the correct balance between greatness and humility, but his intent was not wicked.

By the nineteenth century, most Hasidic movements had become dynastic, an issue that Yehudah Arye Alter (1847–1905), the leader of the Ger Hasidism in Poland in the late nineteenth century, addressed in his *Sefat Emet*, one of the most important collections of Hasidic sermons from that period.[47] Korah's claim that "all of Israel are holy" betrays a misunderstanding of this holiness. The high priest (*kohen ha-gadol*) is the source of holiness, while the Levites, to whom Korah belongs, are merely "pure." The holiness that Korah ascribes to all of Israel is not inherent but rather derived from the high priest. Moreover, the role of the high priest is dynastic, a gift of God from the womb for all generations. Alter seems to be using the biblical text to argue for the dynastic rule of the *tsaddikim*, who have inherited the divine grace previously held by the high priests. Other pretenders to this leadership role need to know their subordinate place, a lesson meted out to Korah.

Finally, the radical nineteenth-century Hasidic leader Mordechai Leiner (1801–54), the founder of the Izbitse Polish branch of Hasidism, had to resolve Korah's role according to his deterministic theology.[48] Everything that happens is the will of God, thought Leiner, in a kind of Hasidic version of Calvinism. So God must have willed Korah's rebellion. Here Leiner tries strenuously to show that there is a distinction between what really is the will of God and what we humans think is the will of God. Korah genuinely thought that his rebellion was the divine will, but he was mistaken. It is an act of hubris to think that our understanding of God's will guarantees the rightness of our actions. Interestingly, though, Leiner is prepared to accept Korah's claim that all of Israel are holy, but this claim will become true only in the messianic age.

These Hasidic texts betray an ambivalence toward Korah, a worthy and intelligent leader who nevertheless failed to understand his place in the divinely dictated hierarchy of Israel. Yet no Jewish text so decisively embraces Korah as the *Interpreter's Bible*, composed by liberal Protestants in the mid-twentieth century:

> We live in revolutionary times. Korah . . . was the first revolutionist among the people of Israel. . . . They declared: "You have gone too far! For all the congregation are holy, every one of them." What else was this but the first foregleam of the universal priesthood of all believers?

... What else was this but a revolt against what seemed to them the political and economic dictatorship of Moses, and with social results that were far from satisfactory to them? ... Today we glory in their two main contentions, viz., ecclesiastical and political democracy. ... In what then did the crime of Korah and his associates consist? Was it not that they failed to see that their timing was wrong? ... The people of Israel were not ready for them.[49]

The authors do not indulge in supersessionism, although they presumably believed that it was the Christians, especially after the Reformation, who were ready for the radical message of Korah. Did they see Korah as the prefiguration of Luther? Either way, this counterhistorical reading of the Bible makes plain what we have already found in the midrash: as much as the rabbis were compelled to bury Korah discursively, just as God buried him literally, they put some radical ideas in his mouth—or in the mouth of his wife—and thereby provided fodder for future rebels.

CHAPTER 3

Counterhistory and Jewish Polemics against Christianity

The Sefer Toldot Yeshu *and the* Sefer Zerubavel

AMOS FUNKENSTEIN DEVOTED A SIGNIFICANT amount of his scholarly attention to polemics between Jews and Christians.[1] He was particularly interested in how each religion borrowed motifs from the other and inverted the other's narrative, a procedure that he labeled "counterhistory."[2] He defined this genre of historical writing as follows: "[Counterhistory's] function is polemical. [Its] method consists of the systematic exploitation of the adversary's most trusted sources against their grain—'die Geschichte gegen den Strich kämmen.' [Its] aim is the distortion of the adversary's self-image, of his identity, through the deconstruction of his memory."[3] Funkenstein was interested in counterhistory as a particular type of historical narrative, which he called an "inauthentic narrative." He wished to examine the line between history and narrative by identifying a category of historical writing that lacked grounding in reality. In most counterhistories, he claimed, historical truth does not "shine through." Counterhistorians, instead of using historical sources, take the sources of their adversaries and turn them on their heads. Historical truth therefore cannot shine through in such narratives because "everything in them is a reflective mirror." The goal of the counterhistorian is to deny the adversary his identity, yet since the polemicist has lost touch with reality, he subverts his own identity as well. This is because those who construct polemical counterhistories must of necessity base their own identities on the denial of the Other.

Funkenstein concludes the section of *Perceptions of Jewish History* in which he deals with counterhistories by arguing that Holocaust revisionism is just such an attempt to rob the Other (in this case the Jew) of his or her memory and, therefore, identity. He also attacks those Zionists who would deny an identity to the Palestinians. Here he himself is engaged in a polemic, since he uses the term *counterhistory* as a weapon to uncover the ethical issues that underlie such forms of historiography. What is not entirely clear in this account is whether these kinds of counterhistories are to be rejected on ethical or historical grounds. Are they unhistorical because of their questionable ethical motivation, or are they unethical because "reality does not shine through"?

To complicate the matter more, Funkenstein allows parenthetically that certain counterhistories, such as those of Augustine of Hippo (whose history of the church is a counterhistory of Rome), Gottfried Arnold (who held that the true Christianity was the history of its heretics), and Karl Marx (who inverted the history of capitalism into an account of the rise of the proletariat), might be excluded from his negative description of the category. On what basis might they be excluded? Does something of reality "shine through" them, or is it rather that their motivation is not the unethical desire to rob the Other of his or her identity?

It is this suggestion that not all counterhistories necessarily fall under the definition given above that I wish to pursue in this essay. Two years before Funkenstein first used the term *counterhistory* in print, I published my *Gershom Scholem: Kabbalah and Counter-history*, a book based on a dissertation that I wrote under Funkenstein's supervision. My use of the term came out of intensive discussions with him, but my own definition departed significantly from the one that he proposed. I distinguished counterhistory from revisionism by claiming that a counterhistory finds the truth in a subterranean tradition that must be brought to light, much as the apocalyptic thinker decodes an ancient prophecy. Counterhistory is a type of revisionist historiography, but where the revisionist proposes a new theory or finds new facts, the counterhistorian transvalues old ones. He or she recognizes the "mainstream" or "official" history but holds that the vital force behind that history lies in a secret tradition. History consists of the dialectic between the normative and the subterranean.

It is in this latter sense that we might understand not only the work of Scholem but also that of Augustine, Arnold, and Marx. In the following remarks, I would like to suggest expanding the concept of counterhistory in two directions from what might at first appear to be an unduly narrow and monolithic definition in Funkenstein's account. I will do so by examining two texts. The first is the *Sefer Toldot Yeshu*, which is Funkenstein's primary example of a Jewish anti-Christian counterhistory. I will show that this scandalous text, although seeming on the face of it to fulfill the criteria for a counterhistorical polemic, might better be read as a satirical folktale that works by substitutions rather than inversions. In the second half of the essay, I will argue that the category of counterhistory might be extended to apocalyptic texts, taking as my example a text from around the same period, the *Sefer Zerubavel*. In this way, I hope to bring together Funkenstein's interest in apocalypticism, which was one of his earliest fields of research,[4] with his later preoccupation with Jewish-Christian polemics. Apocalyptic literature may turn out to be one of the best examples of counterhistorical polemic.

My reading of the *Toldot Yeshu* has been influenced by Erich Gruen's analysis of another of Funkenstein's examples of counterhistory, the genre of ancient "antisemitism" that began with the third-century BCE Egyptian Manetho.[5] According to these Hellenistic and Roman critics of the Jews, many of whose writings were collected by Josephus in his *Contra Apionem*, the Jews are not a genuine *ethnos*, since they originated as a leper people in Egypt, were expelled by the Egyptians, and came to occupy the Land of Israel by force. Their religion lacks legitimacy, some of these writers suggest, because it is simply an inversion of Egyptian practices. Funkenstein argues that Manetho and his successors knew the Exodus account and deliberately inverted it for their own polemical purposes. Manetho and his successors created counterhistories out of the Bible to deny the Jews their identity.

Gruen suggests that this reading of Manetho and the other Hellenistic accounts of the Exodus may be misguided. In a careful analysis of a number of such narratives, he shows that those frequently assumed to be polemically anti-Jewish may not be polemical at all. They often contain a mixture of both positive and negative judgments about the Jews. Moreover, their source may not have been the biblical Exodus account at all, but rather indigenous Egyptian traditions in which the Jews play a minor role at best. Gruen even speculates that some of the sources for these ostensibly anti-Jewish counterhistories may have been alternative Egyptian Jewish stories about the Exodus, midrashim that the Egyptian Jews created to glorify the history of their diaspora community.

Gruen's persuasive argument need not detain us here. The methodological point that I wish to borrow from him is that what may appear on the face of it to be polemical counterhistory could turn out on closer reading to have more complex meaning. This, I want to claim, is the case with the *Sefer Toldot Yeshu*, a text that Funkenstein considers, with Manetho, to be a perfect example of such counterhistory. Although composed of some details from the New Testament and other Christian sources, the *Toldot Yeshu* will turn out to contain many sources from the Talmudic tradition and others that are the sheer invention of the author. We know that many traditions circulated about Jesus in noncanonical Christian texts, and it is reasonable to assume that similar stories, with only tenuous connections to the synoptic Gospels, might be found in Jewish circles as well. In fact, as Samuel Krauss showed nearly a hundred years ago,[6] many of the stories in the *Toldot Yeshu* are based on folklore motifs that were compiled and reworked. Moreover, some of these stories are not simply derogatory or pejorative: often they contain more complex value judgments. Although clearly intended to satirize Christian origins, the *Toldot Yeshu* will emerge as far different from a systematic negative inversion of the Gospels into a counterhistory.

The *Toldot Yeshu* is a compilation of stories about Jesus and the early church. Its original date of composition is unclear but may be either late Talmudic or Geonic, since variants of it appear in Aramaic and Syriac fragments. Interestingly enough, Voltaire thought that it was from the first century and even predated the Gospels. He called it "the most ancient Jewish writing against our religion that has been transmitted to us. This is a life of Jesus Christ completely contrary to our holy evangelists."[7] Voltaire was perhaps the first to give the *Toldot Yeshu* this kind of counterhistorical definition.

On the face of it, the book has all the earmarks of a polemical satire against Christianity based on inversions of New Testament narratives. Jesus is the product not of divine impregnation and a virgin birth but of adultery. In a variant on a Talmudic tradition, according to which the father of Jesus is a Roman soldier named Pandera, the *Toldot Yeshu* holds that Miriam became pregnant when a wicked neighbor snuck into her house while her husband (in some versions referred to as a pious Jewish scholar named Joseph Pandera) was at the house of study. Miriam thinks that the man in her bed is her husband, but when Joseph discovers the pregnancy, he knows the truth and runs away to Babylonia!

Jesus himself is portrayed as a magician who steals the name of God, sews it inside his thigh (genitals?), and uses it for magical purposes, a narrative that has some echoes in rabbinic literature.[8] The Jewish authorities convene to decide what to do about his illicit use of the divine name. They choose a particularly clever sage named Judah Iscariot (!) to sew the divine name into his thigh and to engage in a magical duel with Jesus. They bring Jesus before Queen Helena and confront him. When he sees that he is surrounded, he announces that he wants to go up to his father in heaven and, employing the divine name, takes off in a flight reminiscent of the aeronautical tricks of Simon Magus. Judah lifts off after him and, in a dramatic aerial combat, brings Jesus crashing down to earth by ejaculating on him, thus rendering him and the magical name of God impure. Some of the versions more prudishly have Judah urinate on Jesus, but urine does not cause cultic impurity. For our purposes, however, it is the reversal in which Judas Iscariot becomes the hero, while Jesus is the villain, that signals a possible counterhistory. The text even suggests that this story explains why the sages of Christianity curse Judas: "When they [the Christians] have a conflict or dispute, they say to each other: 'Let it happen to you what Judah Iscariot did to Jesus.' And they weep over this incident throughout the night of the birthday of Jesus."

Yet this last passage suggests the limits of the category of counterhistory for our story. The text either is not aware of or chooses to suppress the Gospel account of Judas's betrayal of Jesus, an account that could have easily served a counterhistorical purpose. Moreover, it invents both a Christian folk saying and a religious practice that have no relationship to any actual Christian custom. If counterhistory requires extensive knowledge and inversion of the original history, the *Toldot Yeshu* turns out to be defective on both counts: it uses only bits and pieces of the Gospel stories, as well as Christian apocrypha, often out of their original context, and it invents complicated narratives that have little to do with the original.

One example is the thirty pieces of silver that Judas received for betraying Jesus, which do, in fact, appear, but in an entirely different context: the Jewish sages buy Jesus's body for thirty pieces of silver from one Judah the Gardener (Yehudah ha-Ganan, who in some versions seems to be identical to Judas Iscariot). This Judah the Gardener secreted the corpse in his garden in order to prevent Jesus's disciples from stealing the body. Here too, a New Testament story, the empty crypt, serves as the backdrop for a fanciful send-up of the Resurrection. The figure of Judah the Gardener may have its source in John 20:15, in which Mary Magdalene sees the resurrected Jesus in the garden, supposes him to have been the gardener, and accuses him of having absconded with the body. The *Toldot Yeshu* has Judah the Gardener in fact steal the body in order to thwart the disciples and then has him sell it to the sages.

Yet this narrative move confuses the polemic more than it supports it. The text begins by saying that the disciples planned to steal the body and pretend that it was resurrected. If the author was intent on simply inverting the original story, it would have made more sense to have the disciples do as they planned. But since it is the Jews who hide the body and then drag it through the marketplace, the Gospel account is not so much inverted as discarded. The *Toldot Yeshu* introduces this narrative in order to give an excuse to the queen to kill the disciples for claiming a phony resurrection, a detail that has no basis in the original.

The claim that Jesus was a magician, of course, is well grounded in the synoptic Gospels, as Morton Smith pointed out many years ago,[9] since many of Jesus's original activities involved exorcism and healing. The *Toldot Yeshu* seems aware of this aspect of the Gospels, but its treatment is more of an extension than an inversion. Moreover, the *Toldot Yeshu* may just as well have relied on Talmudic traditions that treat Jesus as a magician and regard his death as just punishment for blasphemy. At one point, the sages place Jesus in a circle and strike him with sticks to demonstrate that he lacks magical powers. Might this circle story not be an inverted echo of the magical feats of

Honi the Circle Maker, the well-known character from the Talmudic tractate Ta'anit?[10]

Rabbinic tradition appears to be either the source for other stories in the *Toldot Yeshu* or, at least, a reflection of a common, non-Christian source. For example, in a tale somewhat reminiscent of a midrash on the hanging of Haman, Jesus makes all the trees take an oath not to hang him; but the Jews find a thick stalk of cabbage, which does not count as a tree, and they use it to hang him.[11] Indeed, the whole account of Jesus's execution by stoning and then hanging, carried out by the Jews, is also much closer to the Talmudic account than to the New Testament.[12] There are no Romans in the *Toldot Yeshu*; Pilate is replaced by a Jewish queen, named Helene, who converted to Judaism but was attracted to Christianity, a figure that Krauss showed is an amalgam of the wife of the Hasmonean Alexander Yannai; Salome, who was also known as Helene; the proselyte Helene of Adiabene; and the mother of Constantine. There is no trial in front of the high priest, but instead a hearing in front of the queen with the rabbis leading the attack against Jesus. As in one Talmudic story about Jesus,[13] the *Toldot Yeshu* takes place in the time of Shimon ben Shetah, some hundred years or more before the actual time of Jesus.

The text's treatment of key figures is also more complex than one might expect from a pejorative counterhistory. Although Mary is not the holy virgin of Christian tradition, neither is she portrayed with quite the same venom as in later medieval texts, such as the thirteenth-century compendium of anti-Christian polemics, the *Nizzahon Yashan*. In the *Toldot Yeshu*, by contrast, she is the innocent victim of a licentious neighbor and believes that she is having intercourse with her husband in the dark. Why should a text intent on pillorying Christianity resort to such a detail, which softens the inversion of the Gospel account? The answer, I believe, is that the *Toldot Yeshu* is not only a polemic but is also motivated by other narrative impulses.

Jesus himself is presented as a learned sage who "could learn in one day what another lad could not learn in many years." The text brings in this "fact" to demonstrate that "for this reason the sages said that bastards are clever," a distortion of an actual rabbinic saying preferring learned bastards to ignorant high priests. Jesus is one of the rabbinic class whose arrogance turns him into a rebel. He may have stolen the divine name from the Temple, but his magic is based on something the Jews hold to be real. In a sense, what the text tries to do is to turn him into a worthy opponent in terms of rabbinic values, quite the opposite of the simple carpenter portrayed in the Gospels.

The treatment of Paul and Simon Peter is similarly surprising. Both turn out to be, not rebels against Judaism, but rather infiltrators sent by the rabbis to persuade the Christians to divorce themselves totally from the Jews. Thus, anti-Jewish Christian legislation becomes a clever ploy instigated by the Jews themselves to prevent corruption of Judaism. The strategy of the text is to reverse the sense of Jewish powerlessness in the face of Christian enmity by arguing that the Jews really control Christian history after all. A counterhistory this may be, but it is one that turns certain Christian heroes not into villains but into Jewish agents.

I have tried to suggest here that alternative narratives of the opponent's history may be constructed without close attention to the opponent's canonical texts. While we may wish to retain the term *counterhistory* to describe such narratives, we need to recognize them as possibly grounded in alternative folklore traditions rather than in self-conscious inversions. This form of counterhistory does not so much invert the other's story as subvert it by substituting a different narrative. The *Toldot Yeshu* turns the son of God not into the son of Satan, as we might expect from a counterhistory, but rather into an audacious trickster operating within the rabbinic elite, similar, in a way, to Korah in the rabbinic tradition, as I have argued in chapter 2. The categories of folktale and satire do not contradict counterhistory but enlarge the term beyond mere polemic.

It is interesting that Amos Funkenstein did not subject the *Toldot Yeshu* to the same value judgment he attached to Maneto or Holocaust revisionists. Neither did he explicitly exclude it from his negative list of counterhistories, as he did Augustine, Arnold, and Marx. Was the *Toldot Yeshu* an attempt to rob the Christians of their identity, and did it therefore also undermine the identity of its authors and readers? I have no doubt that Funkenstein's view of the text was not this negative. On the contrary, he delighted in the transgressive quality of the *Toldot Yeshu*. Whether strictly a counterhistorical polemic or a folkloristic satire, the *Toldot Yeshu* represented for him the assertive voice of an oppressed minority whose response to its condition was not passivity.[14] It would therefore seem to me important to add a political or social dimension to the evaluation of counterhistories: they mean something different in the hands of a minority as opposed to those of the majority.

If counterhistory can function as a literature of protest, I would like to suggest that apocalyptic texts may sometimes fit into this category. I have in mind the *Sefer Zerubavel*, a seventh-century apocalyptic text from Palestine.[15] Funkenstein mentions the *Sefer Zerubavel* in passing in *Perceptions of Jewish History* in his discussion of apocalypticism but does not investigate how it functions as a counterhistory.[16] However, in his overall description of apocalypticism, he notes that "at times—though by no means always—the apocalyptic vision of history is rooted within a sectarian counterideology."[17] It is precisely this insight that I wish to take up and pursue in relation to Jewish-Christian polemic.

In the nineteenth century, the *Sefer Zerubavel* was generally thought to derive from the time of the First Crusade, based on dates that the author provides. But as Israel Levi showed early in the twentieth century,[18] the correct way of interpreting this numerology points to the struggle for Jerusalem between the Persian Sassanian Empire and the Byzantine Empire in the years before the Arab conquest, with the date of composition probably around 628 or 630. The book is the source for Armilus (probably a variant of Romulus), a satanic figure who would become one of the most popular representatives of Rome and Christianity in later Jewish literature. As David Berger has shown, Armilus combines two other typological figures, Balaam and Aram, and its linguistic derivation may be from the Greek, meaning "destroyer of nations."[19] The typological fusion of these biblical and midrashic characters in a figure associated with Rome turns the Roman Empire into the culmination of all enemies of the Jewish people. The text also develops a complex narrative around the figures of two Messiahs, known already in rabbinic literature: "the Messiah son of Joseph," who is killed in battle by Armilus, and "the Messiah son of David," who kills Armilus, resurrects the first Messiah, and ushers in the final age.

The author of the *Sefer Zerubavel* cleverly exploits and inverts Christian *topoi* for Jewish eschatological purposes. Armilus is the Antichrist not only in a general sense but in the precise sense developed in Christian theology since the first century.[20] The identification of the Antichrist with Rome already appears in the Sybilline Oracles in the first century, where the Antichrist appears to be the Emperor Nero. In the second century, Tertullian would interpret the "man of sin," the Antichrist figure in Paul's (or pseudo-Paul's) second letter to the Thessalonians (2:1–12), as the Roman emperor. The Jewish text simply takes this identification to its logical conclusion by assuming that the Byzantine emperor is the successor to the earlier Roman rulers: by its association with Rome since Constantine, Christianity acquires all the negative connotations that it itself previously attributed to Rome.

A variety of details in the *Sefer Zerubavel* further demonstrate its reliance on Christian materials. For example, in the second letter to the Thessalonians (2:8), Jesus is said to destroy the Antichrist with "the breath of his mouth," a motif based on combining Psalm 2:9 and Isaiah 11:4. The exact same idea recurs at the end of the *Sefer Zerubavel*, where the Messiah son of David kills Armilus with his breath. The physical description of Armilus, although different in details from the various depictions of the Antichrist in Christian literature,[21] has the same general hideous features: his hair is a bizarre "greenish gold," his hands reach down to his feet, and so forth.

Earlier commentators have noticed the influence of the Christian Antichrist traditions on the *Sefer Zerubavel* and its successors, and, in turn, the possible influence of earlier Jewish traditions of an Antichrist-like figure on the Christian *topos*.[22] What has not been sufficiently described is the way a text like the *Sefer Zerubavel* not only reflects Christian motifs but systematically inverts them for both polemical and eschatological purposes. By turning the Byzantine Empire into the Antichrist, it stands another Christian apocalyptic tradition on its head: that the Antichrist will be a Jewish leader who will rebuild the Temple.[23] Since this is precisely what the Jews believed their Messiah would do, one might say that this Christian Antichrist doctrine was itself a kind of counterhistory of Jewish messianism. In the *Sefer Zerubavel*, the Jews counterattack by making the very figure that the Christians would call the Antichrist into the real Messiah.

There is more to this inversion, however: Armilus is not just the Byzantine emperor but in fact Jesus himself. And, on the other side of the coin, the Jewish messianic figures in the text assume some of the characteristics of Jesus, especially those taken from the suffering servant tradition. My contention is that the *Sefer Zerubavel* turns Jesus into the Antichrist and asserts that it is the Jewish Messiah who fulfills the biblical eschatological prophecies usually associated with Jesus.

Let us turn now to the text to see how these remarkable inversions are represented. The *Sefer Zerubavel* is placed in the mouth of Zerubavel, the Davidic heir from the biblical book of Ezra who led a failed attempt to reestablish the Davidic monarchy and rebuild the Temple in the late sixth century BCE. Zerubavel has a vision in which he is transported to the city of Nineveh, later identified as "Rome the Great," almost certainly meaning Constantinople (the Rome of Byzantium). There he is commanded to enter a *bet ha-toref*, a variant on rabbinic terms that mean either a "house of idolatry" or a vagina: the sexual double entendre may in fact be relevant here.[24] In the Byzantine context, the *bet ha-toref* clearly means a church, and there Zerubavel sees a man described as "suffering and familiar with disease" (Isa. 53:3). This is indeed the suffering servant of Isaiah whom Christian tradition most insistently identified with its Messiah. This Christ-like figure introduces himself to Zerubavel with the words "I am the Messiah of God, and I am imprisoned here in this jail until the end of time," partly echoing the midrash in which a suffering Messiah is waiting like a beggar at the gates of Rome.[25] Here the midrashic *topos* is sharpened: the suffering Messiah, so reminiscent of Jesus, is imprisoned in a Christian church!

Zerubavel fulfills the prophecy in Isaiah by hiding his face from the Messiah, but then the figure before him is transformed into a "young man of unsurpassed beauty."[26] Would it be going too far to see in these lines a kind of erotic attraction to the figure of the Messiah? As we shall see, this desire would have its counterpart in Armilus.

Two other messianic figures are then introduced. The first is the mother of the Messiah, Hephzibah, the same name as the wife of the biblical King Hezekiah. In this, as well as in the Messiah's name, Menachem ben Ammiel, there are hints of the rabbinic traditions that associated the Messiah with King Hezekiah.[27] In this case, the implication is that the biblical Hephzibah, who is known to us in the Bible only as the mother of the evil King Menasseh, actually had a second son who was hidden away as the future Messiah. Alternatively, the name Hephzibah is associated with the messianic days in Isaiah 62:4, in which Israel's name will be changed to Hephzibah at the end of time.

In any event, the mother of the Messiah plays a very important role in the *Sefer Zerubavel*, one that is unprecedented for a woman in the Jewish eschatological traditions, at least until Shabbtai Zvi.[28] Hephzibah is given the staff of Aaron, which the rabbis believed would become the Messiah's scepter. With this staff, she plays a leading role in the battle against the Jews' enemies. In one version, she kills two kings. Hephzibah combines the biblical roles of Deborah and Yael from the book of Judges, both leading the Jews and personally slaying their enemies.

Like Deborah, Hephzibah shares leadership in these exploits with a man, Nehemiah ben Hushiel, identified at one point as the "son of Ephraim, son of Joseph." Nehemiah is undoubtedly a version of the rabbinic Messiah son of Joseph who wages eschatological wars and falls in battle before the coming of the Messiah son of David.[29] I have no intention of entering into the scholarly sticky wicket of this "second" Messiah. However, the *Sefer Zerubavel* does not only borrow this tradition and dress it up in its own symbolism. It also adds something that, to the best of my knowledge, is not to be found in the earlier tradition: after dying in battle, Nechemiah, the Messiah son of Joseph, is resurrected in the final days by Menachem ben Ammiel and Elijah. Here one can only wonder if the Christian myth of the executed and resurrected Messiah might have served as foil for the *Sefer Zerubavel*.[30] Perhaps our apocalyptic author might have even made the obvious, if unhistorical, association between Jesus the son of Joseph and the Jewish Messiah son of Joseph. Even if not, it is still quite possible that, just as the *Sefer Zerubavel* gave the Messiah son of David certain Christ-like features, so it attributed to the Messiah son of Joseph the death and resurrection of the Christian savior. Once again, we have evidence of the theft of Christian themes, even where they have Jewish antecedents, for Jewish apocalyptic purposes.

Once it had emptied the Christian Messiah of all his traits and attributed them to the two Jewish Messiahs, the *Sefer Zerubavel* could turn Jesus himself into the monstrous Armilus. This it does in the birth story of Armilus, in which the adulterous birth of Jesus in the *Toldot Yeshu* is transformed into myth. Zerubavel is once again transported into a *bet ha-toref*, where he sees a stone idol in the image of a beautiful woman: "And anyone who gets up the courage to look at her cannot do so, because no man can look in her face due to her beauty." Here the Virgin Mary is turned into a kind of satanic seductress. Zerubavel learns that Satan has had intercourse with this idol, which then gave birth to Armilus.

There is, then, a certain symmetry between the Messiah and his mother, Hephzibah, on the one hand, and Armilus and his stone mother, on the other. In both cases Zerubavel encounters both the Messiah and the idol in a church, and in both cases there is erotic attraction, the first homoerotic and positive, and the second heterosexual and dangerous. The connection between idolatry and illicit heterosexuality has deep roots already in the biblical tradition, as, for example, in the archetypal story of Zimri in Numbers 25, where the cultic practice of idolatry involves a sexual orgy. The *Sefer Zerubavel*'s association of the "house of idolatry" and "vagina" recapitulates this theme by suffusing the Byzantine Church with all the pejorative pollution associated in rabbinic tradition with female genitalia. As do earlier Jewish writers, the author of our text sexualizes the idolatry he identifies with Christianity. In so doing, he inverts the image of Mary from virgin to whore.

The two mothers also both play active roles in the war of Armageddon. In its effort to counter and invert the Christian traditions of Mary, the *Sefer Zerubavel* gives an unprecedented role to a Jewish woman in the redemptive process but, intentionally or not, elevates the role of the satanic Christian woman as well. This parallelism may have its source in the political role of the Virgin Mary in Byzantium. As Vasiliki Limberis has shown, Mary was identified with the fifth-century Byzantine princess Pulcheria, who established several churches dedicated to her.[31] From this point onwards, the imperial cult of Byzantium was inextricably linked to the deified Virgin. Icons of Mary came to be used to protect cities or armies; Emperor Heraklios, who is almost certainly the Armilus of the *Sefer Zerubavel*, was known to have carried a statue of the Virgin into battle. As Martha Himmelfarb has observed: "If, as seems likely, our author was aware of this practice, the military role assigned to Hephzibah represents an attempt to offer a Jewish answer to the Virgin."[32]

There is an additional symmetry as well. The Messiah son of Joseph is slain by Siroe, the king of Persia, a historical figure who killed his father and reigned for less than a year (it is the time of his reign that made it possible for Israel Levi to date the *terminus a quo* of the text as 628–29 and to argue that the author had to have lived close to this time and before the Muslim invasion). The complex historical situation in Palestine in this period found the Jews squeezed between a hostile Persian king and Heraclius, the emperor of Byzantium. A quasi-alliance between the two is reflected in the text. In killing the Messiah son of Joseph, the Persian king thus acts as a kind of "Antichrist son of Joseph," that is, a secondary figure in the pantheon of Antichrists parallel to the Messiah son of Joseph as secondary to the Messiah son of David. The polemic of the *Sefer Zerubavel* therefore operates with a series of symmetries between the forces of light and the forces of darkness.

It is no surprise that an apocalyptic text might have polemical intentions, as Moritz Steinschneider already noticed in the nineteenth century when he included the *Sefer Zerubavel* in a collection of "Apocalypses with Polemical Tendencies."[33] The nature of apocalypses is to divide the world into the "children of light" and "children of darkness," and the satanic forces are never just generic but always refer as well to a specific enemy. The dualistic nature of history in apocalyptic thought also feeds this tendency, creating a "counterideology," as Amos Funkenstein called it, of the sect as opposed to its opponents. It is for these reasons that apocalypses are one of the most fruitful genres for counterhistory, for the apocalyptic writer seeks a world "turned upside down." This does not, however, mean that every apocalypse is necessarily a counterhistory. What we find in the *Sefer Zerubavel* is the required additional ingredient: the appropriation of the enemy's most beloved images for one's own purpose and the transformation of the enemy into the very force that the enemy itself regards as satanic. So the *Sefer Zerubavel* takes the figure of the suffering, dying, and resurrected Messiah from Christianity as its model and leaves the Messiah of Christianity a hideous monster born of the union of an idol and the devil.

As bitingly satirical as are the stories in the *Toldot Yeshu*, they seem relatively defanged in contrast to the savage inversions of the *Sefer Zerubavel*, which bears a message far more systematically subversive. Yet Jews and non-Jews alike have regarded the *Toldot Yeshu* as the epitome of Jewish anti-Christian counterhistory, while the *Sefer Zerubavel*, its message cloaked in esoteric symbols, has generally not been given its polemical due. Indeed, seeing how apocalypses function as polemics adds a new social dimension to their eschatological speculations. If, as Amos Funkenstein argued, a counterhistory is designed to rob the Other of his identity, the apocalypse more than the folk tale accomplishes this purpose most thoroughly. And if the counterhistorian must necessarily end up basing his own identity on that of the Other, the *Sefer Zerubavel* demonstrates how much Jewish apocalypticism owes to its Christian enemy. The *Sefer Zerubavel* thus emerges as a perfect case of Amos Funkenstein's abiding interest in the singular entanglement of the Jewish and Christian traditions, an interest that he pursued with profound knowledge of both sides of the polemical barricades.

Moreover, in the *Sefer Zerubavel* we find a new form of the polemical exploitation of history for ideological purposes: history not as *past* but as *fictitious future*, that singular reorientation of time with which an apocalypse puts historical events into the prophetic mouth of an ancient source. In this way, the understanding of apocalypse as historical polemic adds another dimension to Amos Funkenstein's discovery of the surreptitious functions of historical consciousness in the Jewish tradition, the central theme of his synoptic *Perceptions of Jewish History*.

CHAPTER 4

"The Torah Speaks the Language of Human Beings"

Abraham Ibn Ezra's Radical Interpretation of the Bible

AMONG MEDIEVAL JEWISH BIBLE COMMENTATORS, none anticipated modern biblical criticism as closely as the twelfth-century Spanish philosopher, poet, astrologer, traveler, and exegete Abraham Ibn Ezra. While this fact has been noted in passing by commentators since the seventeenth century, no one has attempted to reconstruct Ibn Ezra's radical exegetical method from his often-obscure commentaries.[1] Like modern critics, Ibn Ezra detected possible interpolations in the Pentateuch that raise questions about Moses's authorship. He further evolved a theory of immanent *literalist* criticism and rejected reading the Bible with philosophical presuppositions. He appropriated the dictum "The Bible speaks the language of human beings" in order to explain difficulties that other commentators, while using the same expression, allegorized to suit their philosophies. But in contrast to the biblical criticism that began with Spinoza in the seventeenth century, Ibn Ezra did not want so much to sever the Bible entirely from philosophical speculations as to harmonize it with the Neoplatonic and Aristotelian vocabulary with which he operated.[2] By selective application of science to scripture, Ibn Ezra tried to save the Bible from a scientific critique. As we shall see, the complex rejection and application of philosophy in exegesis was expressed by Ibn Ezra in a theory that the Bible represents a *dual perspective*: human and divine, colloquial and philosophical.

Our reconstruction of Ibn Ezra's exegesis will take the following form: we will first discuss some features of his exegetical theory, primarily his discovery of interpolations and his rejection of philosophical allegories. We will then point out the difficulties and ambiguities in the method and, finally, attempt to resolve them with recourse to Ibn Ezra's cosmology.

THE EXEGETICAL THEORY OF IMMANENT CRITICISM

In his commentary on Deuteronomy 1:1–3, Ibn Ezra lists a number of obscure passages in the Bible that might be interpreted as interpolations.[3] For example, in his commentary on Genesis 12:6, Ibn Ezra notes that the passage "And the Canaanite was *then* in the land" can be construed two ways. It might refer to a relationship between past and distant past: *before* Canaanites conquered the land of Canaan, there were other inhabitants. Or "There is a great mystery and the wise will remain silent." The mystery is not difficult to guess: the passage might refer to a relation between the present and past. The author wrote the verse *after* the Canaanites had been expelled from the land, namely after the death of Moses. Since the textual evidence in Genesis 10 implies that Canaan was the first to inhabit the land, Ibn Ezra seems convinced that the verse was written after the death of Moses. Indeed, there is little doubt that Ibn Ezra believed that all of the passages he lists in Deuteronomy 1:1–3 were interpolations.[4] However, as Richard Simon already pointed out in the seventeenth century and as Orthodox Jewish commentators also argue, Ibn Ezra by no means rejected Moses's authorship on the basis of these few interpolations.[5] His scathing remarks against Rabbi Yitzhak, who thought that the verse "And these are the kings who reigned in the land of Edom" (Gen. 36:31) was written during the reign of Yehoshofat, conclude that Yitzhak's blasphemous book should be burned. The best we can argue on the basis of scanty evidence is that Ibn Ezra was willing to explain certain passages by a theory of interpolation but rejected those who applied this principle of "modern criticism" too freely when another explanation might work as well. This is not the only context in which Ibn Ezra appears as a cautious radical.[6] In any case, his predilection toward unorthodox interpretations led him to include commentaries even more radical than his own, if only in order to refute them. Thanks to him, we have become aware of the startling range of opinions in the scholarly Jewish world of his time.

But Ibn Ezra's theory of interpolations is only a part of a wider theory of literal exegesis, or attempts to understand the text immanently. His rejection of excessive allegorization in favor of literal exegesis rests on an attack against some the exegetes of his day, notably a Rabbi Isaac[7] and Sa'adia Gaon.[8] Excessive allegorization results from the desire to harmonize the Bible with the conclusions of medieval science and philosophy. For example, in his desire to show agreement between the biblical story of Creation and Ptolemaic astronomy, a certain Spanish scholar distorts both the literal meaning of the text and astronomical science. In discussing Genesis 1:14 ("And God said, 'Let there be lights in the sky of the heavens'"), he thinks that the sky is divided into eight spheres, seven for the planets and one for the fixed constellations. But the text plainly says that there are heavens above this sky. Now, if the Spanish commentator understands the text literally, then his cosmology is faulty, since twelfth-century cosmology did not recognize anything above the sphere of the fixed constellations. But if he wants to preserve scientific precision, he must allegorize a text that seems absolutely clear. Ibn Ezra does not oppose insertion of any scientific ideas into exegesis; rather, he objects to distorting the text by inserting science, or misinterpreting science in order to fit the text. Thus, on the same passage in Genesis: "And in this path rose Sa'adia Gaon of the Exile, and in his commentary on 'Let there be light' he inserted opinions contradicting the knowledge of astronomy according to the astronomers."[9]

Ibn Ezra's attack on the use of foreign science is part and parcel of a general criticism of excessive allegorization.[10] In opposition to those who try to fit the text to their philosophical preconceptions, "We will not search along the wall like blind men in order to pull out things according to our needs. And why should we turn the obvious into the hidden?"[11] The first task of exegesis is to discover the literal meaning of the text.[12]

Ibn Ezra accepts the medieval aversion to anthropomorphisms but rejects excessive allegorization of them. For instance, on the verse "And God said, 'Let there be light,'" Sa'adia Gaon wants to elicit proof from the text for his theory that there is no mediation between God and creation. Hence, he interprets "and God said" to mean "and God willed." Sa'adia presupposes that God's will is not mediated as an efficient cause. Ibn Ezra criticizes Sa'adia on the grounds that, grammatically, the text could not have meant "and he willed" or else it would have said, "And he said there to be" (infinitive as opposed to imperative). This ostensibly trivial grammatical point conceals a deeper argument: if the literal sense of the text contradicts a proposed allegory, then the allegory is invalid. However, far from suggesting that God actually speaks, Ibn Ezra also allegorizes the text, but not by substituting another expression. He understands the phase "God said" in everyday terms: if a king orders his servants to do something, his verbal command indicates that he need not physically exert himself. The allegory serves a pedagogical rather than philosophical purpose: to teach that no matter *how* God creates, he does not exert himself.[13] The allegory is permissible because the very usage of language in the Bible suggests it; Sa'adia's allegory imports a philosophical preconception into the text and thus distorts the literal (and grammatical) meaning of the verse.

Ibn Ezra's method is, then, one of immanent allegorization. In distinction to Sa'adia Gaon, he takes his metaphors from the language of the Bible itself, rather than substituting another, externally derived expression. Sa'adia's error is in searching for philosophical precision in the Bible. Ibn Ezra argues instead for a nontechnical exegesis: "The Bible speaks the language of human beings."[14] The application of human adjectives to God is part of the Bible's nontechnical, colloquial language. For instance, the Bible itself admits that "the Eternity of Israel will not lie or change his mind, for he is not a man to change his mind."[15] But in another place it clearly states that "God changed his mind."[16] No allegorical substitution can solve the contradiction without a gross distortion of the text; instead, Ibn Ezra explains that in the latter verse "The Bible speaks the language of human beings." We are not permitted to infer anything positive about God (for example, whether he changes his mind) from the use of any given colloquial metaphor. In fact, this dictum is the most common explanation in Ibn Ezra's commentaries for passages suggesting that God has a body[17] or emotions.[18]

Since the purpose of the Bible's author was pedagogical and not philosophical, he accommodated his work to the language and understanding of common men. The perspective from which the Bible observes the world is also human. For instance, the creation of the world must be understood from an earthly point of view: the heavens in the Creation account are merely the heavens we see, the direction upwards, and not the "heavens above the heavens" (*shmay ha'shamayim*—the supralunar world). Here again, the words *heaven* and *earth* are colloquial rather than scientific. At least in its discussion of Creation, the Bible is concerned only with the sublunar world that is observable by men; a description of the supralunar world can be found in the books of the astronomers. Only by understanding Creation from a human perspective can we account for the scientifically puzzling implication in Genesis that the moon is larger than the stars.[19] Only by our principle that the Bible speaks not just the language of human beings, but indeed from the human perspective, can we resolve the tensions between science and scripture. In answer to Sa'adia's school (and, in fact, much of medieval thought), Ibn Ezra boldly asserts that the Bible does not contain all knowledge; its pedagogical focus is man in his everyday needs. Hence, its limited scope, its earthly perspective, and its ordinary language.

To be sure, the subject matter of the Bible is holy, but its means of communication is worldly. Although excellent knowledge of Hebrew is necessary for exegesis, the status of the biblical language is no different from that of any other language. For Ibn Ezra, language is purely instrumental. No philosophical conclusions can be drawn from minor word variations, as long as the essential meaning is preserved.[20] For instance, the differences in language between the Exodus and Deuteronomic versions of the Decalogue are differences in form but not in meaning: "Know that the words are like bodies and the meanings are like souls and the relation of the body to the soul is like a tool."[21] Ibn Ezra's doctrine that the Bible speaks the language of men is a commentary on language itself. Man uses metaphors that are taken "neither from the worlds above him nor below him." Hence, such expressions as "the mouth of the earth" and "the hand of the Jordan."[22] The search for knowledge begins with man himself: "The principle is: how can man search to know what is above him if he doesn't know his own body and soul."[23] The Bible is the beginning of all knowledge, but it is not in itself all knowledge.

We are now in a better position to understand Ibn Ezra's rejection of philosophical allegories in favor of immanent metaphors. Unlike a univocal philosophical vocabulary, the biblical language is ambiguous like any other ordinary language. Only when an ambiguity in language exists is allegorization permissible, and then the nonliteral meaning must be taken from the Bible's own use of language. For instance, the verse on circumcision of the flesh defines circumcision. But the phrase "uncircumcised of the heart" (Deut. 10:16) contradicts man's reason, since literal circumcision of the heart would clearly be fatal. Now, in order to avoid this absurdity, the terms *heart* and *circumcision* must be understood as ambiguous: they can stand for thoughts (i.e., as metaphors) as well as for their literal significations. This allegory is suggested by the biblical language itself, which often uses parts of the body to refer to two things (the actual organ and something metaphorically implied). Similarly, the Tree of Knowledge is puzzling, for surely Adam and Eve were created with some faculty of reason. But in biblical Hebrew *knowledge* is an ambiguous expression, since it can also stand for carnal knowledge. The only way to understand the passage is by means of the second, metaphorical meaning.[24] In both cases, man's reason acts as a negative litmus test to determine where there is an absurdity and where to suspect an ambiguity.

To conclude our reconstruction of Ibn Ezra's method, we have seen how the doctrine that the Bible speaks the language of human beings provides an alternative to philosophical allegorization of the Bible, while still avoiding unthinking literalism. Given Ibn Ezra's belief in the fundamentally human nature of the scriptures, it is no surprise that he suggested (implicitly) a historical approach to the question of the Bible's authorship in its hints of interpolations.

TENSION IN THE METHOD

The particular linguistic analysis necessary for the literal understanding of the Bible is based on a faculty of reason that can detect the ambiguities of biblical language. We have called this a *negative* litmus test for immanent ambiguities: reason does not dictate what the text should say, as Sa'adia would have it, but rather detects where the text is problematic, contradicting man's reason: "Every matter of a commandment, small or large, is weight on the scales of the heart, since there is in the heart a faculty of reasoning implanted from the wisdom of God. And, if reason will not tolerate the matter, or if it contradicts the evidence of the senses, then it is permissible to search for an allegory."²⁵ What is the nature of this faculty of reasoning (*shikul ha-da'at*) that is necessary for exegesis? Is it the property of the philosophic elite or of all human beings? If we examine the above statement from Ibn Ezra's Introduction to the Pentateuch, we are puzzled by the use of the word *heart*. Does it refer metaphorically to the highest soul (*neshama eliyona*), as it does in his commentary on Genesis 1:1?²⁶ Or does it refer literally to the physical organ? An examination of the other texts gives us the answer that it is, indeed, the second, literal meaning. Basing himself on Sa'adia's tripartite correspondence of parts of the body to psychological faculties, Ibn Ezra writes in his commentary to Exodus 23:25–26: "The *neshama* is wisdom, and it is situated in the brain.... The spirit [*ruah*] is in the heart and man lives through it, and it is the faculty that seeks strength to overcome all that stand against it and it is the master of anger ... and the *nefesh* is in the liver and it is the urge to eat." Furthermore, we learn from the commentary on Ecclesiastes 7:3 that "man has three souls. One is the vegetable soul, ... and it is the soul of desire and need to drink and eat. The second soul is the animal soul, and it is the seat of the five senses and of locomotion, and this soul is also in man. But only man has the third soul, which is called *neshama*; it distinguishes between truth and falsehood and is the seat of wisdom. The second soul is the intermediary between the two other souls, and God gave *reasoning* to man, which is called 'heart.'" *Heart*, then, is a precise term for the second soul, which governs the senses and the passions. Apparently, *shikul ha-da'at* is a type of practical reasoning that coordinates the evidence of the senses (*common sense* in the medieval use of the term). This faculty is universal: "the reasoning ability that God has implanted in the heart of every man."²⁷ Yet the wisdom to distinguish between truth and falsehood is situated in the brain, and although perhaps present *in potentia* in all men, it is developed only in the philosopher. There is, then, a distinction between two types of reasoning and, by implication, two types of knowledge: philosophical speculation that leads to knowledge of truths, and practical reason, which provides, among other things, a universal moral sensibility.²⁸ It is this latter *shikal ha-da'at* that is necessary for exegesis. As we have noted, it is not a positive philosophic reasoning but a universal sensitivity to what is ambiguous in ordinary language.

Can a person with a good knowledge of Hebrew then be a perceptive biblical interpreter? The truth is not that simple. As we have already seen, limited allegorization is permissible in the case of crude anthropomorphisms ("And God *said*, 'Let there be light'"). But does a conception of God without human characteristics belong to common knowledge or only to philosophers? If all people possessed an abstract notion of God, then the "language of human beings" would have no recourse to anthropomorphisms at all in describing God. Clearly, Ibn Ezra did not hold that all humans innately know God to be without human features; this knowledge is a *secret* possession of philosophers. If this is the case, then it seems that Ibn Ezra does not rigorously maintain his distinction between philosophical and practical reasoning; philosophical preconceptions *are* allowed to dictate exegesis in detecting anthropomorphisms.

Our suspicion of a possible ambiguity in Ibn Ezra is reinforced when we find that certain passages of the Bible are comprehensible, in his view, only with the aid of scientific philosophy. For example, in his commentary on Psalm 19:2–8, he claims that the text is obscure without the aid of astronomy: "'The heavens relate the glory of God and the sky tells of the work of his hands'—this psalm is very honored and it is connected with the workings of the heavens, and now I will explain it briefly, but he who has not learned astronomy will not understand it." Unquestionably, the meaning of the word *heavens* is different in Genesis and in Psalms, since in one it is limited to the visible sky, and thus precludes the aid of astronomy, while in the other it requires it. While in the first, the literal meaning of the text is obscured by the insertion of a scientific discourse, in the second, it is meaningless without it. In the first the word has vernacular meaning, while in the second it has a technical scientific sense. In this latter case, reason, as Ibn Ezra has defined it, is insufficient for understanding the passage; external scientific knowledge is required. Moreover, in this passage at least, the Bible speaks from a *heavenly* rather than *human* perspective.[29] Our faith in the consistency of meaning is undermined by this sudden switch in perspective and vocabulary.

RESOLUTION OF THE TENSIONS: THE DUAL-PERSPECTIVE DOCTRINE

We have discovered a serious tension and potential inconsistency in Ibn Ezra's exegesis between the rejection of philosophy and use of philosophy; at times, it seems, the Bible speaks in the vernacular language, while at other times it uses words in a precise technical fashion. I shall try to prove that this *dual perspective* is a result of the very nature of the cosmos as Ibn Ezra understood it and that it becomes consistent only once we understand his cosmology.

In Ibn Ezra's cosmos there are three worlds, arranged hierarchically: upper, middle, and lower.[30] The upper world is that of the incorporeal angels, who control the other two worlds.[31] The middle world (supralunar) contains the spheres of the stars and the planets. Each sphere is controlled by an intelligence or angel and obeys fixed laws. The combination of the planets and constellations in different configurations directly influences events in the sublunar, or lower, world: "The middle world of the stars and planets has many changes, due to which creatures in the lower world change in their essences and also in their accidents. But the essences and the light [i.e., accidents] of the bodies of the middle world do not change."[32] The sublunar world is fundamentally different from the supralunar world, since its four elements are continually subject to dissolution and recombination; the sublunar world is characterized by change, while the upper worlds are characterized by permanence.[33] In another formulation, "The general is preserved while the particular is lost."[34] The term *general* here refers to both the form of a species and the laws that govern it; *particular* signifies the accidents that distinguish one individual in a species from another (i.e., the tangible modifications of the essence such as shape and color). Now, as we have seen above, the source of these accidents is also the constellations: "The stars are the cause of visible images."[35] But they are transmitted to the sublunar world indirectly, by mediation of the moon.[36] Somewhere in the process of mediation, the fixed number of combinations of the constellations proliferates into an infinite variety of accidental possibilities in the sublunar world: "Although I cannot count the individuals [in the sublunar world], their genera [in the supralunar] are preserved, known, and counted."[37]

This apparent tension between the finitude of forms and the infinitude of individuals in the sublunar world is reflected in the Bible itself.[38] In his interpretation of Ecclesiastes 1, Ibn Ezra agrees with the pessimistic passage "There is nothing new under the sun." But on Psalm 19:3, he gives a mathematical analogy to the constant flux of the world, an arithmetic series that he claims cannot be predicted by a formula. So it is with the world "because there is something new every day." Nonetheless, there is no contradiction between the two passages: "And there is no claim that Ecclesiastes contradicts this, since there it speaks of the general [*klal*]."[39] The Bible speaks from two different but noncontradictory perspectives: "The movements of the spheres are fixed from one perspective and changing from another; they move on straight paths *in relation to themselves* and not on straight paths *from the viewpoint of the inhabitants of the earth*."[40] From the perspective of the general (the supralunar world), the stars are fixed, their combinations infinite, their paths constant; from the perspective of earth, their combinations are infinite and their paths variable.

The laws of nature that we derive by observing the world around us are relative because they are prejudiced by our limited perspective. However, the objective laws of nature, derived through philosophical reasoning, may seem to contradict our observable laws. Nonetheless, we are dealing, not with two contradictory set of laws, but instead with two perspectives. Consider the following analogy: Newtonian physics is a precise description of rectilinear motion on earth. But applied to motion in space approaching the speed of light, it is inadequate. From a *general* perspective, Newtonian physics appears to contradict Einsteinian physics. From an earthly perspective, it is a sufficiently accurate approximation. A similar principle applies to the Bible itself. Certain passages allude to the *general*, while others refer to the *part* or human perspective. To return to a previous example, the moon is called one of the "greater luminaries" from the viewpoint of man. Similarly, David is called *gadol* (large) by Samuel in relation to his brothers, not because of his physical size, but by virtue of his moral stature.[41] Size has two meanings: technical (absolute physical dimensions) and relative-metaphorical. The colloquial usage derives from man's subjective perception, whether of the moon or King David. Hence, if one should ask: "Haven't the astronomers shown that all the stars with the exception of Venus are larger than the moon, and yet it is written 'the large luminaries,'?" the answer is that the meaning of "large" is not by virtue of the physical body but only because of the light.[42]

The relation of man to an object is through perception of its accidents: "The senses perceive the accidents,"[43] and "The eye does not see the sun but the rays emitted by it."[44] The limit on man's ability to perceive the *klal* (the general) is part of the limit on his practical reason, namely, that his information comes through his senses. His knowledge of the supralunar world is indirect. That which appears to be changing in the constellations is really just a change in the perceiver himself: "The changes in causes are a result of changes in the nature of the perceiver, and the thoughts of each man change according to the nature of his body . . . [as affected] by the constellations . . . and the states . . . and foods."[45] This geographical and dietary explanation for different mentalities also explains why men have different conceptions of God. Since God is one, "foreign gods" must refer to a distorted but not necessarily completely false concept of God. Interestingly, Ibn Ezra hints that the physical conditions of the land of Israel may allow a purer perception of God there than in other places.[46]

Everyday language is drawn from this ethnographic perspective: since human beings perceive only the accidents tangible in the sublunar world, their language is drawn from their images of that world. Hence, the names of God that describe his perceivable attributes (Shaddai, Elohim) are borrowed from the language of human beings as opposed to God's essential name (YHVH).[47] The language of the Bible is an accommodation to man's limited perception. But since perception varies according to geographical factors, it is likely that colloquial language also varies according to location. Much of the Bible—and particularly certain of its commandments—is accommodated to the specific understanding of the Jews and their language.[48]

But is man forever doomed to his shadowy cave, incapable of understanding the fixed laws that govern the perceived chaos of his world? Certainly not. The philosopher is able to view the universe from a universal perspective and to grasp the laws of the supralunar world that govern the sublunar world. Knowledge of the sciences is necessary for man to rise above his human perspective and reach God. Certain passages in the Bible teach us that the way to God lies in progressive accumulation of knowledge: "'Let us pursue knowledge of God because his origin is like the dawn'—pursuit of knowledge of God is the secret of all the sciences, and only for this reason was man created. But he cannot know God until he has learned many sciences, which are like a ladder that rises to the highest level. And the meaning of 'dawn' is that in the beginning, the wise men will know God by his deeds [i.e., events in the sublunar world] like the dawn, and, minute after minute, the light grows until he knows the truth."[49]

Humans need not remain landlocked because they are not merely creatures of the sublunar world. As man is a "microcosm of the universe,"[50] his highest soul corresponds to the soul of God, while his vegetative soul corresponds to the sublunar, material world. The process of overcoming the lower soul is often dialectical, since the principle of one soul may be the very opposite of its competitor. Hence, Ecclesiastes says that "anger is better than joy" but also that "anger is the providence of fools." Yet the two passages are not contradictory, says Ibn Ezra in response to rabbinical objections.[51] The first refers to the conflict between the joyful vegetative soul and the angry animal soul. The accumulation of knowledge corresponds to a progressive purging of passions from the soul until one reaches the ideal of contemplation.

But philosophical contemplation is not itself knowledge of God; the philosopher cannot by himself attain this knowledge. The best he can hope for is a stoic resignation to the determined actions of the constellations: "The philosopher who has no inheritance of money will be happy in his knowledge and will not be angry at his poverty because his destiny was already decreed from the creation of the world . . . and he who has a corrupt horoscope in matters of money or other matters has no redress."[52] At this stage in our inquiry, it seems as if an unbridgeable chasm lies between the human and philosophical perspectives. While the uneducated man makes value judgments about events in the sublunar world, the philosopher understands that "the constellations were not created to do good or evil, but they only proceed in their course."[53] While for the uneducated, miracles are possible, the philosopher recognizes that all changes in our world are explainable by laws. The common person thinks she sees God's hand in the world, but the philosopher tells her that she is simply ignorant of astrology.

It is certainly true that Ibn Ezra tries to explain miracles as unusual, but still natural, phenomena. For example, he explains the parting of the Red Sea by a meteorological theory. In his discussion of the "wind of God" in

Genesis 1:1, the wind is to be understood literally; God uses the wind as his angel or messenger. With the exception of the creation of human beings, the creation of the sublunar world is a natural separation and reordering of the already-existing four elements. Ibn Ezra's treatment of the word *creation* (*briyah*) hints that it means molding or cutting from preexistent matter, rather than *creatio ex nihilo*. The "letters and signs" that are so often taken to be miracles are only apparently so in the lower world. They therefore do not appear in texts such as Ecclesiastes, which are concerned with the fixed laws of the upper worlds.[54] Those miracles often associated with the prophets are usually just natural *signs*, which do not contradict natural law.[55]

Are miracles then simply an illusion of the human perspective? Ibn Ezra's negative answer to this question lies at the heart of his attempt to synthesize the human and universal perspectives in a religious vision of exegesis. According to Ibn Ezra, the totality of the universe includes a principle higher than even the constellations and their governing intelligences. This is the "essential name of God acting as an attribute name."[56] God can intervene in the operation of general providence and thus improve or damage the fate of an individual: "God said to Abraham before 'I will multiply your seed,' 'I am El Shaddai,' which means the director of the highest constellations. Not that he alters the constellations, only when a man knows and adheres to his name, he will do him good that is not in his constellation ... and that is the secret of the whole Torah."[57] The value-free operation of the constellations is given value standards not only by the judgment of man but also by the action of God. An alliance between man and God against the indifferent action of the heavens is possible. However, God does not abrogate natural laws when he performs miracles, but rather circumvents or moderates them, often with the aid of natural causes.[58]

Ibn Ezra's attempt to harmonize deterministic astrology with God's special providence leads him to a reinterpretation of the rabbinical doctrine "Israel has no constellation." In the Talmudic Tractate Shabbat (156a), a long discussion of the worth of astrology is concluded with the admonition to a believer in the stars: "Abandon your horoscopes, since Israel has no constellation." By implication, the rabbis rejected astrology as a form of idol worship. But according to Ibn Ezra, all nations, including Israel, are under the influence of the stars. Only Israel has the ability to escape by direct appeal to God himself. The appeal to special providence is possible only by direct communion with God, a uniting of man's reason with God's, independent of any intermediaries. Among the prophets, only Moses attained this personal contact with God. Nonetheless, Moses provided the Jews with a way of reaching God without the gift of prophecy: the Bible itself. Even the uneducated Jew who follows the commandments can apparently escape his or her predetermined fate.[59]

The God who performs miracles is not a transcendent being who suspends the fates with a bolt of lightning. Special providence is a result of the very nature of God himself: "God is one, he creates all and he is all."[60] God differs from everything in the universe in that he is the whole, while everything else is only a part. The universe is not separate from God; it *is* God. The angels discussed in Genesis 1:1 (*Elohim*) are not just natural phenomena harnessed as God's messengers. Because they carry God's name ("My name is in him"), they are emanations of God.[61] At this juncture, Ibn Ezra falls squarely in the Neoplatonic tradition in which the universe emanates from God.

We can now understand the peculiar relationship between those names of God drawn anthropomorphically from the sublunar world and the essence of God. "A speaker cannot compare the works of God to anything else except his works, since everything is his works."[62] When we describe God with anthropomorphisms, we do not contradict God's essence, because those accidental terms are reflections or emanations of his essence. Hence, anthropomorphisms are not total falsehoods. They express a partial view of God, since, indeed, every element of the universe is part of God. On a pedagogical level, the language of men has a limited (although crucial) status. But philosophically, everyday language is as important as a technical, scientific vocabulary, only its object is this sublunar world.

While the individual part of the universe consists of necessary essence and contingent accidents, only God is necessarily both essence and accidents together. From an earthly perspective, change is a perception of new accidents. But in relation to God, change is essential. This is what Ibn Ezra means when he says that "the part cannot change the part, only the whole can change the part."[63] In this sense, the astrologer may predict the future as Balaam does, but he cannot change fate; only the man of faith, in his communion with the whole, can evoke miracles. When linked by faith to God, our perceptions of infinite multiplicity and change in this world are not illusions but an integral part of God's dialectical emanations into parts of the universe. Only by starting with the earthly perspective of biblical knowledge can human beings rise to knowledge of the supralunar spheres. Only by dialectically combining both types of knowledge can they overcome fate and unite themselves with the whole of the universe.

We have now reached the end of our effort to reconstruct Ibn Ezra's exegetical theory on the background of his philosophy. We are in a position to understand the doctrine of accommodation as a synthesis between the human and cosmological perspectives. The Bible contains certain passages where cosmological knowledge is necessary for exegesis, while other passages must be understood in everyday language. However, our ability to distinguish between the two perspectives depends on our understanding of philosophical truths. We know that the Creation account must be understood as the creation of only the sublunar world, because philosophy describes the supralunar world and we do not find it in the literal story before us. Ibn Ezra's exegetical theory is built on a circular argument: to understand the pedagogical parts of the Bible, one does not need philosophy, but philosophical knowledge is necessary to discover which passages require philosophy and which do not. To follow the Bible's teaching, and thus circumvent astrological fate, one need not be a philosopher. But the biblical commentator who teaches the common people how to read the Bible requires a philosophical education. The Bible does not contain all knowledge, but neither, for that matter, does philosophy. Only a synthesis of the two brings salvation.

CHAPTER 5

Between Melancholy and a Broken Heart

A Note on Rabbi Nahman of Bratslav's Depression

THE CORRELATION BETWEEN AFFECTIVE DISORDERS and creative genius now seems reasonably well established.[1] While by no means all creative spirits suffer from disturbances of mood, and, conversely, not all victims of such disease are geniuses, there nevertheless appears to be a strong, if still-unexplained, causal relationship between elevations and depressions of mood and creativity. Perhaps a relatively greater amount of attention has been paid to bipolar disorders—commonly called manic-depression—than to unipolar (depression), since it is easier to understand how manic and hypomanic states might lead to outbursts of creativity, while major depression would seem by its very definition to preclude the kind of mental exertion necessary for artistic, intellectual, or spiritual expression. But for those who experience episodes of depression with partial remissions, it may be possible to plumb the depths of melancholy and to turn the experience into expression and representation. In some cases, the very transformation of the experience into expression may itself constitute at least a transient cure.[2]

In the sphere of religious spirituality, depression may play a particularly important role, since it can provide a gifted spiritual person with acute insight into the nature of suffering. By turning individual experience into theology, he or she may be able to give meaning to a universal human condition. In this way, a psychological condition that we might call a deviation from the norm—a "disorder"—may become the source for understanding and responding to what is existentially universal. From this point of view, psychological analysis of a religious figure does not diminish the resonance of his or her creative insight but, on the contrary, exposes the dialectical relationship between individual pathology and universal experience.

The figure in the history of the Jewish religion who perhaps lends himself best to such an analysis is Nahman of Bratslav (1772–1810), the great-grandson of the Baal Shem Tov, the putative founder of Hasidism. Nahman founded his own sect of Hasidism, which continues to this day as a virtually unique, even paradoxical phenomenon: a Hasidic sect without a living charismatic leader.[3] Nahman's teachings focused deeply on his own inner struggles, many of them around questions of sexuality and the body. He subjected his own shifting moods to profound analysis and tried to understand them in terms of the Kabbalistic theology that permeated Hasidism. While he did not necessarily prescribe that his followers emulate his own tormented soul, his psychological struggles were obviously viewed as very significant by his Hasidim. Thus, in one place, he remarks: "Do not learn from me as I appear. Even though you generally see me with a sad demeanor, you should not copy this.... In truth I am happy. It is only because I am clearing a path for you in the wilderness, cutting away the underbrush, [that I appear this way]."[4] The "true zaddik," as Nahman frequently referred to himself, takes on the suffering of the world and, through his suffering, gives meaning to the human condition. Not without justification, many twentieth-century Jewish thinkers, including Martin Buber,[5] have seen Nahman as a precursor to contemporary religious existentialism.

Since Nahman made his own moods so central to his teachings, his biographers have a wealth of reasonably reliable information for describing his psychological condition. While attempts at psychoanalytic study have not been lacking,[6] the most cautious of modern commentators have been content to describe his pathology without necessarily identifying its cause. Thus, Joseph Weiss, who pioneered the critical study of Bratslav Hasidism, claimed that Nahman was a manic-depressive and that the dialectic in his theology between opposing principles reflects the movement in his soul between these two poles.⁷ Arthur Green, in his magnificent biography of Nahman, *Tormented Master*, generally avoids a clinical diagnosis, but his reading seems to emphasize more the persistent guilt, self-doubt, and depression that recur in the sources.⁸ Whatever Nahman's precise diagnosis, there can be little doubt that he did suffer from severe bouts of depression that served as an important source for much of his theology.

Hasidism is often considered a movement that elevated joy to the highest religious position. Although not every Hasidic master uniformly made joy the central principle of his teaching, Nahman must have labored under a particular burden, as the great-grandson of the Baal Shem Tov, in struggling to reconcile his own melancholia with the joy taught by his illustrious forebear. Some of Nahman's discourses seem to reflect this struggle: "The main thing is that one must struggle with all one's strength to be joyous always. It is the nature of man to be drawn into melancholy [*marah shekhorah*] and sadness [*atzvut*], because of the things that happen to him; every man is filled with sorrows. Therefore, one needs to force oneself with great strength to be joyous always."⁹ One has the impression that joy for Nahman had to be purchased with an enormous effort, that it contradicted the core of his being. Yet he must have also sensed the necessity, not only personally but also as the scion of a great Hasidic dynasty, of retaining for joy its theological pride of place.

Nahman's biographer and disciple Nathan of Nemirov attempted to understand Nahman's chronic depression as the sign of his messianic lineage and, in so doing, perhaps to harmonize it implicitly with the joy central to Hasidism: "It is known that his family was descended from the House of David. That is why they generally go about with a broken heart [*be-lev nishbar*] and without a laughing countenance. For King David wrote the Book in Psalms, the bulk of which is filled with remorseful statements that come from a broken heart; in fact, all his words are brokenhearted outcries and supplications. That is why his descendants, even now, generally have broken hearts."¹⁰ This novel analysis of King David's affective state of mind was an extraordinary attempt to identify what we might today call a genetic history of depression in the Davidic dynasty. By retrojecting Nahman's depression onto the author of Psalms, Nathan was able to turn his master's pathology into a proof of his messianic identity.

What interests me most in this quotation from Nathan of Nemirov is less the messianic association than the phrase with which Nathan describes Nahman's condition: brokenhearted (*lev nishbar*). A close reading of a number of Bratslav texts demonstrates, I believe, that Nahman attempted to solve the contradiction between his depression and the Hasidic teaching of joy by distinguishing between different types of melancholia. It would, indeed, be no surprise that someone of his remarkable sensibility suffering from chronic bouts of depression would become acutely sensitive to the gradations and colorations of his condition. In making these kinds of distinctions Nahman was attempting to find a spiritual solution to the demons that plagued his soul.

In the passage quoted above in which Nahman prescribes the necessity of forcing oneself to live in joy despite the sorrows of daily existence, he continues: "Nevertheless, a broken heart is also a very good thing, even though for a limited time. It is desirable therefore to fix a particular time of the day to break one's heart and to commune with God, as is our practice. But for the rest of the day, one should be in joy, since a broken heart can easily become melancholy [*marah shekhorah*]."[11] Nahman is referring here to the Bratslav practice of *hitboddedut* or solitary prayer, during which the adept would seclude himself, often in nature, and address God directly. This prayer would typically take the form of shouts and cries rather than coherent words, and it was the occasion for a kind of emotive confession in front of God. The essence of such prayer, for Nahman, was the broken heart. Only when one experiences the sorrow of the broken heart can one address God from the depths of one's soul. It is particularly fascinating that Nahman uses the transitive "to break one's heart" to describe how one engages in *hitboddedut*. One must induce this affective state at will during a defined period each day. In this way, what must have been originally, for Nahman himself, a means of externalizing his feelings of depression now became a practice even for those who might not be experiencing depression themselves. Indeed, this term became a virtual emblem of the Bratslav sect; even today, one can find Bratslav bumper stickers in Jerusalem that read: "There is nothing more whole than a broken heart."[12]

Nahman is, however, very concerned to prevent the deliberate state of brokenheartedness from becoming full-fledged depression or melancholy (*marah shekhorah*, which literally means "black bile"). The two are obviously related, but while the former is a positive or useful emotion, the latter is extraordinarily dangerous. In fact, Nahman repeatedly refers to sadness (*atzvut*) or melancholy as a force that is "very destructive [*mezik*] and gives power to that evil inclination [*yetzer ha-ra*] which is coarse materiality."[13] Given the associations of the evil inclination and materiality with uncontrolled sexual desire for rabbinic culture in general and for Nahman in particular, this passage suggests that the sexual forces that Nahman feared so much and that he struggled so hard to subdue were linked in his mind with the evil side of his depression.[14]

In another text, Nahman spells out in more detail the difference between these two types of depression:

> A broken heart and sadness are not the same thing at all, since a broken heart is in the heart, while sadness comes from the spleen. This sadness from the spleen is the evil side [*sitra ahra*], and God hates it, while a broken heart is favored by God, since a broken heart is very, very dear to God. . . . .
>
> The one who experiences sadness is like one who is angry and raging against God for not fulfilling his wishes. But he who has a broken heart is like . . . a baby who whines and cries when his father leaves him.[15]

Following medieval psychology, the black bile (*marah shekhorah*) of melancholy or sadness comes from the spleen. The heart, on the other hand, is the seat of emotions and is the organ through which one communicates directly with God. Nahman clearly holds that the emotions connected with a broken heart can lead to melancholy, although he does not furnish a physiology for this progression. But the two are essentially different. Melancholy is associated with anger, a profound insight into the nature of depression.

Brokenheartedness, on the other hand, is sorrowful and is connected with a sense of abandonment by God, similar to the abandonment of the child by its father. This particular emotion is positive and useful because it serves as the springboard for trying to recapture intimacy with the transcendent God. As has been extensively documented, this was the great theological challenge that Nahman sought to overcome.[16] As opposed to other forms of Hasidism that emphasized God's immanence, even to the point of pantheism, Nahman's theology was plagued by doubts arising from God's seeming absence. The sense of abandonment or brokenheartedness that the adept experiences within his own soul can be harnessed as a spiritual force for seeking this absent God. Indeed, God loves this emotion because it brings the worshipper into proper communion with him. Although it might have been desirable to try to maintain this feeling throughout the day, so that one would always experience the alienation of an absent God, Nahman limits it to the set hour of *hitboddedut* lest it open the door to the destructive forces of melancholy.

In using the term *broken heart* to refer specifically to abandonment by the beloved parent, Nahman may have intuited what James Masterson has called "abandonment depression."[17] This is depression that results from an early experience of abandonment by a parent and that often manifests itself in a splitting between a "real self" and a "false self." The false self is a construct to defend against the feelings of abandonment, and it is often perceived to be waging war on the true self. Without entering into what would be a fruitless search for causes in Nahman's early life, it may well be that the struggles that Nahman describes between his twin natures as zaddik and as sinner reflect just such a war between true and false selves. If so, then his persistent guilt, loathing of his body, and preoccupation with death may all be linked to the abandonment depression he describes as a broken heart.

The distinction that Nahman draws between melancholy and a broken heart may point to a difference in gradation between depression so deep as to paralyze, on the one hand, and a less severe depression, technically labeled "dysthymia,"[18] in which one experiences a sense of loss and alienation but not the full paralysis of major depression. In such a dysthymic state, one might still be able to mobilize the affective disorder against itself by turning the sense of despair into a vehicle for overcoming despair. This is the practice that Nahman developed for the hour of *hitboddedut*, first for himself and then, by extension, for his Hasidim.

The mobilization of one's moods during *hitboddedut* requires a set of physical practices that resemble the Tantric goal of emptying the body of all feeling.[19] The adept emits groans and sighs (*krekhtzin* in Yiddish) while, for instance, holding his hand on table until he is unable to lift the hand from the table. In this way, he separates himself from the physicality of his hand. He then proceeds to carry out this procedure with each external limb of the body. By emptying the life force from the external limbs, one also affects the internal organs of the body. In the end, one empties the blood (that is, the life force) from one's heart until the heart becomes an empty chamber (*halal be-kirbi*). This procedure is clearly very dangerous, since one verges on death in this exalted state. Since Nahman elsewhere equates melancholy with death,[20] it seems that the practice is designed to gain control of the fear of death by deliberately simulating a near-death experience. Given Nahman's hostility toward the body, the technique also promises a kind of pure spirituality within this material world.

This Tantric-like practice is related directly to the type of depression Nahman calls "brokenheartedness," as he reveals in a parable that he tells in the middle of the text on *hitboddedut*.[21] The parable concerns a king who sends his son out to learn wisdom. When the son returns, full of wisdom, the father commands him to take a large rock, like a grinding stone, and carry it up to the attic of his house. The son is unable to fulfill his father's command and becomes very dejected over his failure. Finally, the father reveals to the son that he never intended for him to carry the stone up as it was, but rather to take a hammer and break it into small pieces that he would then be able to carry. Nahman then explains the meaning of the parable: "Similarly, God commands us to carry our hearts up to him in the heavens, but our hearts are like the heart of stone, which is very large and heavy and impossible to bring up to God in any way. We can do so only by taking a hammer and breaking and smashing the heart of stone, and then we will be able to raise it up. The hammer is speech." The hammer of speech most probably refers here not to normal speech but to the cries and groans prescribed for *hitboddedut*.

The paradox of the parable is that only he who suffers from the depression called a broken heart can commune with God. Only he who feels abandoned by God can find God. Therefore, if one's heart is not already broken, one must first break it. All the wisdom that the son has acquired, wisdom that must refer to standard rabbinic learning or perhaps even Kabbalah, is inadequate to solve the father's command. The true wisdom is the wisdom of the suffering zaddik, a wisdom earned by painful years of self-exploration and despair.

The technique of using one's broken heart as a vehicle to God cannot, however, be described as a self-cure, for the very dialectic of Nahman's theology precluded the possibility of permanently transcending the gulf between humans and God. Put differently, if Nahman was able to mobilize his depression in the service of his theology, the theology demanded that the depression not be overcome: if one's heart were no longer broken, one would have to break it anew in order to reach God. Rather than a cure, I would prefer to see this technique as a dynamic way of living with depression by erecting a high wall between the destructive and creative poles of the disease and by taking partial control of the disease through the simulation of the out-of-body and death feelings that depressives often describe as controlling them.

In his magisterial survey of the history of the Kabbalah, *Major Trends in Jewish Mysticism*, Gershom Scholem argued that rather than creating new and original forms of Kabbalah, Hasidism turned Kabbalah into a mystical psychology: "Kabbalism [became] an instrument of psychological analysis and self-knowledge."[22] By this he did not mean—as I do not here—that the profound myth of the Kabbalah was reduced to psychological states. In the case of Nahman of Bratslav, not only did Kabbalism become an instrument for self-knowledge, but also, conversely, self-knowledge became a source for what must be considered—Scholem's statement notwithstanding—an original contribution to Kabbalistic theology. As I have tried to suggest in these brief remarks on Rabbi Nahman's depression, theology may acquire its deepest meaning when it resonates against the lived experience of a spiritual genius struggling with those inner demons that are also our own.

PART TWO

AMBIVALENT MODERNITY

CHAPTER 6

The Kabbalah in Nachman Krochmal's Philosophy of History

THE EMERGENCE OF SECULAR JEWISH historiography in the beginning of the nineteenth century took place among the competing stars of ascending romanticism and waning rationalism. On the one hand, the early German Wissenschaft des Judentums must be considered a romantic movement to reconstruct the shattered Jewish identities of German Jews by recovering their lost history. To this end, the young intellectuals of the Verein für Kultur und Wissenschaft der Juden were as much attracted to suppressed and even heretical traditions within Judaism—Hellenistic Jewish philosophy, Spinozism, and the Kabbalah—as to the mainstream.[1]

At the same time, however, this movement, which gave impetus to the rise of Jewish historiography, was pulled in the other direction by the forces of eighteenth-century rationalism, under whose lengthening shadows its adherents still stood. Eager to prove that the Jews were as "rational" and "modern" as the German society they sought to enter, they searched Jewish history for rational models and tended to delegate to the dustbin those parts of the past, such as the Kabbalah, which seemed to them most alien to them and to their age. They believed that as the Jewish people progressed, they had gradually discarded expressions of "false consciousness" such as Jewish mysticism and were in the process of realizing the purely rational concept of

God that had been hidden in Judaism from the outset.² It is curious and indicative that in early nineteenth-century Germany, perhaps the most serious student of the Kabbalah was Franz Josef Molitor, a Christian deeply influenced by the mystical romanticism of Franz von Baader.³ In eastern Europe, however, where Jews were much less subject to the pressures of assimilation stemming from emancipation, the young "science of Judaism" took a more nationalist and all-inclusive form. Yet even here, such scholars as S. Y. Rappaport (1790–1831) and Judah Leib Miesis (1798–1831) took an exceedingly dim view of Jewish mysticism.⁴ In Italy, where the Jewish Enlightenment took a roughly similar course, S. D. Luzzatto—perhaps its main proponent—was as hostile toward the Kabbalah as his eastern European contemporaries.⁵ To be sure, there were significant exceptions to this rule. Eliakim Milzahgi (1780–1854) and D. H. Joel (1815–82) wrote important defenses of the Kabbalah as legitimate parts of Jewish history and theology.⁶ Milzahgi's most important work remained in manuscript and probably had little influence until the twentieth century, but Joel's attempt to demonstrate the parallels between medieval Jewish philosophy and the Kabbalah is instructive. Only by the establishment of the philosophical legitimacy of the Kabbalah could Jewish mysticism be rescued from excommunication.

Joel's treatment of the Kabbalah points to the work of the most important exception to the general hostility toward Jewish mysticism in the nineteenth century: Nachman Krochmal (1785–1840).⁷ Like Joel's, Krochmal's positive attitude toward the Kabbalah could find expression only by transforming mysticism into philosophy. Yet a study of the precise status of the Kabbalah in Krochmal's thought is of much greater interest than in the case of Joel, for Krochmal's attitudes toward irrationalism were inextricably linked to his coherent and subtle philosophical system.

Born in Galicia, where he lived his whole life, Krochmal was part of the nascent eastern European Jewish Enlightenment.⁸ He wrote exclusively in Hebrew, and his translations of the jargon of German Idealism into Hebrew served as an important conduit for the transmission of Western ideas to the East. Unlike many of his Western contemporaries, Krochmal remained Orthodox throughout his life, but he recognized that the spirit of his times was historicism, which demanded that theological commonplaces, such as the claim that the Pentateuch was the work of one author, must be subjected to historical criticism. Krochmal was equally aware that historical thinking constituted perhaps the greatest danger to traditional Judaism, for it alienated the Jew from his tradition. But he believed that only by adopting and transforming secular historical thought could traditional Judaism be defended against the attack of history. As opposed to the emerging extreme Orthodoxy of such rabbinical authorities as Moses Sofer, Krochmal realized that retreat was no solution: only by engaging the enemy with its own weapons could Judaism be saved. Without a doubt, however, Krochmal's adaption of historicism profoundly altered traditional Judaism itself in the process.

Krochmal tried to harmonize the traditional category of *netzach yisrael* (eternity of Israel), which is manifestly antihistorical, with an understanding of the Jewish people as a historical entity, as a people that changes through history. Since the Jewish people are guaranteed eternal existence even as they change, their past intellectual products must share something in common with their current self-consciousness. Even a speculative movement like the Kabbalah, which might seem particularly alien to us today, must contain some seeds of truth, since, as a product of Jewish self-consciousness, it has contributed to the preservation and development of the Jewish people. Krochmal's sympathetic treatment of the Kabbalah was, therefore, intimately related to his attempt to bridge the gap between traditional modes of thought and secularism.

I will argue in the following pages that although Krochmal did indeed accord the Kabbalah—and irrationalism generally—a more reputable place in Jewish history than did his contemporaries, his argument is laden with seeming contradictions that reflect the ambiguities of a historical approach to Judaism informed by rational idealism. The uneasy position of irrationalism in Krochmal's system illuminates the problematic nature of his attempt to rescue traditional Judaism with the weapons of its ostensible enemy, historical thought. Moreover, an examination of Krochmal's view of the status of irrationalism in Jewish history will throw light, if obliquely, on some of the inherent problems that the nineteenth-century Wissenschaft des Judentums as a whole encountered in its historical reconstruction of the Jewish experience.

THE PROBLEM

In his *Guide for the Perplexed of Our Time* (*Moreh Nevukhe Ha-Zeman*), Krochmal seems to say rather contradictory things about the Kabbalah. In chapter 6, he suggests that all speculative movements, including the Kabbalah, Gnosticism, Neoplatonism, Maimonidean philosophy, and nineteenth-century Idealism, are somehow related.[9] At one point he seems to equate the Kabbalists' "secret of the unity and the faith" (*sod ha-yihud ve-ha-emunah*) with Maimonidean philosophy and Idealism. Krochmal saw his own work as a modern-day version of Maimonides's *Guide for the Perplexed*, based, in part, on German Idealism.[10] By association with these philosophical traditions, the Kabbalah seems to gain philosophical status. Moreover, and in anticipation of Gershom Scholem's later arguments, he suggested the similarities between Gnosticism and the Kabbalah, such as their common notions of a hidden God and the hypostatization of God's attributes.[11] Since he also tried to demonstrate the connections between Gnosticism and Neoplatonism, whose metaphysics he himself partially appropriated,[12] one senses that, by implication, the Kabbalah would also have to be considered close to Neoplatonism, and therefore a respectable philosophical movement.

In other places in the *Guide*, however, Krochmal does not take such a charitable view of the Kabbalah. He opens chapter 1 with a diagnosis of three interrelated psychological maladies of religion.[13] He calls mysticism the first malady into which religion can degenerate. Mysticism by nature fosters a mad attempt at ecstatic unification with God, which in turn leads to antinomianism. It is clear that in his reference to antinomianism as the inevitable result of mysticism, Krochmal had in mind the Sabbatian movement of the seventeenth century. Although in chapter 1 of the *Guide* he gives only an ahistorical typology of religious degeneration, he suggests elsewhere that Sabbatianism, the most cogent example of antinomianism in Jewish history, was a product of the Kabbalah.[14] Again foreshadowing Gershom Scholem's analysis of the analysis of the Gnostic character of Sabbatian Kabbalah,[15] Krochmal maintains that Sabbatianism was a Gnostic movement. By associating both the Kabbalah and Gnosticism with Sabbatianism, which remained an unspeakable heresy even in his own day, Krochmal seems to have demoted these speculative movements from their formerly elevated status.

RESOLUTION BY RECOURSE TO KROCHMAL'S PHILOSOPHY OF HISTORY

One way of resolving this contradiction in Krochmal between a "positive" and "negative" Kabbalah is by recourse to his philosophy of history. As I have already noted, Krochmal historicized Israel's religious life. Like all nations, the Jews undergo inevitable processes of rise, maturity, and decline. The non-Jewish nations each undergo only one cycle of rise and decline, since national spirits are necessarily finite. Only Israel, because it embodies Absolute Spirit, overcomes this fate and regenerates after each cycle.

Krochmal was, therefore, able to historicize the traditional concept of *nezsach yisrael* by suggesting that while the Jews are subject to immanent historical laws of rise and decline, the transcendent spirit of their nation guarantees that they will not decline permanently.[16] As Nathan Rotenstreich has pointed out,[17] this view of history, which attempts to combine immanent laws with a transcendent guiding spirit, is highly problematic. It did, however, allow Krochmal to preserve Jewish uniqueness while arguing that Israel was subject to the same historical laws as any other nation.

Krochmal speaks of three cycles in Jewish history since biblical times. Only the third cycle interests us here, since it encompasses the history of the Kabbalah. The third cycle began, according to Krochmal, after the Bar Kokhba revolt in the second century, reached maturity roughly in the Gaonic period, and began to decline after the death of Nachmanides in the thirteenth century. It came to a final nadir with the 1648 pogroms and Sabbatianism.[18]

Krochmal's history of the Kabbalah follows precisely the course of this third cycle and is, in fact, dictated by it. The Kabbalah flourished from the time of Alexandrian Jewish philosophy until Nachmanides and then began to degenerate. It achieved maturity during the Gaonic period, precisely when Jewish history as a whole reached its high point in the third cycle. In an argument remarkably similar to Scholem's,[19] Krochmal advances the theory that Kabbalists in Babylonia had already developed the doctrine of the *sefirot* in the Gaonic period and that their speculations were carried westward via Italy to Spain in various "scrolls and small pamphlets" (*megilot ve-kuntresim ketanim*). The *sefirot* system then surfaced in the classical literature of the Spanish Kabbalah: the *Sefer ha-Bahir*, *Zohar*, *Sefer Ha-Temunah*, and

Sefer Razi'el. Krochmal, therefore, joined a school of thought, originated by Yehuda Arieh Mi-Modena and Jacob Emden and later subscribed to by Heinrich Graetz and Gershom Scholem, that dated the classical pseudepigraphic works of the Kabbalah to the thirteenth century. For Krochmal, the classical literature was derived from the Babylonian "scrolls" but was a degenerated form of the earlier literature.[20] Works like the *Zohar*, which he believed to have been written after Nachmanides's death (1270), were already part of the decline phase of the third cycle of Jewish history. Ultimately, this late Kabbalah became the prime cause of Sabbatianism. Gnosticism and Kabbalah were sound doctrines during the early period, which corresponded to the growth phase of the third cycle, but they became distorted and even heretical in the phase of decline. The fate of the Kabbalah was, therefore, an integral part of the general development and denouement of Jewish history during this cycle. This historical explanation for Krochmal's varying evaluations of the Kabbalah, already recognized by Fischel Lachover,[21] leads to certain difficulties. If the Kabbalah as a philosophical movement had originally possessed a perfectly clear conception of Absolute Spirit, it should not have degenerated, since Absolute Spirit presumably guarantees eternity. It follows that Kabbalah did not have at any time in its history an entirely true idea of God and that we must therefore reexamine the initial claim that Kabbalah, Maimonidean philosophy, and Idealism are conceptually identical.

THE KABBALAH AS A "SCIENCE OF FAITH"

In chapter 6, we learn that these three "sciences of faith" were indeed similar in function but not necessarily in content. Krochmal explains that "the divine Torah has instructed us with general and faithful principles in order to arrive with their aid at the goal and clarity that is in knowledge and worship."[22] These principles constitute the "sciences of faith" and are the conceptual apparatus by which man converts sensual images (*tzi'urim*) into "concepts of the understanding" (*musagim sikhliyim*) and, finally, into the most abstract "concepts of the reason" (*musagim tevuniyim*).[23]

Krochmal borrowed these technical epistemological terms from Kant, but whether he used them in precisely the same sense as Kant cannot be explored in detail here.[24] For our purposes we must note that according to Kant, every man is endowed with the same potential conceptual apparatus.

Krochmal, on the other hand, did not maintain that all men are blessed with the same capacity for abstract conceptualizations of their sense perceptions. Each nation has its own "science of faith" that determines its capacity to conceptualize experience. These "sciences of faith" are *revealed*, as Krochmal indicates by the quotation from the *Mekhilta* with which he opens chapter 6: God has given his creatures "a sign known to them to attune the ear to what it is capable of hearing." This statement is immediately perplexing, since it suggests that the conceptual ability of each nation is at once innate and also acquired through revelation: the spiritual quality of a revelation will determine the ability of its recipient to conceptualize it. Krochmal does not seem to have resolved this conflict between the innate and the revealed "spirits" of the nations. In any event, his argument is clearly quite different from that of Kant, for whom the nature of our perceptual experiences does not determine our innate ability to generalize perceptions into abstract concepts. While Krochmal did indeed adopt Kant's epistemology, his Jewish philosophy led him to qualify severely Kant's epistemological universalism: only the Jews are capable of the most abstract conceptualization of Spirit, since only the Jews have a revelation from Absolute Spirit.

The other nations receive only partial revelations of Absolute Spirit, or, more precisely, revelations of only a partial spirit. Every religion, no matter how primitive, possesses some form of spirituality, and therefore every group of people has its own "science of faith."[25] However, since the "sciences of faith" of the non-Jewish nations are all based on incomplete revelations, they cannot ever conceptualize Absolute Spirit. As soon as these nations become conscious of their own limited national spirit, they begin to decline, since their "science of faith" has reached the end of its potential.

As opposed to the Gentile nations, Israel's "science of faith" should be perfect, since only Israel enjoyed a revelation of Absolute Spirit. Surprisingly enough, however, when the Jews first received their revelation, their understanding was only an intuition of the level of "the beginning of conceptualization" (*tehilat ha-mahshavah*). This level was certainly higher than the merely sensual revelation perceived by polytheists, but it was not yet on the level of pure abstraction. Instead of arguing that the Jews possessed an immediate understanding of the Absolute Spirit, Krochmal subjects the Jewish religion to the same laws of history as he does the nations: the Jewish "science of faith" developed historically. In Daniel's time, for instance, the prophet had to "posit the existence of a particular guardian angel for our nation as well" (in contradiction to an unmediated relation to Absolute Spirit) because of the "image of the beginning of conceptualization" (*tziyur tehilat ha-mahshavah*) of the generation. The generation of Daniel was capable only of representing sense perceptions in crude pictorial images.[26]

The various "sciences of faith"—Kabbalah, Maimonidean philosophy, Neoplatonism, and modern Idealism—were therefore all suited to their particular generations. The history of Israel's spiritual development is the history, not of successively more abstract revelations of God, but of ever more refined "sciences of faith" for conceptualization of the original revelation. Because its original revelation gave it an intuitive perception of Absolute Spirit, Israel survived the vicissitudes of history. This intuition guaranteed it the potential to conceptualize revelation as abstractly as possible, although its "sciences of faith" realized this potential only gradually, as they developed through history. Israel went through cycles of growth and decline throughout its history because during each period its "science of faith" was not yet fully developed. Each representation of revelation, however, carried sufficient truth to guarantee survival into the next cycle.

To understand Krochmal's view of the precise status of the Kabbalah as a "science of faith," we must now examine how the Kabbalah conceptualizes revelation. In his account of mysticism in chapter 1 of the *Guide*, Krochmal suggests that the mystic rejects the sensual world and relies solely on the "internal eye." If the goal of reason is to achieve greater abstraction and distance from the sensual world, then the mystic does not seem so irrational. Indeed, Krochmal notes that mysticism "begins with reason."[27] However, the mystic quickly slips from his rational speculations into "feverish imagination" (*retihat dimyonam*). His "inner eye" begins to conceive angels and other beings "with pure or no matter," and with which he tries to unite himself. At the end, the mystic imagines he is one with God.

Why does mysticism degenerate from a promising rational beginning to a potentially heretical imagination? The name of the chapter about Kabbalah, "The Path of Externals" (*derekh ha-hitzonim*), suggests an answer. The title seems to refer at first to Krochmal's method of learning about ancient Kabbalah by consulting "external sources," such as the Christian texts on

Gnosticism.[28] However, it might also hint at Krochmal's real evaluation of the Kabbalah as a "science of faith." Krochmal appears to use the term *devarim hitzoniyim* (external matters) to refer to the sensual world (*hanoflim mi-tahat la-hushim*).[29] The tendency of mysticism to turn inwards is illusory abstraction that conceals mysticism's fundamental sensuality. The "inner eye" of imagination is misleading because it does not adhere to the proper rationalist epistemology that Krochmal borrowed from Kant.[30] Imagination leads us to believe in things without matter that can still be comprehended. Correct epistemology, however, however, does not renounce sense perceptions but abstracts *from them*. From concrete, particular houses, the mind abstracts the general concept of a house.[31] In its facile rejection of sense perceptions, the mystical imagination actually becomes entangled in sensual representation, such as the hypostatization of God's attributes as angels. Krochmal presumably believed that the Kabbalah's vivid symbolic pictures of God's emanations were just such sensual products of the imagination. The rationalist, on the other hand, is able to rise above sensual modes of representation by rooting his conceptualizations in sense data to begin with. The Kabbalist takes the seemingly easier path of a direct flight to the divine but paradoxically remains very much grounded in sensuality, while the rationalist attains greater heights by his slow and systematic ascent.

The Kabbalah may have asked the proper questions, but it arrived at an inadequate answer because its way of conceptualizing was imaginative rather than rational. The Kabbalah necessarily declined during the third cycle of Jewish history because its epistemology was inherently flawed. Nevertheless, Jewish mysticism played an important preservative role in Judaism during the early part of the third cycle as a partial "science of faith."

The Kabbalah's ambiguous position as a partially correct "science of faith" is due to the intermediate status that Krochmal assigned to imagination in his epistemology. Like Spinoza and Kant, Krochmal seems to have believed that imagination was an unclear but not entirely untrue form of reasoning. Through imagination, one might arrive at an unclear representation of truth. Even if the Kabbalah was the product of imagination, it was a *partial* manifestation of spirit, as was the case with the polytheistic religions. Krochmal actually suggests a hidden comparison between the Kabbalah and the religions of the Gentile nations. He refers to the various partial spirits of the nations with the biblical attributes of God such as "splendor" (*tiferet*), "courage" (*gevurah*), "wisdom" (*hokhmah*), and "understanding" (*binah*).³² With minor changes, his list corresponds to the names of the Kabbalistic *sefirot*. The Kabbalah was, then, a kind of compendium of all the divinities of the nations; it was on a higher level than the religions of these nations because it included all of their partial spirits, but its mode of representation was equally sensual.

Why did a modern philosopher of Judaism devote so much of his work to examining earlier "sciences of faith" when they were only inadequate representations of Absolute Spirit? Why are there lengthy chapters in the *Guide* on the Kabbalah, Gnosticism, Neoplatonism, Maimonides, and Abraham Ibn Ezra? The answer is that, for Krochmal, the modern "science of faith" is historical criticism: the modern philosopher is obligated to investigate older "sciences" as part of his own historical "science." Krochmal tells us that the way to fight the "perplexity of the times" is with its own weapons. In the time of Maimonides, the danger to Judaism was Aristotelian philosophy, which Maimonides effectively countered with a reinterpretation of Aristotle. In the nineteenth century, the danger is historicism, which must be fought with Jewish historicism. In his introduction, Krochmal gives an example of this approach by showing how a historical interpretation of the Bible can render it more relevant to an enlightened generation. The example from biblical scholarship is meant to set the stage for all of the *Guide* as a historical interpretation of Jewish sources from all of Jewish history. The modern philosopher must be a philosopher of history whose task it is to extract the partial reflections of truth from earlier "sciences of faith." The implication is that the philosopher of history does not so much develop a new "science of faith" *sui generis* as reconstruct such a science from the shards of previous generations. He takes the various expressions of consciousness from the past and synthesizes them historically: where previous generations engaged in reflection, the philosopher of history achieves the highest abstraction: self-reflection.

Did Krochmal see his own "science of faith" as historically relative, as he thought older sciences were, or was his science absolute? Was Jewish history open-ended, or would it come to an end after the three cycles he explicitly postulated? There is evidence that Krochmal believed his own "science of faith" to be absolute and final. In chapter 11, he claims that the rabbis themselves knew that much of the wisdom literature attributed to Solomon was written many centuries after Solomon.[33] He suggests that the guarded character of these references shows that the rabbis felt compelled to suppress their "modern" historical interpretation. There was, then, an underground tradition of the correct "science of faith" that was not suited to the understanding of the masses. In his own time, however, these esoteric doctrines might be revealed: "What remains of [these esoteric doctrines] is spoken of and explained in the proper place in the chapters of this work [because] in the end of many days [*be-aharit ha-yamim ha-rabbim*] which is our time, the oath of suppression [*neder ha-alamah*] has been lifted."[34] Historical criticism is able and even obligated to make the hidden historical interpretation of the rabbis public because we live in the "end of days." Krochmal's clearly deliberate use of the traditional eschatological expression in conjunction with his own historical philosophy suggests that when historical science, as the most abstract expression of original revelation, becomes public, we enter messianic time. Historical science is proof of the end of days.[35]

To be sure, the catastrophic break in history usually associated with Jewish eschatology is notably absent from Krochmal's account, as are other traditional motifs such as the return to Zion and the rebuilding of the Temple. For Krochmal, the "end of days" does not seem to usher in a new era in the everyday world; it remains a theoretical achievement of the philosophic spirit. Yet in the light of Krochmal's idealism we might suspect that the arrival of speculation at its ultimate destination might also have practical consequences: once Judaism can express its original revelation in its most abstract form, it can presumably avoid further cycles of rise and decay. But on this significant point, Krochmal was vague at best.[36]

From the vantage point of historicism as the ultimate "science of faith," Krochmal was able to treat the Kabbalah as a historical source while still restricting it to an inferior, but not entirely false, level of cognition. As an intermediate science of faith—between pure sensuality and pure abstraction— the Kabbalah occupied a "middle" stage in Jewish history. Unlike many of his contemporaries, Krochmal did not exclude the Kabbalah from the history of Judaism, but he subordinated its imaginative or irrational epistemology to his own rational idealism. His ambiguously sympathetic treatment of the Kabbalah was certainly unusual for the Wissenschaft des Judentums, but it demarcated the furthest limits to which the nineteenth century was prepared to go. In light of his own rationalism, Krochmal was not able to accord irrationalism autonomous status of its own: the Kabbalah remained the unwanted stepchild of the history of Jewish philosophy. The consideration of Jewish mysticism in its own right would have to await the historiography of Gershom Scholem in the twentieth century.

CHAPTER 7

Masochism and Philosemitism

The Strange Case of Leopold von Sacher-Masoch

IN THE HISTORY OF NINETEENTH-CENTURY sexuality, the erotic novels of Leopold von Sacher-Masoch occupy an important place as the literary source for the term *masochism*. Writing primarily in the 1860s, 1870s, and 1880s, Sacher-Masoch won a wide audience for his pornographic tales. But it is less well known today that in the same period he also wrote a long series of "tales of the ghetto" that are distinguished by ardent philosemitism. In the following remarks, I shall investigate the congruence between eroticism and philosemitism in the writings of this peculiar Austrian author.

The rapid industrialization of central Europe in the second half of the nineteenth century brought with it the destruction of traditional village life and a corresponding nostalgia for this vanishing idyllic world. The literary genre of *Dorfgeschichten*, pioneered by the German-Jewish author Berthold Auerbach, was part of the attempt to recapture through fiction what modernity had destroyed. Within the category of *Dorfgeschichten* literary historians have identified a particular subgenre called *Ghettogeschichten*, which sought to satisfy the thirst of the German-reading public for medieval romance with stories of the still-traditional Jewish communities of eastern Europe.[1]

The discovery of the "ghetto" (a romantic misnomer from a strictly historical point of view)[2] must be understood as a kind of literary mirror image to the rise of modern antisemitism. While nineteenth-century antisemites since the Enlightenment saw in the Jews a backward and primitive people still mired in the Middle Ages, the authors of the *Ghettogeschichten*—Leopold Kompert, Karl Emil Franzos, Berthold Auerbach, Aaron Bernstein, and Eduard Kulke (to name but a few of the best known)—turned these medieval characteristics into quaint virtues. These stories were not really meant to portray the Jews with historical or anthropological accuracy, although some of the authors were well acquainted with the folk customs of their subjects. Rather, we have here what Henry Wassermann has called "Judaism as a sentiment."[3] For example, although romantic love played practically no role in the ethos of traditional Jewish life, the *Ghettogeschichten* revel in stories of beautiful "semitic" girls and their romantic problems. What interested the readers of the *Ghettogeschichten*—Jews and non-Jews—was therefore not so much the Jews as they really were but more a sentimentalized and romanticized community that might satisfy their need for a *récherche du temps perdu*.

The philosemitic nature of these stories should not, however, be exaggerated or misunderstood. The authors—most of whom were Jews—were for the most part liberal enlighteners whose sympathy for the eastern European Jews was inextricably mixed with harsh criticism of religious obscurantism and economic slothfulness. In addition, the stories frequently go beyond medieval romance and deal with very contemporary problems of the ghetto in confrontation with modernity. Many of the writers were intensely concerned with problems of conversion and intermarriage, and in some cases we sense that they projected their own problems and those of their readership on the eastern European Jews, who also, of course, faced such issues but to a much lesser extent than one might assume by reading the *Ghettogeschichten*.[4] The stories of the ghetto are therefore distinguished by tensions between romantic and critical views of the Jews and between a kind of escapism into the past and an impulse to confront contemporary problems.

One of the strangest of the writers of *Ghettogeschichten* was Leopold von Sacher-Masoch. Born in Lemberg, Galicia, in 1836, he taught history for a period in Graz but spent most of his life as the writer of second-rate erotic fiction. After a somewhat nomadic existence, he finally settled in Lindheim,

Germany, and died either in 1895 or in an insane asylum in Mannheim in 1906.[5]

Sacher-Masoch belonged to the minority of *Ghettogeschichten* authors who were not Jews, yet his philosemitism in many ways surpassed that of his Jewish colleagues. For example, in a time when such writers—and especially the Jews among them—were extremely critical of Hasidism, Sacher-Masoch took a much more sympathetic position. In 1889, he published an account of a visit in 1857 to the rabbi of Sadagora in which he describes in great detail the court of the Hasidic master.[6] The article claims, among other things, that the rabbi even had a good many non-Jewish admirers, including Sacher-Masoch's uncle. Sacher-Masoch agrees with the critics of Hasidism that the Hasidim appear to be frequently misled by various hallucinations, but he emphatically denies that they are "tricksters" (*Betrüger*) as their enemies claim. The "madness" of the Hasidim can be attributed to the influence of the physical geography of Galicia ("the wide, limitless plains"), and Sacher-Masoch favorably compares the Hasidic fantasies to those of Hamlet and Faust. He boasts that he is the first author to try to understand Hasidism from a sympathetic point of view.[7]

Sacher-Masoch's philosemitism had its roots in his lifelong attachment to the Galician atmosphere in which he was born and raised. His family lived in Lemberg (Lviv), now a part of Ukraine. The population of this territory was a mixture of Austrian officials, Polish aristocrats, Ukrainian and Ruthenian peasants, Jews, and a host of other nationalities. Most of Sacher-Masoch's stories feature one or another of these ethnic groups and take place in the Galician setting. This fascination with eastern Europe as an area of exotic romance and passion was by no means unique to Sacher-Masoch, and it forms an important motif in modern German literature (one thinks immediately of Thomas Mann's *Magic Mountain*). In Sacher-Masoch's case, identification with the ethnic mix of Galicia led to an internationalist philosophy in opposition to exclusivist nationalism. Such an antinationalist position naturally favored the Jews, the quintessential example of a people without a nation-state.

In fact, Sacher-Masoch was singled out for a vituperative antisemitic attack in 1885 as a result of his editorship of a short-lived literary journal, *Auf der Höhe,* which was published by a Jew. The journal expressly declared itself an "international revue," but the anonymous critic entitled his pamphlet "Auf der Höhe—ein Beitrag zur Charakteristik der philosemitischen Presse."[8] He accused Sacher-Masoch of championing Jewish, French, and Slavic principles against those of *Germantum*. Here, then, is a striking example of a typical theme in modern antisemitism: the notion that "internationalism" is intrinsically Jewish or philosemitic. In Sacher-Masoch's case, the charge appears to be justified.[9] Sacher-Masoch had ample opportunity to become acquainted with Jews in his native Lemberg, which was the capital of Galicia, one of the most dynamic areas in modern Jewish history. Part of the Kingdom of Poland until the latter was partitioned in the late eighteenth century, Galicia was ceded to the Austro-Hungarian Empire. It was at once part of the traditional Jewish community of eastern Europe (the bulk of which was annexed by Czarist Russia) and also a window to the West through its political annexation by Austro-Hungary. Caught in this fashion between East and West, Galicia became the battleground for the first great clashes between the Jewish Enlightenment and Orthodoxy, especially between the Hasidim and their opponents. Sacher-Masoch's father, who was the chief of police in Lemberg in the 1830s and 1840s, took an active role in the controversies between Hasidim and Maskilim (enlighteners). Unlike his son, he was hostile to Hasidism and wrote a number of quite negative memoranda on the Hasidim at the prompting of Joseph Perl, one of the foremost Galician enlighteners.[10]

Sacher-Masoch's stories are filled with detailed knowledge of the Galician Jews among whom he grew up. In fact, his acquaintance with Galician-Jewish folklore appears to have been much deeper than that of his Jewish contemporary Karl Emil Franzos. While he does not seem to have known Hebrew, he made extensive use of written materials in German on Jewish history and customs and—more important in terms of folklore—he also seems to have had oral informants among Galician Jews. Hence, his stories have a certain value for folklorists in addition to historians of literature. A few examples will suffice. In the story "Pintschew and Mintschew," he explicitly compares his heroine, Esterka, to the heroine of the traditional Esterka legend, the Jewish girl who was the lover of the Polish king Kasimir.[11] He also uses the Yiddish word *puretz* (the orthography suggests immediately that his source was the Galician dialect of Yiddish).[12] According to any standard

Yiddish dictionary that Sacher-Masoch might have consulted, *puretz* (or *poretz*) means any aristocrat (typically Polish or Russian). Yet in a footnote he defines it as "an elegant Christian who has no money, a ruffian horseman [*lumpiger Cavalier*]." This definition betrays real knowledge of vernacular folk usage. *Puretz* invariably has a negative connotation, and in Galicia in the second half of the nineteenth century would most probably refer to the lower class of the nobility, which was on the road to impoverishment.[13]

Another example of such knowledge of Yiddish folklore is his use of the word *dalles*, which means "poverty." In two stories ("Der Prostek" and "Des Dalles des roten Pfeffermann"), he defines the word as "personified misfortune, a figure from Jewish folklore."[14] Although such a definition does not appear in the dictionary, eastern European Jewish folklore does, in fact, contain stories of poverty or misfortune as a person.[15]

A final example, for which, however, Sacher-Masoch's sources do not receive corroboration, is his claim that the Hasidic opponents of Jacob Frank (the eighteenth-century Messianic pretender who was active in Poland, Austria, and Germany) greet each other with the phrase "What's new in Pinczow?" (Sacher-Masoch claims that Frank first appeared in the town of Pinczow in southeast Poland).[16] The obligatory answer is something like: "The devil is doing his work." None of the sources on Frank refers to Pinczow,[17] nor have I been able to find any confirmation of the use of this phrase among Hasidim. Even his claim that the Hasidim were opponents of Frank is historically questionable, since it is not clear to what extent they even knew of each other. Yet even if Sacher-Masoch's information is historically inaccurate, it seems unlikely that he could have fabricated it out of whole cloth, and it may well reflect certain folktales about Frank current in nineteenth-century Galicia.[18]

These examples suggest Sacher-Masoch's intimate knowledge of Jewish folklore, but his stories also demonstrate knowledge of Jewish history and literature. His biography of Shabbtai Zvi (the false Messiah of the seventeenth century) is based on Peter Beer's *Geschichte, Lehren und Meinungen aller bestandenen und noch bestehenden religiösen Sekten der Juden* (1823–24) and possibly also on Francois Pétis de la Croix's seventeenth-century *Memoires de l'Empire Ottoman* (Paris, 1684).[19] Although Beer's work has been shown by modern scholarship to be fairly unreliable (Beer was an Austrian

Jewish enlightener), Sacher-Masoch had every reason to believe it accurate. His biography, as we shall see here, is highly romanticized, but it is at the same time firmly grounded in the facts of Shabbtai Zvi's life as far as they were known in the nineteenth century.

Sacher-Masoch also showed an impressive knowledge of Jewish religious sources. His story "Pintschew and Mintschew," which is a somewhat sentimentalized tale about two Jews who carry on perennial Talmudic disputations (a subject that other authors typically treated with far less sympathy), is replete with authentic arguments from the Talmud. He seems even to have knowledge of the contents of specific Talmudic tractates such as Berakhot.

Yet despite Sacher-Masoch's relatively precise knowledge of Jewish life and customs, his stories share with all the *Ghettogeschichten* the conflicting tendencies to romanticize and criticize. On the one hand, his portrayal of the ghetto has a highly idyllic element. Jews and Gentiles invariably live together in harmony. The one story about antisemitism ("Frau Leopard") makes it clear that the antisemite is an exception, and in the end the Jews get their revenge on him. Reflecting a kind of Enlightenment ideal, the Jews are typically patriotic ("Der letzte Mann," "Judith von Bialopol," "Die Deborah von Nagy Nemethy," "Abe Nahum Wassertrug"). In one case ("Abe Nahum Wassertrug") the Jews' patriotism seems to be based on historical fact. The historical setting is the 1846 Polish uprising in Galicia against Austria, a theme that occurs repeatedly in Sacher-Masoch, most probably because he himself witnessed these bloody events as a child. His Jewish hero saves the community from the rebels, and this Jewish allegiance to the Austrian government seems borne out by the information we have of Jewish attitudes toward the revolt.[20] "Der letzte Mann" and "Die Deborah von Nagy Nemethy" offer models of Jews as soldiers, the last featuring a Jewish woman leading Hungarian patriots into battle.

On the other hand, there is a strong critique of certain aspects of traditional Jewish life in Sacher-Masoch's stories that may well reflect the influence of those Maskilim with whom he was in contact. In "Des Dalles des roten Pfeffermann," a poor Jewish family is haunted by the ghost of poverty, who turns out in the end to be none other than the father himself. He has become a drunkard and wife-beater and does not work to support his family. But once unmasked, he reforms and the family escapes poverty.[21] The

Enlightenment message is clear: the Jews themselves are to blame for their poverty, and if they reform and work hard they can transform themselves. The theme of Jewish productivization, a favorite of the Haskalah, is the message of another story, "Rabbi Abdon."[22] The Kabbalist's son, Simon, becomes enlightened, marries a poor girl against the wishes of his father, and runs away from home to become a soldier and then a farmer. He returns home as a solid peasant after many years and takes his aged father to live with him on his farm like a "true patriarch." The typical Enlightenment themes of patriotism, agricultural productivity, and a return to the biblical ethos are all woven together in this story.

Like many of his Jewish colleagues, Sacher-Masoch took a rather negative view of poor Jews. In "Der Handel um der Namen,"[23] which relates how the Jews paid the Austrian officials to be given aristocratic and beautiful surnames, the protagonist, Absalon, who cannot afford a respectable name, is meant to evoke sympathy but is also portrayed with typical antisemitic stereotypes as a dickering Jew. If Sacher-Masoch's attitude toward the poor was ambivalent at best, his philosemitism is invariably strongest with regard to wealthy Jews, and particularly Jewish women. Upper-class Jews are his heroes in most of the stories and are attractive and romantic, while the lower class is pathetic and in need of reform. There is a historical dimension to this as well. In "Die Judith von Bialopol," he describes one of his heroes as having all the characteristics of the proud nobility of biblical times, which "are being increasingly lost as Israel has developed from a free people of shepherds and fighters into a people of shopkeepers and servants."[24] As in the historical romances of Abraham Mapu and other eastern European writers of the Jewish Enlightenment, Sacher-Masoch tries to recapture a certain biblical type, which he believes still exists among the Jews even if Jewish society as a whole has degenerated. It is therefore no surprise that his stories are frequently about characters he admits are "exceptions."

It must be emphasized that this double image of the Jews characterized many of the Jewish enlighteners, who adopted bourgeois and capitalist values and judged Jewish society accordingly. Their heroes were drawn from the mercantile class, and the targets of their criticism were "hewers of wood and carriers of water." Sacher-Masoch does not seem to have shared these capitalist values, and his heroes are drawn more from an imagined Jewish aristocracy, although it is an aristocracy whose economic base is clearly in commerce. Yet even if these characters are merchants, their behavior is aristocratic. The Jewish enlighteners also leveled substantial criticism at the representatives of traditional religion, especially the Hasidic leaders. Sacher-Masoch did not share these concerns, for his stories rarely deal directly with the burning questions of religion that were so primary to the Jewish enlighteners. For instance, his treatment of Talmudic casuistry is surprisingly mild, and in some stories he portrays enlightened Jews who are thoroughly Orthodox in their religious practice.

At this point in our discussion, we must return to those writings of Sacher-Masoch that, as I mentioned at the beginning of this essay, made him most famous: his pornography. Like most pornographic literature, these stories are tediously repetitive, and they are distinguished by one persistent motif: they invariably feature domineering, aristocratic women dressed in furs (Sacher-Masoch's particular fetish). These women enslave and torture their male companions in scenes with strong erotic undercurrents, even where the eroticism itself may not be fully explicit. The nature of these erotic relationships led the late nineteenth-century psychologist Richard Krafft-Ebing to coin the term *masochism* after our subject, just as he labeled *sadism* after the Marquis de Sade.[23] It is in fact fascinating to compare Sacher-Masoch with the Marquis de Sade.[24] Both were members of the aristocracy, and both had rather anarchistic philosophies of society in which their sexual predilections played a central role. Both sought to play out their sexual fantasies in real life and turned to fiction as a release from those fantasies whose very nature made realization impossible. The line between fiction and reality is sufficiently blurred in both de Sade and Sacher-Masoch for it to be unclear whether their fiction was a substitute for frustrated reality or reality a theatrical extension of their fiction. It is, however, beyond our scope to examine closely the precise nature of Sacher-Masoch's erotic writings or of his own peculiar psychology. What is of interest to us is how his sexual concerns informed his philosemitic writings.

The most cursory survey of Sacher-Masoch's work confirms that most (although by no means all) of his Jewish stories are obsessed with Jewish women and many of them permeated with masochistic motifs such as his fetish with furs. Even his seemingly factual account of the Hasidim of Galicia resonates with his favorite themes. Thus, he lingers over a description of the rabbi's wife and daughters who lounge about the foyer of the mansion dressed (as his women invariably are) in sumptuous furs.

Fascination with Jewish women was one of the hallmarks of the *Ghettogeschichten*. Dark, sensuous, and exotic, the women in many of these stories seem to convey an erotic message, even when well hidden behind the obligatory stereotypes of chastity.[26] At the same time, these romantic females are frequently at the cutting edge of social change. Many of them are tempted by intermarriage and conversion. For writers such as Leopold Kompert and Karl Emil Franzos, the romantic alliance was often the fictional focus for criticism of traditional Jewish society.[27] Thus, one of the frequent themes of these stories is the desire of a couple to wed against the wishes of parents and community, a desire that often ends in tragedy.[28] While this literary stock-in-trade can be found in almost every bourgeois novel from the late eighteenth century on, it has particular significance in the Jewish context, in which arranged marriages (often through a marriage broker) were a cornerstone of traditional Jewish society. The "discovery" of Jewish women by the authors of the *Ghettogeschichten* (although there were certainly earlier authors—such as Shakespeare and Lessing—who made polemical use of the "beautiful but innocent" Jewish daughter) was a crucial aspect of their dual attempt to sentimentalize and criticize traditional Jewish life.

Sacher-Masoch's treatment of Jewish women shares some of these stereotypes, but in a much stranger and more radical way. Problems of intermarriage and romantic love tend to play less of a role in his stories, despite certain exceptions.[29] The stories typically feature beautiful and domineering Jewish women—usually with weak husbands—whose powerful personalities are the motive forces in the plot. The image of the Jewish woman as dynamic and powerful, which can be found in other *Ghettogeschichten*, perhaps reflects the social reality of eastern Europe, where women tended to be much more active in economic life than men. But Sacher-Masoch combined this literary *topos* with his own sexual fantasies. His women are the Jewish variants of the half-demonic creatures of his non-Jewish erotic novels.[30] To be sure, the erotic element in the Jewish stories is more often than not camouflaged in allusions and hints (even in his straight pornography, Sacher-Masoch is only really explicit about sadomasochism, while erotic scenes as such are treated with greater reticence). Nevertheless, the erotic suggestiveness of the Jewish tales certainly went far beyond anything else of his day. Yet before we dismiss Sacher-Masoch's Jewish stories as simply a bizarre mixture of *Ghettogeschichten* and pornography, we must investigate more closely the possible hidden message of his stories.

I believe that we shall find behind these erotic tales a fascinating philosemitic ideology with a strong polemic for the emancipation of women. In Sacher-Masoch's own terms, we shall discover a "philosemite in furs." If Sacher-Masoch used his Jewish stories as a vehicle for his erotic fantasies, he also adopted eroticism as a cloak for a statement on the Jews. There are a number of indications that Sacher-Masoch was aware that his Jewish women did not exactly represent social reality. For instance, he begins the story "Die Venus von Braniza" by suggesting that Talmud scholars typically have unattractive wives because "God saves for his dearest ones, the Talmudists, those women whom no one else would like." His story, he tells us, is about an exception, a true "Venus," who, like the heroine of his most famous erotic novel (*Venus in Furs*), is "born to rule" and dresses in fur coats.[31] The explicit statement that his fiction deals with exceptional rather than representational women is important, for it suggests that Sacher-Masoch was less interested in portraying social reality in his treatment of women than in presenting an ideal type. He surely knew full well that most Jewish women were neither wealthy nor domineering, nor did they dress in extravagant furs. But the erotic symbolism of such women served a crucial function in his Jewish fiction.

In a number of the stories, women are the representatives of Enlightenment and emancipation from backward men. The "Deborah of Nagy Nemethy" is a Hungarian patriot, while her husband is a weak-willed coward who refuses to fight for his country. She ultimately accuses him of spying against the Hungarians (a charge that is never fully proven in the story), arrests him at gunpoint, and has him turned over to the Hussars. Similarly, in "Des Dalles des roten Pfeffermann," it is the drunkard husband who brings poverty upon his family, and the wife is portrayed as the heroine. While this story lacks the erotic and masochistic elements of the Deborah tale, the criticism of the man and glorification of the woman suggest the same relationship between the sexes (when the family achieves wealth at the end of the story, the wife appears decked out in furs, the symbolism of which we already recognize). Perhaps the most striking example of "modern" women versus "medieval" men is in "Der Scheidebrief" ("The Writ of Divorce").[32] The story concerns a young man, Eliam Goldreich, who asserts that women are of inferior intelligence and that a Talmud scholar should not marry for love. As a result of these "chauvinistic" views, he is rejected as a husband by the daughters of the Orthodox yet enlightened Kalmus Feuerstein. However, a friend of the daughters, Afra Rabinowitsch, who is introduced as "an enlightened [woman], who preaches . . . that there is no such thing as love . . . and whom all men fear because she is as evil as she is beautiful," surprises all by suddenly agreeing to marry Eliam. "I shall marry him in order to punish him," Afra tells her friends, "[and] when I wish, I will force him to give me a writ of divorce." Following the marriage, she torments him by forbidding him to touch her and humiliates him by besting him in Talmudic arguments. Through superior Talmudic knowledge and clever reasoning, she proves to him why she need not cut her hair as do Orthodox Jewish women after their marriage (this was one of the bones of contention between the enlighteners and their opponents). She finally forces him to give her a writ of divorce once he has learned his lesson and become a docile husband. In the end, however, she discovers that she has now come to love her transformed husband and she tears up the writ.

In this story, the sadistic character of the heroine is verbal as opposed to the more explicit scenes of physical punishment in Sacher-Masoch's purely erotic novels. Yet verbal humiliation—even if with Talmudic arguments—is characteristic of such sadomasochistic fiction. In any event, the sadistic nature of Afra should not obscure the Enlightenment message of the story. Sacher-Masoch opposes the traditional Jewish marriage in which the woman is neither consulted nor given power within the family. Once the woman is emancipated (which, in Sacher-Masoch's world, means that she dominates), both parties discover the romantic love they previously denied. Yet the solution does not involve an escape from Judaism: Afra transforms her marriage by acquiring knowledge of the Talmud, a traditionally male domain.

The most dramatic eroticism in Sacher-Masoch's Jewish stories is undoubtedly in his novelette *Sabbathai Zewy* (1874).[33] As I have already noted, the work is based on Peter Beer's history from the early nineteenth century, and with the exception of the erotic scenes, it follows Beer's account almost word for word. Sacher-Masoch's chief literary interest in writing about Shabbtai Zvi seems to have been erotic, and he strictly avoided using his imagination for the other details of the life of the seventeenth-century Messiah. The result is a startling combination of detailed historical fact and outrageous fancy.

The figure of Shabbtai Zvi had already attracted a number of novelists, including the anonymous author of the Hebrew novel *Me'orot Zvi* (1814), S. Meschelssohn, whose German romance *Sabbathey Zwy* appeared in 1856, and the Hebrew novelist Abraham Mapu, whose unpublished fragment *Hoze Hezyonot* was written around 1858.[34] In general, however, most nineteenth-century Jewish writers steered clear of Shabbtai Zvi, since the Sabbatian movement still constituted a heinous heresy for the Orthodox and a degenerate form of mysticism for the enlightened. Mapu's novel, which seems to have been censored as a result of pressure from the Orthodox, is more a polemic than real fiction. He uses the Sabbatian movement as a symbol for how fanatical religion can break up the Jewish family. Sacher-Masoch's biography represents a relatively early attempt to romanticize the figure of the would-be Messiah, an approach that was as yet unthinkable for most Jewish authors. Only at the end of the nineteenth century, as I will discuss in chapter 9, would writers such as Jacob Wassermann and, later, others under the influence of Jewish nationalism explore the fictional possibilities of Shabbtai Zvi from a more sympathetic point of view.

Shabbtai Zvi's biography already contained much historical material with erotic potential. His first two marriages ended in divorce when he refused to have any sexual contact with his wives. His third marriage, which was given mystical significance by his followers, was to a strange Polish-Jewish girl of dubious reputation named Sarah.[35] Sarah was thought to have been raised in a nunnery, and some accounts considered her a prostitute. Sacher-Masoch naturally made the most of these hints. Beer had suggested that Shabbtai Zvi chose beautiful women as his first two wives in order to put his ascetic vows to the test. Sacher-Masoch embroiders on this suggestion and describes in erotic detail how the first two wives, Sarah and Hannah (the names are his own inventions), attempt in vain to seduce the young Kabbalist.

It is with the third wife, whom Sacher-Masoch mistakenly calls Miriam, that the story reaches its climax and where we can also discern between the lines a kind of Enlightenment interpretation of Shabbtai Zvi's biography. Unlike the previous wives, Miriam takes the initiative and haughtily forbids Shabbtai Zvi to touch her. This naturally increases his erotic attraction. Shabbtai is subsequently imprisoned by the Turks, and the sultan threatens him with death if he refuses to convert to Islam. Miriam takes it upon herself to "transform Shabbtai from a saint into a man." To convince him that he is not the Messiah—as she herself now believes—she must force him to sin. She does this in a manner that we by now recognize as vintage Sacher-Masoch. Claiming to be overcome by the spirit of God, she leads Shabbtai to the river and forces him to bathe with her in a scene the eroticism of which is unmistakable. She then leads him into a garden where she binds a crown of thorns around his head until he bleeds and proceeds to flagellate him with a thorn branch. When he finally recovers, he asks Miriam what she has done to him. She replies: "I have made you a man, you saint ... and this is the great miracle I have accomplished. Shabbtai Zvi, you are not the savior of Israel, you are not the Messiah."[36] Shabbtai then converts to Islam and lives out his days as a Moslem practicing the Jewish religion.

Once again, we have a bizarre mixture of sadomasochism and allegory. Sacher-Masoch seems to regard Shabbtai Zvi as deluded primarily because of his sexual asceticism. He must be transformed from an ascetic saint into a man, and this can be done only by a domineering woman. Miriam brings the wayward mystic down to earth by corporal punishment. Interestingly enough, the release of Shabbtai Zvi's sexuality, which symbolizes his return to humanity, is connected with a sin: conversion to Islam. The message of the story seems to be that Jews must give up their more ascetic and mystical tendencies in order to realize their humanity. Could it be that Shabbtai's conversion to Islam, while still retaining Jewish practices, might signify Sacher-Masoch's conviction that Jews must at least partially assimilate?

We must not, however, ignore the Christian allusion in the story that is suggested by the crown of thorns with which Miriam tortures her husband. For Sacher-Masoch, Christ seems to have represented the incarnation of God in an inverted sense: the turning of religion into worldliness. In the introduction to his projected, but never completed, magnum opus, *The Legacy of Cain*, he presents the outlines of a peculiar philosophy that is a mixture of social Darwinism, utopian Christianity, and a kind of protoexistentialism.[37] All men are descendants of Cain and are condemned to wander in a cruel world in atonement for the sins of the first humans. Life is a brutal struggle for power and possession, at the origin of which lies woman's dominance of man. No wonder, then, that *Venus in Furs*, Sacher-Masoch's most famous sadomasochistic novel, was to be the first part of *The Legacy of Cain*. Cruel nature dictates this relationship between men and women. Human institutions, which Sacher-Masoch regarded as perverted, such as work, property, and the state, were all consequences of women's demands upon men. Sacher-Masoch planned volumes in *The Legacy of Cain* that would advocate an end to exploitation in work and property and a new international order in place of chauvinistic nationalism. Yet he does not seem to have believed that erotic relationships, which were the cause of these perversions, might be transformed. In this cruel world, the only possibility for true happiness lies in the full acceptance of death, and Christ represents such a philosophy in his voluntary acceptance of his crucifixion. Christ is the culmination and fulfillment of the legacy of Cain, namely, acceptance of the world as it is. By bringing Shabbtai Zvi back to humanity with a crown of thorns, Sacher-Masoch seems to be saying something about the Christian Messiah as well: his greatness lies precisely in his acceptance of his humanity.

Sacher-Masoch's fascination with Shabbtai Zvi may well have had something to do with the antinomian aspects of the Sabbatian movement, which were frequently given sexual expression, especially in the polemics of the opponents of Sabbatianism. Sacher-Masoch seems to have been aware of this antinomian tendency, since, at the end of his story, he quotes the Talmudic saying from the Tractate Sanhedrin according to which the Messiah will come only when the world is either totally virtuous or totally sinful. Since the former is impossible, the followers of Shabbtai Zvi argued that they were justified in converting to Islam in order to realize the latter.

Sacher-Masoch combines this antinomian suggestion with explicit eroticism in another story that we have already mentioned, "Die Venus von Braniza." Here the beautiful young wife asks her husband, a Talmudic scholar, when the Messiah will come, and she receives the above answer. One day, when her husband is away, she sleeps with a local cavalry officer and explains to the husband, upon his return, that she did so in order to bring the Messiah.

It does not seem to me that Sacher-Masoch wrote this strange little story in order to satirize the Talmudic saying. Instead, he seems to find within Jewish belief a certain erotic potential, even if it exists on the periphery of normative practice. This story, like that of Shabbtai Zvi and many of the others discussed here, represents an attempt to eroticize Jewish life *from within*. Sacher-Masoch exploits hints within Jewish tradition and practice to portray an erotic reality utterly foreign to actual Jewish life. In many cases, the purpose of this eroticization of the Jews is to promote certain specific goals such as the emancipation of Jewish women. In a larger sense, however, to treat the Jews as subjects of eroticism means to treat them as normal human beings, and there can be no doubt that whatever the peculiarities of Sacher-Masoch's sexual vision, his Jewish stories have this philosemitic intention.

The most philosemitic of Sacher-Masoch's stories are perhaps those that feature a powerful Jewish woman as the savior of her people. This theme was not uncommon to the *Ghettogeschichten* as a whole, if one may judge by such stories as Kompert's "The Second Judith" and Franzos's "Two Saviours of the People." Sacher-Masoch infuses this motif with his own particular tendencies. In "Frau Leopard,"[38] the Jews of Zamosto are persecuted by an anti-Semite, Agenor Koscieloski. A beautiful Jewish widow, Frau Leopard, seduces the antisemite and tricks him into coming to her house disguised as the tailor Weinstock who has been sentenced by the local rabbinical court to a beating by his creditors. The creditors lie in wait and, taking the antisemite for their debtor, set upon him with their cudgels. Sacher-Masoch can barely hide his delight in describing the humiliation of the antisemite at the hands of the widow.

Another such story, "Die Judith von Bialopol," has a historical setting: the Turkish invasion of the Ukraine in the 1670s.[39] Despite minor historical inaccuracies in the story, it is indeed likely that the Jews took an active role in the defense of their towns as they do in Sacher-Masoch's Bialopol.[40] The heroine is a beautiful woman named Judith, and the story is an explicit imitation of the apocryphal book of Judith. Sacher-Masoch was not the first to use the figure of Judith (see Kompert's "Die zweite Judith"), but she seems to have special erotic significance for him. Thus, *Venus in Furs* commences with the author reading the book of Judith and halting over the verse: "God punished him and delivered him up to the hands of a woman" (a reference to Holofernes's bloody death at the hands of Judith, the Jewish woman who seduces the enemy general in order to kill him). In our story, the Judith of Bialopol smuggles herself out of the besieged city and seduces the Turkish pasha. Her husband—portrayed typically as weak and almost unmanly—comes looking for her and is captured by the Turks. In order to convince the Turkish general of her loyalty, Judith recommends all sorts of bizarre and brutal tortures for her husband. Having deluded the enemy of her true intentions, she sneaks into the pasha's tent and kills him. The Turks withdraw after the death of their general, and the city is saved.

In both of these stories, a brave and powerful Jewish woman saves her people (and, in Judith, the non-Jews as well) from their enemies by the combined use of eroticism and sadism. This is perhaps the place to raise the question of just where Sacher-Masoch stands in such stories of the Jews and their enemies. One might think that as a non-Jew he must, in some sense, identify with the enemies of the Jews and derive masochistic pleasure at their defeat and degradation. Yet from all the biographical data we possess, the evidence is that Sacher-Masoch identified strongly with the Jews themselves. Many of his business and personal relationships were with Jews. Without entering into the treacherous waters of psychology too deeply, we may have here a case of "identification with the aggressor" or displaced sadism, which some theorists believe characterize the masochist.[41] According to this view, the masochist identifies not only with the victim in his fantasies but also with the sadist. Thus, by turning the Jews into the aggressors, Sacher-Masoch may well have expressed his identification with them in their struggle against antisemitism. Given the nature of his erotic fantasies, it is possible that the only way he could express his philosemitism was by portraying the Jews—through their women—not as victims but as powerful and victorious. If it is no surprise that a masochist could identify with oppressed people such as the Jews, it is more significant that he turns them into heroes.

The psychological dimensions of Sacher-Masoch's work, debatable as they are, interest us less than the symbolism of sadomasochism for his pro-Jewish position. The literary consequence of his individual psychology was the reversal of antisemitic stereotypes of the Jews. By presenting the Jews as the heroes—or, more precisely, the heroines—of his erotic fiction, he, like the other writers of *Ghettogeschichten,* tried to make his subjects more human and thus to promote their acceptance by European society.

CHAPTER 8

Historical Heresies and Modern Jewish Identity

IN *THE HERETICAL IMPERATIVE*, PETER Berger argued that modernity, characterized as it is by a plurality of choices, necessarily embraces heresy, for heresy, as he defines it (going back to *hereisis* in Greek), means "to choose." In the Hellenistic *oikumene*, the word most commonly referred to a "faction" or "party," from which, in the letters of Paul, for example,[1] it eventually developed the pejorative meaning of factionalism or sectarian disagreement. With the gradual emergence of an "orthodox" church, heresy came to mean dissent from dogma, and indeed orthodoxy constructed itself precisely by naming and categorizing heresies. Berger contrasts the world of "tradition" with modernity in the following terms: "For premodern man, heresy is a possibility—usually a rather remote one; for modern man, heresy typically becomes a necessity. Or again, modernity creates a new situation in which picking and choosing becomes an imperative."[2]

Berger's equation of secularism with heresy is a singularly interesting attempt to describe the dialectic of modernization in religious terms. Yet it seems to me to fail, at least in the Jewish case, one that Berger himself quotes repeatedly. Jewish tradition does not conform to his definition of tradition, the static character of which probably applies to *no* historical tradition. Consequently, the relationship of modern Jews to heresy is not quite the diametric opposite of tradition. Rabbinic culture, which represents tradition for Berger, certainly developed a concept of heresy and even a lexicon of terms (*min, kofer, epikores*) by which to label the heretic. But the process of marking the boundaries turns out to have been much more difficult and complex than Berger's polarities would admit. Rabbinic culture constructed the category of heresy by a process of simultaneously naming and erasing the heretic. Thus, the Hebrew name for Jesus, *Yeshu*, was understood traditionally as an acronym meaning "May his name be blotted out." But even as traditional authorities sought to erase the heretic by naming him, the very process ensured a kind of recuperation. Jesus himself, for example, appears in a discussion of capital punishment as a case from which one might learn the law (the rabbis have no difficulty here in taking full ownership of his execution!).[3]

Elisha ben Abuya, perhaps the most famous heretic in the Talmud and a figure, like Jesus, to whom we shall return, is renamed, in one tradition, as Aher or "Other." But this renaming also hardly succeeds in "blotting him out." Far from it. Elisha is declared a heretic and "rabbinized" at one and the same time. Interestingly enough, it is a prostitute who, in the Babylonian account, names him Aher: "He went and found a prostitute and asked for her. She said to him: Are you not Elisha ben Abuyah? When he tore a radish [or turnip] out of the ground on the Shabbat and gave it to her, she said: 'He is another [*aher hu*].'"[4] We need not detain ourselves with the possible (Freudian?) meaning of the tubular vegetable that Elisha plucks on the Sabbath. More significant is that it is a woman who first recognizes and names his "otherness," his transformation from a rabbi into a heretic. Yet the way in which the editors of the Babylonian Talmud compiled the Aher stories immediately reverses the process. Aher engages his disciple Rabbi Meir in a series of typically rabbinic exegetical exchanges that would seem to suggest the possibility of his repentance, except that Elisha says that he heard from behind the *pargod* (the "veil" that separates heaven from earth) that only for Elisha was repentance denied. Following Elisha's death, Rabbi Meir and Rabbi Yohanan vow that upon their own deaths, Elisha will be punished and forgiven. Then another female figure is introduced, this time Aher's daughter, who asks Rabbi Judah ha-Nasi to support her. Judah rejects her when he learns her identity, but she replies: "Remember his Torah and not his deeds," whereupon "a fire came down and enveloped the rabbi's bench."

Without entering into a detailed analysis of these stories,[5] it is clear that the Talmud struggles mightily to reverse Elisha's apostasy and even turn it into the occasion for a classically rabbinic discourse.

Whether or not these stories have any historicity behind them, they attest to a singular struggle within rabbinic culture over how to define orthodoxy versus heresy. There can be little doubt that the rabbis were aware of similar debates among the Christians, especially in Palestine. By the fourth century CE, the Council of Nicaea codified a process in development for at least two centuries when it elaborated the dogma that would differentiate between orthodox and heretical Christians. Shaya Cohen has argued that the Council at Yavneh represents the diametric opposite to Nicaea: "The sages of Yavneh . . . created a society based on the doctrine that conflicting disputants may each be advancing the words of the living God."[6] The real question that faced the rabbis was whom exactly to include within the magic circle of "disputants" granted the authority to advance "the words of the living God." Within that circle, all disagreements were "for the sake of heaven," but at the same time the rabbis clearly recognized categories of heretics who were outside (see the discussion of Korah in this context in chapter 2). The ambivalence evident in the stories around Elisha ben Abuya attests to the fuzziness of the boundary between who was in and who was out. If this argument is correct, then Berger was surely wrong, or at least too extreme, when he asserted: "Whatever else may be the problems of a traditional society, ambivalence is not one of them."[7]

I have used Berger as perhaps too easy a foil for an investigation of the category of heresy in modern Jewish culture. In what follows, I want to argue that modern Jewish writers often unconsciously replicated this process of distancing and recuperation in their attitudes toward three of the most important heretics in Jewish history: Jesus, Shabbtai Zvi, and Elisha ben Abuya.[8] Rather than fully embracing these heretics, as an extrapolation from Berger's argument might suggest, modern Jewish culture often celebrated them, but only after reinterpreting the meaning of their heresies. I also want to argue that the very definition of terms like *tradition* and *modernity* relies, in part, on how these historical figures are represented.

I have suggested the term *counterhistory* to designate a type of historiographical inversion practiced by such figures as M. Y. Berdichevsky, Martin

Buber, and Gershom Scholem for recovering a Jewish past different from the rational or legal "establishment" traditions.[9] Much like the eighteenth-century German pietist Gottfried Arnold, who held that the true history of the church was the history of its heretics,[10] these Jewish writers, in very different contexts, searched for the true Judaism in subterranean mystical and messianic traditions. The term *counterhistory* may, however, require some rethinking in light of the material I will present here. What will emerge is perhaps a more complicated and ambivalent relationship to Jewish heretics from history. Moreover, insofar as interpretations of history are crucial components in the construction of contemporary identities, the ambiguities in the way these heretics were treated will suggest a more complex understanding of what constitutes a secular or modern Jewish identity.

One figure who will loom in the background of this study is Spinoza, the icon for other modern heretics and a figure whose nineteenth- and twentieth-century Jewish reception is the subject of Daniel Schwartz's *The First Modern Jew*.[11] Spinoza enjoyed a renaissance among German Jews in the nineteenth century,[12] but only after the fin de siècle did he become a hero for eastern European Jews revolting against tradition (one thinks of Isaac Bashevis Singer's heretical characters who obsessively read Spinoza, a practice that Singer borrowed from earlier Yiddish and Hebrew writers). It is interesting that Heinrich Graetz, in his binaries of Jewish history (philosophy vs. mysticism, Mendelssohn vs. the Baal Shem Tov), pairs Spinoza with Shabbtai Zvi: "Without dreaming of it, Spinoza possessed in the East an ally, diametrically his opposite, who worked hard for the destruction of Judaism."[13] The extremes met: the heresy of excessive rationalism was just as costly to Judaism (as Graetz understood it) as the heresy of irrationalism. But as the "non-Jewish Jew" par excellence, Spinoza might serve as a palimpsest for a variety of constructions of modern Jewish identity. Thus, David Ben Gurion's suggestion that the *herem* against Spinoza be lifted stemmed from a Zionist interpretation of the famous passage in the *Tractatus* where Spinoza speculates on the possibility of the reestablishment of Jewish sovereignty. Whether or not Spinoza would have had any interest in the Zionist movement had he lived three centuries later, he served Ben Gurion as a model of a secular but potentially nationalist Jew.[14]

JESUS AS RABBI

The historical heretics that I want to take up here are not, however, like Spinoza, obvious precursors to modern secularism but rather heretics whose dissent might more properly be termed religious (although Spinoza's own secularism was itself thoroughly grounded in an internal critique of Jewish biblical exegesis). We begin with Jesus, the most famous of Jewish heretics, whose heresy points not to secularism but to the foundation of a competing religion. As is well known, Jesus appears very infrequently in classical rabbinic sources, but his image could not be avoided, especially by Jews living in Christian lands. The *Sefer Toldot Yeshu*, a folkloristic and satirical retelling of the life of Jesus, appears on first glance to be a classic "counterhistory."[15] But, as I discussed at greater length in chapter 3, it is not so much an inversion of the Gospel as an alternative narrative. Jesus himself is turned into a rabbi gone bad, a black magician with a yeshivah education. Jesus is one of the rabbinic class whose arrogance turns him into a rebel, and thus not so far from the midrashic interpretation of Korah discussed in chapter 2. He may have stolen the divine name from the Temple, but his magic is based on something the Jews hold to be real. What the text tries to do is to turn him into a worthy opponent in terms of rabbinic values, quite the opposite of the simple carpenter portrayed in the Gospels. The Jesus of the Gospels has to be recuperated as a rabbi in order to turn him into a heretic.

It was, then, not such a major step for Jacob Emden, in the eighteenth century, to argue that Jesus did not preach abrogation of the law but instead developed a form of Judaism for the Gentiles.[16] Emden's "tolerance" of Christianity has to be understood, of course, in the context of his obsessional campaign against Sabbatianism: where the Sabbatians break the law, the Christians come to uphold it: "It is recognized that also the Nazarene and his disciples, especially Paul, warned concerning the Torah of the Israelites to which all the circumcised are tied. And if they are truly Christians, they will observe their faith with truth, and not allow within their boundary this new unfit Messiah Shabbtai Zvi who came to destroy the earth."[17] Emden thus enlisted Christianity as an ally against the antinomian Sabbatians: true Christians are better than heretical Jews. Emden's Jesus was no heretic, as he was for the earlier tradition, but the fact that tradition could consider him a rabbi, albeit an aberrant one, laid the dialectical foundation for Emden's position.

It was an even smaller step from Emden to Moses Mendelssohn, who was in communication with Emden and clearly knew his work. In *Jerusalem*, Mendelssohn insists that even a Jew who converts is still bound by the law, and, like Emden, he enlists Jesus as his ally: "Even if one of us converts to the Christian religion, I fail to see how it is possible for him to believe that he thereby frees his conscience and rids himself of the law. Jesus of Nazareth was never heard to say that he had come to release the House of Jacob from the law. Indeed, he said, in express words, rather the opposite; and, what is still more, he himself did the opposite."[18] Jesus demarcates the border between Christianity and Judaism: he is at once a Jew and a Christian, but as a Jew he still follows the law.

Mendelssohn set the tone for what was to become a relatively common nineteenth-century Jewish position,[19] articulated most polemically for liberal Jews by Abraham Geiger. As Susannah Heschel has argued, Geiger was the first Jewish scholar to reclaim Jesus as a Jew, and he did so in order to construct a polemical counterhistory of Christianity.[20] This counterhistory made the Jews the true subjects of world history, as the source for all that is true in Christianity and Islam and as the carriers of the pure message of revelation. Jesus was a Pharisee whose messianic mission found support among the lower classes, especially in Galilee: "He was a Jew, a Pharisean Jew with Galilean coloring. . . . He did by no means utter a new thought; nor did he break down the barriers of nationality."[21] But with his death, the church, which derived from the Sadducees, developed a doctrine of fulfilled messianism that short-circuited the open-ended, future thinking of the Jewish messianic teaching. This new religion proclaimed love, but in thoroughly hypocritical terms. Geiger thus recovered Jesus for Judaism by divorcing his life from the teachings of the church. Jesus's teachings represented a legitimate form of Jewish messianism that the church corrupted. By returning to the Pharisees, of whom Jesus was a prime representative, modern Jews might recover the messianic mission that had remained in a state of quasi-concealment since the dispersion. Of course, for Geiger, the Pharisees were not equivalent to the rabbis of the Talmud, who, very much like the church fathers, had distorted their predecessors' pure teachings. They were, not surprisingly, the precursors of modern Reform. What is most arresting in Geiger's position is the way Jesus is pressed into service as a spokesman for the messianic message of the Pharisees. Judaism emerges as the true Christianity, a startling polemical reversal of the classic Christian *theologumenon*. Conversely, true Judaism—meaning Reform Judaism—is the religion of Jesus, a contention unlikely to make Geiger popular among his more traditional Jewish compatriots.

Yet far from a kind of assimilationist transformation of Judaism into a version of Protestantism, Geiger's intention was assertively Jewish. Indeed, as Heschel has documented, Geiger's reappropriation of the Jewish Jesus provoked venomous Christian rejoinders, which suggests that some Christian thinkers, at least, understood the subversive import of his position. Jesus as Pharisee was clearly the opposite of the traditional Jewish interpretation of Jesus as black magician or hypocritical bastard in the medieval polemical literature, but it shared with that literature the view that Jesus was a member of the rabbinic caste. In reclaiming Jesus as a rabbi, Geiger explicitly challenged Christians over who was the true heir of biblical messianism, and in so doing, for all his desire to modernize the Jewish religion, he continued a characteristically medieval polemical tradition.

Jesus, of course, captured the imagination of many Jewish writers and artists during the nineteenth and twentieth centuries, and it is not my purpose to review this extensive material.[22] He became a figure upon whom one could project one's own philosophy, but typically with some caveat that would explain where Christianity went wrong: one could recuperate Christianity's founder only by divorcing him from the religion bearing his name. One example is Joseph Klausner, who followed other Jewish writers in arguing for the parallels between Jesus's teaching and that of Jewish sources of the period. He did not, however, as did many Jewish apologists, see Jesus as primarily preaching an otherworldly messianism; Jesus, too, believed in a political transformation of this world. Where Jesus departed from Judaism was in the extremity of his ethical demands. As such, his movement could never be political in the full sense, that is, as anything more than a marginal group of individuals. Christian ethics, says Klausner, can work only for individuals, not for collectives.[23] Christian nations therefore have been historically barbarous, since Christianity is unable to teach true social justice. Only Zionism, for Klausner, a Revisionist Zionist himself, combined nationalism with social ethics.

Another strategy involved inversion of Christian imagery. For Lamed Shapiro, whose story "Der tzeylm" ("The Cross") occasioned a ferocious debate among eastern European intellectuals writing in Yiddish, the cross symbolized violence: the victim of a pogrom is marked on his forehead like Cain, but with a cross.[24] This savage act releases all his inhibitions, and he himself becomes as violent as his persecutors.[25] The meaning of the cross is inverted: it redeems not through love but through violence. Yet the cross as a symbol for suffering is, of course, central to Christianity, and Jewish writers and artists, responding to the pogroms of the late nineteenth and early twentieth centuries, saw an inversion of persecutors and victims: where traditional Christianity accuses the Jews of deicide, this Jewish interpretation, in David Roskies's phrase, put "Jews on the cross."[26] Artists like Marc Chagall found Christian imagery the most evocative for expressing the suffering of the Jews.[27]

Yet here too, a seemingly revolutionary appropriation of Judaism's most famous heretic had traditional resonance. In seeming response to the Christian interpretation of the suffering servant of Isaiah 53 as Jesus, Rashi argued, probably in the wake of the First Crusade, that it is the Jewish people as a whole to which the suffering servant motif refers.[28] Although of course the source, the Bible, is itself Jewish, Rashi's interpretation was driven by Christian exegesis. Similarly, the Hebrew Crusader chronicles, as Shalom Spiegel pointed out in his famous essay, appropriate the *akedah* of Isaac in a way that suggests full awareness of the Christian use of this biblical motif as a prefiguration of Jesus.[29] When one reads the Jewish chronicles of the Crusades, one is struck by how often the theology of the texts sounds explicitly Christian, with the tales of martyred women that resonate with the cult of the Virgin Mary or with the claim that the blood of the martyrs atones not only for the sins of their own generation but for the sins of all the generations.[30] Filled with extraordinarily violent language denouncing Christianity and its founder, the chronicles nevertheless derive much of their imagery, including the language of blood vengeance and atonement, from those they explicitly call heretics.

Yet the modern appropriation of Jesus differed significantly from the medieval in several crucial respects. While medieval writers might borrow Christian motifs, they never revealed their source, while the modern writers and artists are only too willing to put the Nazarene at the explicit center of their projects. Moreover, if in central Europe and the United States the recuperation of Jesus was limited to the theological realm, writers like Shapiro, Zhitlovsky, and Sholem Ash, as well as artists like Chagall, had thoroughly secular agendas. Indeed, one might argue that once detached from his Christian moorings, Jesus served as an unlikely source for a secular Jewish identity.

Turning now to Shabbtai Zvi, not all Orthodox opponents of the seventeenth-century Messiah followed Emden in dissociating Christianity from the more recent heresy of the Sabbatians. The hagiographical collection of stories about Israel Baal Shem Tov, *Shivhei ha-Besht*, first published in 1814, contains some fascinating material on the Besht's relationship to Shabbtai Zvi:

> Rabbi Joel told me . . . that Shabbtai Zvi came to the Besht to ask for redemption. Rabbi Joel said in these words: "The *tikkun* is done through the connection of soul with soul, spirit with spirit and breath with breath." The Besht began to establish the connection moderately. He was afraid as Shabbtai Zvi was a terribly wicked man. Once the Besht was asleep and Shabbtai Zvi, may his name be blotted out, came and attempted to tempt him again, God forbid. With a mighty thrust the Besht hurled him to the bottom of hell. The Besht peered down and saw that he landed on the same pallet with Jesus.[31]

This is a thoroughly subversive teaching that the editor of *Shivhei ha-Besht* tries to efface by claiming, "I was reluctant to write it down, but nevertheless I did so to show to what extent pride can be dangerous." Pride, however, has little to do with the matter at hand. Instead, if a *tikkun* can be done only by someone in the same "soul family" as the one being redeemed (a principle that has its origins in Lurianic Kabbalah), then Jesus, Shabbtai Zvi, and the Besht are all related. Whether one can infer that they are therefore all related to the soul family of the Messiah remains unclear, but what is indisputable is that the line between the hero and the heretics is not quite as distinct as the text proclaims. On the very eve of modernity, a work that would become canonical for a movement that has served as one pillar of Ashkenazic Orthodoxy hints, perhaps not fully conscious of the implications, that certain heretics might lie as much "inside" as "outside." I will take up the modern secular recovery of Shabbtai Zvi in the next chapter.

RECUPERATING THE "OTHER"

Aher or Elisha ben Abuya is perhaps the archetype of the Jewish heretic: unlike Jesus, he did not found a monotheistic religion, or, like Shabbtai Zvi, convert to another monotheistic religion. Instead, according to some of the rabbinic accounts, he denied the very essence of Judaism and perhaps even the existence of the divine.[32] One text holds that he believed in two divinities (*shtei reshuyot*), but in another he proclaims, "There is neither justice nor a judge." And in yet another he denies the validity of the law. He reads the heretical books, chases after "evil culture" (*tarbut ra'ah*), and pursues a hedonistic life. For all or some of these reasons, he proved an attractive figure for those modern Jews rebelling against traditional Judaism. Richard Rubenstein, the post-Holocaust theologian who proclaimed the death of God when it became briefly fashionable to do so in Protestant theological circles, quoted Aher: after the Holocaust, the only justifiable position is that "there is neither justice nor a judge."[33]

Elisha was the subject of a number of scholarly studies in the nineteenth century.[34] The first of these was Heinrich Graetz's doctoral dissertation, "Gnosticismus und Judenthum," published in 1846. For Graetz, who assumed that Gnosticism was an actual religious philosophy, Judaism in late antiquity was virtually defined at its core as the opposite of Gnosticism: where the Gnostics believed that law derived from an evil demigod, Judaism held that the law was revealed by a good, transcendent God.[35] Where Gnosticism preached hedonism and communism of property and women, Judaism insisted on strict sexual morality. Although in his "Structure of Jewish History" Graetz was to argue against reducing Judaism to a single essence, his doctoral dissertation is driven by exactly that impulse. Thus, Aher, in Graetz's hands, does not merely become alienated from Judaism but adopts a "type of opposition against the essence of Judaism."[36] And that opposition can only be Gnosticism. Indeed, Elisha's other two companions, Ben Azzai and Ben Zoma, who come to a bad end after entering the *pardes*, are also infected with forms of Gnosticism, although not to the same extent as Elisha. For Graetz, then, Aher's licentious and antinomian behavior flows directly from the religious philosophy he adopts in place of Judaism. Aher is a critical figure for Graetz because he is the heretic who establishes by negation the very truths of Judaism.[37] It is entirely possible that Graetz's treatment of Aher was designed as a warning against the perils of nineteenth-century Reform: denial of the law would lead to Elisha's fate. And his interpretation leaves no room for recuperation; in fact, he dismisses the stories of Rabbi Meir's attempt to rehabilitate Elisha as unreliable and unhistorical.

Graetz was not to have the last word, however. Like Jesus and Shabbtai Zvi, Aher attracted the attention of writers of fiction and drama, among them (in Yiddish) Leon Feinberg's *Got fun Tsorn* and Jacob Gordon's *Elisha ben Avuyo—drama in fir akten*. Here, however, I want to look at one particular work in English that actually had wide influence: Milton Steinberg's *As a Driven Leaf*, first published in 1939 but still in print as of the present writing.[38] Steinberg was a Conservative rabbi deeply influenced by Mordecai Kaplan's Reconstructionism.[39] It is perhaps not a coincidence that Kaplan was perhaps the only public figure among American Jews to have been declared a heretic by Orthodox rabbis.[40] As one of Kaplan's most prominent disciples, Steinberg could not avoid the question of what heresy might mean in a modern, American Jewish context.

Steinberg was a middlebrow writer whose *Basic Judaism*, first published in 1947, became a virtually canonical text for several decades after World War II and is also still in print. His novel about the life of Elisha ben Abuya needs to be read against (or with) *Basic Judaism*. In the latter book, Steinberg takes a middle-of-the-road position on the contradictions between what he calls "the traditionalist" and "the modernist" views. While allowing each of these movements their voice, he tries to demonstrate that "the two groups, traditionalist and modernist, have more in common than apart. Their viewpoints make up not two religions but variants of one."[41] The Jewish religion is nondogmatic and tolerant of different doctrinal points of view. One can be a good Jew, as well, by following a variety of ritual practices, from the traditional to the modern. For Steinberg, "basic" Judaism is a very large tent with room for all parties and opinions: while it lacks a single essence, in the nineteenth-century meaning of the word, it can still be reduced to a common set of principles.

The purpose of Jewish monotheism is not just repudiation of idol worship; it is even more the claim that "reality is an order, not an anarchy; that mankind is a unity, not a hodge-podge; and that one universal law of righteousness holds sway over men, transcending borders, surmounting all class lines."[42] Note how little this formulation relies on the existence of a divinity! Polytheism, on the other hand, by assuming a different deity for each object in nature, "tore reality to shreds and then, to confound confusion, assumed that each spirit had no other role except to look after its own. Under this construction there was no order, either logical or moral to things."[43] We will need to keep these two quotations in mind as we turn to the novel.

In his *Partisan Guide to the Jewish Problem*, Steinberg laments the lack of Jewish fiction in English.[44] He clearly saw his own work as an exception. The novel about Elisha is a rather well-written reconstruction of Jewish culture and religion in late first-, early second-century Palestine, ending with the Bar Kokhba rebellion. There are, of course, many ways in which Steinberg created an overly idealized portrait of the rabbinical class: the Sanhedrin sounds like a cross between an American university academic senate and a court. To be fair to Steinberg, he included an "Author's Note" in which he explains which sections of the novel were based on historical sources and which were his own invention.[45] But my purpose in discussing the novel is not to evaluate its virtues and vices but rather to examine the uses to which Steinberg puts the life of Elisha.

The first question that the novel raises is why Steinberg chose to portray the history of the early rabbinic period through the lens of its greatest heretic. Elisha clearly represents not only the possibility of ancient heresy but also a prototype of the modern assimilated Jew. Yet Steinberg's own position on Elisha is much more complicated than that: the book is not simply a sermon against assimilation. Elisha's father is a Hellenizer who tries to avoid his son's circumcision and raises the boy with a Greek tutor. But when the father dies, Elisha is adopted by his uncle, Amram, a pious Jew of the rabbinical caste, who is presented as a harsh and unbending patriarch. The figure of Amram casts a rather dark shadow over rabbinic Judaism and makes Elisha's earlier Greek education seem comparatively more benign by contrast. Thus, even in the early pages of the novel, the seemingly obvious dichotomy between good Orthodox Jews and evil Hellenizers becomes much more blurred.

Steinberg presents Elisha throughout as a sympathetic figure whose decision to abandon Judaism does not come easily or without ambivalence. Elisha endorses the *pax Romana* that "provided security for the individual and the opportunity to live out his life without hindrance in pursuit of the dreams of his heart,"[46] a formulation suspiciously like the American creed of individualism and equal opportunities for all. But he is repelled by the slave market and the fact that the empire is built upon the labor of slaves (perhaps a hint of Steinberg's own moderate socialism). He makes cogent arguments against the Bar Kokhba rebellion, but his collaboration with the Romans against the Jews, which is suggested by one rabbinic source,[47] is a consequence, in the novel, of blackmail: Elisha saves his friend Pappas from death by cooperating with Tinneas Rufus. Elisha is a reluctant traitor.

The most important element in the Talmudic Elisha ben Abuya stories is, of course, the four who entered the *pardes*, of whom only Rabbi Akiva comes out unharmed, while Elisha "cut the saplings." Just what this experience was and just what Elisha is said to have done have both been the subjects of intense debate among scholars since the nineteenth century. Steinberg reduces what many consider a mystical journey to a graduate seminar: Akiva, Elisha, Ben Zoma, and Ben Azzai convene as a kind of special study circle, and Elisha convinces them that they should examine the very roots of Jewish faith in order to construct defenses against skepticism. Ben Azzai specializes in Gnostic mysticism, Ben Zoma in biblical exegesis, and Akiva in "reasoned theology," while Elisha raises the skeptical questions. Unlike Graetz, Steinberg sees Elisha not as a Gnostic but as a student of Greek philosophy. Akiva, no less than Elisha, reads Greek philosophy, but as a kind of prototype for Maimonides, he studies Aristotle side by side with Jewish texts: Akiva is not surprisingly Steinberg's role model for the committed Jew who also immerses himself in worldly knowledge. Ben Azzai's mystical speculations lead to his death, and Ben Zoma goes mad. Following one of the most prevalent interpretations of the mysterious "cutting the saplings," Steinberg has Elisha attend a schoolhouse and voice heretical opinions.

But it is not the *pardes* that causes Elisha to begin his heretical path in Steinberg's narrative. Instead, it is the death of his disciple Meir's twin sons, a story from the midrash that does not, however, include Elisha.⁴⁸ Here Steinberg introduces an erotic element in his tale. Elisha's marriage lacks true love: his wife, Deborah, is a greedy social climber. Elisha is attracted to Bruriah, Meir's wife and, famously, a woman learned in Torah. Elisha confesses his lust for her, but he restrains himself from doing anything about it. It is somewhat puzzling that Steinberg does not make more of Bruriah's learning, since, as a follower of Mordecai Kaplan, he must have envisioned a more equal role for women. But it is Elisha's love for Bruriah, as well as for his disciple Meir, that makes the death of the twins his theological watershed.

Steinberg follows up this erotic incident with the story of Elisha and the prostitute. But here the prostitute, whom he names Manto, is really a courtesan in Antioch, a woman of considerable learning who holds a salon in her elegant house. After Elisha irrevocably breaks from Judaism, he flees to Antioch, where he commences his Greek philosophical studies in earnest. He is invited to Manto's house for a soirée, and, still hesitant to eat nonkosher food, he eats what he takes to be an anchovy but what is actually a turnip cut to look like an anchovy, as Manto explains to him. This peculiar scene makes absolutely no sense if one doesn't know the original Talmudic story, but it suggests the degree to which Steinberg softens Elisha's heretical behavior. True, in the end he becomes Manto's lover, even though she is officially linked to Tinneas Rufus, but he hardly leads a dissolute life.

Quite the opposite: he undertakes a philosophical project—a kind of unified field theory of philosophy—based on geometric proofs. Here it is impossible not to think of Spinoza, whose *Ethics* was just such a geometric construct, organized around axioms and theorems. Without mentioning the seventeenth-century heretic, Steinberg implicitly equates the two. Both sought absolute truth outside of Jewish belief, and both (at least in Steinberg's account of Elisha's life) remained solitary and isolated, bereft of family and friends.⁴⁹ Elisha's project fails when he discovers that even the truths of Euclid can be subverted by non-Euclidean geometry. His faith in reason disintegrates, just as his Jewish faith did earlier. Crushed by his defeat, he returns to Palestine from Antioch and, finding his old disciple, Rabbi Meir, confesses: "And now ... here I am with nothing—no God, no friends, no home."⁵⁰ A tragic figure at the end, he is ready to repent, but, as the Talmudic account itself states, "All may repent, save only Elisha the son of Abuya."

His journey has led him in a circle, so that he is now ready to return to the point of his departure: "And yet I may not enter. For those who live there insist, at least in our generation, on the total acceptance without reservation of their revealed religion. And I cannot surrender the liberty of my mind to any authority."[31] The relevant phrase here is "at least in our generation." For Steinberg clearly wanted to construct a Judaism that would allow liberty of the mind to coexist with revealed religion. Rather than a heretic intent on destroying Judaism, Steinberg's Aher seeks what in Steinberg's view will become possible only two millennia later.

In my examination of the treatment of these heretics, I have tried to show that Peter Berger's dichotomy of tradition and modernity fails to hold true, as he defines it, at least for modern Jewish culture. Traditional or rabbinic Judaism had its own ambivalence toward those it declared heretics, and modern recuperations of Jesus and Elisha ben Abuya were not free from similar ambivalences. In the modern cases, these ambivalences found expression by projecting back on heretical figures from history the conflicts of modernity and transforming these heretics into useful building blocks of modern identities. To label these modern treatments "counterhistories"—that is, thorough inversions of the heretics into heroes—may too easily elide the ambiguities that attend the representations of even the most "heretical" of them. In this light, the polar opposition of heretics versus heroes breaks down and yields a much more complex and dialectical relationship between them. And in an age when secular ideologies have often hardened into orthodoxies by labeling dissenters heretics, modernity does not always appear to be defined by absolute freedom of choice. In constructing modern identities, whether Jewish or not, the hold of tradition, with its now-complicated categories of orthodoxy and heresy, remains a subterranean reality.

CHAPTER 9

Shabbtai Zvi and the Seductions of Jewish Orientalism

IN ONE OF HIS EARLIEST diary entries, dated just before the outbreak of World War I, Gershom Scholem describes a trip to the Swiss Alps.[1] There he engaged in a series of romantic meditations that include a reference to Shabbtai Zvi, who, he says, astonished the people by going into the marketplace in Ismir and pronouncing the four-letter name of God. Despite the popular belief that he should have been struck by lightning, nothing happened. Scholem uses this historical anecdote as a rather surprising way of demonstrating the deluded nature of the Jewish people, who cannot recognize the metaphysical meaning of the grandeur and beauty of the high mountains. Whatever this obscure text may have actually meant to him, one has the distinct feeling that Scholem is comparing himself to Shabbtai Zvi, a comparison that gains some support from his later claim in the diary to be the Messiah.[2]

How and what did Scholem know about Shabbtai Zvi in 1914? He certainly might have encountered him in Heinrich Graetz's history, which, as he tells us in his memoirs, he had already read in 1911.[3] What I wish to argue in this essay, however, is that Shabbtai Zvi was in the air in many different forms in the late nineteenth and early twentieth centuries. In the first sentence of his great essay "Redemption through Sin," Scholem says that "no chapter in the history of the Jewish people during the last several hundred years has been as shrouded in mystery as that of the Sabbatian movement."[4] Despite the common belief today, cultivated in part by Scholem himself, that he had rescued the Sabbatian movement from obscurity and turned it into the major watershed between the Jewish Middle Ages and modernity, there was a rich historical and imaginative literature about Sabbatianism available in German, Yiddish, Hebrew, English, and Russian when Scholem was a young man. In his biography of Shabbtai Zvi, Scholem refers occasionally in passing to this literature and generally dismisses it as historically worthless, an accusation that is largely accurate, if exaggerated. But regardless of their historical validity, these novels, biographies, and essays created a climate of interest in Sabbatianism that must have caught the young Scholem's attention and suggested certain themes for his later investigations.

Some of this literature about Sabbatianism was surveyed by Shmuel Werses in his book on Sabbatianism and the Haskalah.[5] But Werses ends where I propose to begin: with the late nineteenth and early twentieth centuries, which witnessed perhaps an even greater profusion of writing about Sabbatianism than had been the case earlier in the nineteenth century. Werses concludes with a short chapter on the way Jewish nationalist writers transformed attitudes toward Sabbatianism from the negative stance of much of the Haskalah to a new appreciation. Although some of the material that I will cover overlaps with this chapter—and some with material that he covers in other chapters—I want to look at literature written not only by Jewish nationalists but also by some who are often labeled as assimilationists.

Beyond staking out a somewhat different literary territory from that of Werses, I am interested in some very different issues. Sabbatianism functioned as a kind of cultural code for authors working on the borders between Judaism and modernity, as a projection back onto the seventeenth century of modern problems of Jewish identity and assimilation. The most interesting literature of the fin de siècle period was neither pro- nor anti-Sabbatian in the sometimes dichotomous sense we find in Werses. Instead, these works often involve ambiguities that point in suggestive ways to the ambivalence of their authors toward a whole host of contemporary issues: rabbinical authority, heresy, conversion, and messianism, among others.

JEWISH ORIENTALISM

One issue that I want to address in particular is Sabbatianism as a vehicle for constructing a kind of Jewish Orientalism at a time when the Orient was exerting a particularly complex fascination on Jews. As I shall try to show, ambivalence about the Jewish Orient captured many of the other ambivalences of these writers about contemporary Jewish culture. It is in the context of this Jewish Orientalism that I also want to situate the young Scholem's fascination with Sabbatianism, a context quite different from where he is usually located.

In his now classic work *Orientalism*, Edward Said suggested that the range of European associations with the Orient, such as "the Oriental character, Oriental despotism, Oriental sensuality and the like,"[6] are really projections or constructions by Westerners, primarily during the age of imperialism. The power to construct the Orient as a field of knowledge in certain stereotyped ways was part and parcel of the projection of Western power into the area of the Near East. Yet because Orientalism had little to do with the actual Orient, it tells us much more about those doing the constructing than about those being constructed: "Orientalism is—and does not simply represent—a considerable dimension of modern political-intellectual culture, and, as such, has less to do with the Orient than it does with 'our' world."[7]

The history of Jewish Orientalism remains to be written,[8] and I can only offer the barest outlines here, insofar as they connect to the theme of this essay. Paul Mendes-Flohr has suggested that Jewish views of the Orient shifted with Jewish attitudes toward assimilation. In the middle of the nineteenth century, Jews sought to distance themselves from their ostensibly "Oriental" behaviors; with the rise of Zionism and other forms of Jewish self-affirmation at the fin de siècle, many Jews, following Martin Buber,[9] enthusiastically embraced their Oriental heritage in rebellion against the bourgeois West.[10]

Without disputing this overall picture, I believe that even those Jews who affirmed the Oriental in themselves did so in ways that were often quite ambivalent, an ambivalence typical of the way the Western imagination generally depicted the Orient. Although Jewish attitudes often resembled those of other Europeans, Jewish treatments of the Orient were complicated by several factors. Jewish Orientalism, as opposed to non-Jewish, involved constructing an object that was also in some sense ostensibly one's self, the subject that was doing the constructing: those who imagined a Jewish Orient were always conscious of the fact that they themselves were being imagined by non-Jews as Orientals. If the Orient became the classic site of the Other, Jewish Orientalism involved a complex dialectic of projection and displacement of oneself onto an object that was never really other. The fact that the Jewish people originated in the Orient as well as the presence of real Jews in the contemporary Orient aroused contradictory feelings among European Jews of identification and alienation.[11] These Oriental Jews might represent the vestiges of biblical Jews or, alternatively, primitive Jews still mired in medieval obscurantism and irrationality. If one imagined Jewish identity to be primarily European, the Oriental Jews were an inconvenient embarrassment; on the other hand, if one wished to see in Judaism the "spirit of the Orient," one might represent both the Orient and the Orientals in far more positive terms. What has not been sufficiently noticed is the way these contradictory attitudes might exist simultaneously even in those eager to affirm their Oriental "otherness."

When Zionism emerged as both a political and settlement movement, the question of the Orient took on great urgency.[12] Zionist Orientalism, undoubtedly indebted to both European and Jewish Orientalism of the nineteenth century, developed its own peculiar dynamic, especially once European Zionists confronted real Oriental Jews, such as the Yemenites, who came to settle in the Land of Israel. Since the Zionists proposed to take the Jews out of Europe and back to the Middle East, ambivalence about becoming once again "Levantine" turned into a touchstone for the tension in early Zionism between Eurocentric modernism and anti-European antimodernism. Was Zionism to be part of the Orient, or was it to be a movement of European modernity projected into the Middle East?

European Orientalism itself can be divided between those who had actual contact with the Orient and those whose images were constructed much more out of sheer imagination. The French and the English fit loosely into the first category and the Germans into the second. Similarly, Jewish Orientalism divides between those who had direct contact with the Jews of North Africa and the Middle East and those who did not. Because of the French involvement in the region, French Jews were among the first to develop complex direct relationships with Jews in North Africa, Turkey, and other areas of the Ottoman Empire. This new interest in the Orient was awakened by the Damascus Blood Libel in 1840 and, as Aron Rodrigue has shown, was expressed in the educational network of the Alliance Israelite Universelle.[13] The Alliance's project of bringing French Enlightenment to the backward Jews of the Ottoman Empire was the product of Orientalist images of these Jews, but it also contributed toward the production and dissemination of these images.

German and eastern European Jews had less direct contact with Jews of the East, but the images were often similar. Much, although not all, of the late nineteenth- and early twentieth-century literature on Sabbatianism was produced in German. As we will see, these German Jewish authors often conflated images of the Orient with images of the Ostjuden, who, as Steven Aschheim has shown, functioned for German Jews in a similar cultural fashion as Oriental Jews.[14] An additional aspect to the German Jewish literature about the Orient is the curious role of the Sephardic Jew. As Ismar Schorsch argued more than thirty years ago and as John Efron has elaborated more recently, Sephardic Jews often served for enlightened German Jews as models of acculturation without assimilation; the Sephardic Jew represented a kind of Jewish nobility, as opposed to the obscurantist and vulgar Ostjuden.[15] With the discovery of the "degraded" Oriental Jews as an ostensible offshoot of the Sephardim, the image of the Sephardim shifted to a contradictory mixture of nobility and degeneration, a mixture that is particularly evident in the representations of Sabbatianism.

SABBATIANISM AND THE ORIENT

One example of this ambivalent representation can be found in a 1932 travelogue written by the German-Jewish newspaper publisher Esriel Carlebach, under the title *Exotische Juden*.[16] For Carlebach and, one presumes, his readers, the "exotic" was the Orient, defined primarily as the Mediterranean. The first chapter treats the "proud Spaniards" (*stolze Spanier*), the Sephardic Jews of Salonica. Following the long tradition described by Schorsch, Carlebach contrasts the nobility and pride of these Jews with the "hunchback" (*gebeugten-Rückens*) Jews of the North. The Spanish Jews of Salonica set the stage for Carlebach's journeys to other exotic communities of the Orient, including Morocco, Tunis, Tripoli, Yemen, and Smyrna. There he found a variety of "exotic" Jews, exotic not only because of their geographical location but also because of their heterodox beliefs: Karaites, Marranos, and Sabbatians.

Carlebach's Sabbatians were the remains of the Dönmeh sect in Ismir. He describes the "half-darkened" synagogue, mysterious and virtually ruined, where he encounters old men and women, the vestiges of the community. In contrast with this contemporary scene of decay, Carlebach describes the birth of Sabbatianism in almost revolutionary terms. Shabbtai Zvi was a "sensitive, ecstatic young man" who dared to duel with God in protest against the slaughter of the Polish Jews by Chmielnitski. Anticipating Scholem and in line with most of the other descriptions of the impact of Sabbatianism, Carlebach claims that the movement swept the whole Jewish world. Yet Carlebach blames the failure of Sabbatianism on Shabbtai Zvi, who, he says, thought more about himself than about redemption; he was a Messiah not fully committed to messianism.

Carlebach sees the continuing faith of latter-day Sabbatians like Jonathan Eibeschütz and the Dönmeh sect not as a belief in Shabbtai Zvi himself but as a belief in the spiritual phenomenon represented by Sabbatianism. Therefore, he says, it is curiously positive and even prescriptive for modern European Jews: the Donmeh Sabbatians read Maupassant and Voltaire, but when they pray they put away Western literature, just as they do the Koran, speak only Hebrew, and refer only to sacred Jewish texts. Like European Jews, many of the sect "became Greek and married foreigners." Those who have remained faithful have learned the art of dissembling, of seeming to be Muslims while actually remaining Jews. To be able to believe in Shabbtai Zvi nearly three hundred years after his apostasy is a "trick of the soul" not that different from that required to be a Jew in modern times. Thus, the movement that began in ecstasy but failed due to the weakness of its leader still holds a message for Jews facing the challenge of assimilation. In this conclusion, the Sabbatian community of Smyrna represents for Carlebach a peculiar mixture of antiquated decay and stubborn national pride, a combination typical of others of Carlebach's exotic Jews of the Orient.

The role of the Orient as the birthplace of Sabbatianism is evident as well in Josef Kastein's vivid biography *Shabbtai Zewi: Der Messias von*

Ismir, published in Germany in 1930. Kastein's book resembles much of the nineteenth-century literature discussed by Werses in combining historical sources with fictional embellishment. Although Scholem dismissed Kastein's work as little more than a novel, his bibliography includes many of the sources in Hebrew and European languages from the time of the events. Even if Kastein did allow himself poetic license, he did so after fairly extensive historical research.

Seeking to explain the widespread impact of the movement, Kastein argues that Shabbtai Zvi "succeeded, for the people he was addressing were not only credulous Jews but also Orientals. In this connection, one should not forget that there were two factors that did much toward increasing credence for the reports that were circulated—in the Orient the fickle receptivity toward fantasy [*die leichte, phantasiebegabte Empfänglichkeit*], and in the West the allure of the alien [*der Reiz der Entfernung*] and respect for the written word."[17] If the movement's attraction in the East had to do with Oriental irrationalism, the Western Jews were drawn in by two contradictory impulses: a kind of rationalism connected with respect for written reports, and the enchantment of the exotic. Kastein is describing a kind of seventeenth-century Jewish Orientalism as the source for Western Sabbatianism. But he also captures the reasons for contemporary fascination with Sabbatianism. In the twentieth century, the Orient still represented the exotic, as it did in the seventeenth, but knowledge of the Orient, mediated through the written word (that is, Kastein's own book), gives this exoticism a veneer of scientific respectability. This is exactly the combination that Said describes in his analysis of nineteenth-century European accounts of the Orient.

Despite the impression that a passage like this might leave, Kastein was not at all hostile to Sabbatianism. In fact, his attitude was generally quite sympathetic, since he saw Sabbatianism as a legitimate response to Jewish homelessness, a theme that he repeats almost like a litany in his introductory chapter. As a central European Jew, Kastein needed to account for how the more "rational" and "skeptical" Jews who were his ancestors were attracted to the movement in a way different from the alien Oriental Jews. For example, in Venice the news was received with skepticism: "Here is intelligent soil, where much is investigated and much is doubted. Here is no more of the fantastic Oriental imagination."[18] Similarly, in Hamburg and Amsterdam the descendants of the Marranos were more fully equipped with spiritual or intellectual (*Geistigen*) qualities than the Polish Jews, because their suffering was "sublimated." These Jews, who are clearly Kastein's heroes, "regarded [Sabbatianism] from a more worldly, concrete and *political* point of view than the Oriental and Polish Jews. To the other Jews it was a fresh beginning; to them it was a continuation on a higher and clearer plane. And in their response, they showed passionate joy and unfettered exuberance rather than dark and painful penitential practices."[19] The East—whether eastern Europe or the Middle East—is dark and ascetic, while the West is joyful and worldly, a theme to which I will return.

Among the political responses to Sabbatianism, Kastein includes Spinoza's famous "Zionist" passage in his *Tractatus Theologico-Politicus*: Jewish sovereignty might in fact be restored under the proper political constellation.[20] In connecting Spinoza with Sabbatianism in this positive sense, Kastein turns Graetz's association of the two on its head: where Graetz saw Spinoza as the mirror image of Shabbtai Zvi—rationalism versus irrationalism—Kastein brings them together under the category of politics.[21] Spinoza understood the import of Sabbatianism politically. While it is unlikely that Spinoza was in fact commenting on Sabbatianism in this passage (although he was aware of the movement), Kastein may well have been onto something interesting. Following Scholem, much of the work on Sabbatianism has focused primarily on mystical ideas and less on the overtly political side of the movement, such as the persistent use of royal titles for Shabbtai Zvi and the way the movement unfolded within the political relations between the Ottoman Jewish communities and the Turkish state. Interestingly, this fruitful direction for research was anticipated by some of the literature that Scholem dismissed, such as Kastein's work, which focuses much more on the political than on the mystical.[22]

Despite his identification with the ostensibly reasoned position of the Amsterdam and Hamburg Jews, Kastein was by no means a dogmatic rationalist. In language reminiscent of Martin Buber, he notes that "an Age is ripe for a great experience [*Erlebnis*], when it has the courage momentarily to abandon the lamentable control of the brain and surrenders oneself to necessities of the heart."[23] This distinction between brain and heart corresponds to Kastein's dichotomy in his introductory chapter between the Bible, which stirs the emotions, and the rationalism of the Talmud. He sees the Talmud as a legal system of "endless interpretations, reflections, speculations, and theories" that weaned the Jews from the emotional sustenance of the Bible. He even surprisingly claims that the rabbis forbade Jews from reading the Bible before age twenty![24] The Kabbalah attempted a synthesis between the Bible and the Talmud, and Shabbtai Zevi represented the great experience in which the dictates of reason were suspended in favor of a higher law. For a secular Jew like Kastein (and Scholem), Sabbatianism was a precursor of the modern revolt against rabbinic legalism.

As for Carlebach, the failure of Sabbatianism was the failure of its leader, who was not himself transformed by this great experience. Here Kastein becomes rather obscure: Shabbtai Zvi "emulated a historical form of leadership without any adequate spiritual equipment." He never truly transcended the religion against which he rebelled. In a sense, Kastein holds that Sabbatianism was not radical enough: it did not address the universal desire for redemption, "the fundamental fact that a whole world wished to become to be reconciled with its God and its own existence." This desire for redemption continued to echo weakly in movements like Hasidism and Zionism, but it succeeded in neither; writing in 1930, Kastein, who was himself a proponent of Zionism and ended up emigrating to Palestine in 1935, declared that "in Zionism, which was an attempt at a partial solution on the plane of reality, it [redemption] met with defeat."[25]

Interestingly enough, it was only in the philosophy of Martin Buber that Kastein found the true realization of the idea of redemption, and as we have just seen, there are several places in his book where such Buberian terms as *Erlebnis* and *Zweisprache* appear. Arguing that "nothing can so disfigure God's countenance as religion,"[26] he seems to have believed that Shabbtai Zvi was not able to translate his antinomianism into a true spirituality of dialogue. Might it be that, for Kastein, Shabbtai Zvi's Oriental origins precluded the possibility of such philosophical messianism? Only the spiritual equipment of the central European Jews, and not the fantastic imaginations of the Oriental or eastern European Jews, could provide the necessary synthesis between emotion and reason.

If Kastein saw in Shabbtai Zvi's Orientalism the fatal flaw of the movement, the same perhaps was true for Theodor Herzl. A number of early

Zionist writers, such as Shai Ish-Hurwitz, drew explicit comparisons between Zionism and Sabbatianism and between Herzl and Shabbtai Zvi.[27] Herzl himself was evidently uncomfortable with such associations, although he devoted relatively little attention to his ostensible seventeenth-century forerunner. At one point in his diaries, Herzl says, "The difference between Shabbtai Zvi and myself is that he made himself great to be like the great ones of the world, whereas I find the great just as small as I am."[28] This is a rather enigmatic entry, given Herzl's megalomania attested in other places in the diaries.

A more decisive statement of his position on Sabbatianism, and one more relevant for our purposes, can be found in his utopian novel, *Altneuland*. When his two protagonists return to Palestine after twenty years on a desert island, they tour the now-thriving Jewish utopia. At one point, their hosts propose attending one of the cultural offerings of the colony. The choices are a play about Moses at the "National Theater," which they reject as too pietistically uplifting, several popular Yiddish farces, which they dismiss as beneath them, and an opera about Shabbtai Zvi, advertised as "the most beautiful of all modern Jewish operas." Curious about this figure of whom they claim ignorance, they are told: "Shabbtai Zvi was a false Messiah who appeared in Turkey at the beginning of the seventeenth century [*sic*]. He succeeded in gathering a great following among Oriental Jews, but later he became a Moslem and met a sorry end."[29] The visitors declare, "The perfect villain for an Opera," and off the party goes to see the performance.

This brief passage deserves some careful attention. The opera about Shabbtai Zvi stands culturally somewhere between pious "high" religion, represented by the theatrical treatment of Moses, and the low culture of the Ostjuden, represented by the Yiddish farces. In light of Herzl's dismissal of religion and patronizing attitude toward the Ostjuden, only the theme of a messianic movement can be said to have "national" significance. The opera treats a theme out of Jewish history whose value, Herzl suggests, is as a cautionary tale about the pitfalls that Zionism must avoid: although initially sincere, Shabbtai became a "villain" as the mob began to follow him. Here is an example of Herzl's own ambivalence about leading a popular movement; his own theory of Zionism as a vanguard suggests rather a certain elitism.

Unlike other contemporary treatments of Sabbatianism, Herzl sees the movement as primarily an Oriental affair, thus implicitly contrasting it with his own movement. In one place in his diaries, Herzl insists that while Sabbatianism was based on utopian fantasy, his movement will succeed, since "we have machines,"[30] that is, Western technology. For the Jews of the Middle Ages, only fantasies based on charismatic figures might inspire action, while in modern times, when the people are able "to gauge their own strength," miracles and charismatic leaders are no longer needed. Here, once again, we encounter a certain ambivalence on Herzl's part about his own status as a charismatic leader.

Despite Herzl's explicit distancing from Sabbatianism expressed in his narrative description of the movement, the capsule libretto of his fictional opera tells a somewhat different story. Shabbtai is persecuted by a "choir of angry rabbis," but his "strong personality charmed even his opponents and they fell back before him." Here Herzl may have in mind his own controversies with Orthodox authorities who opposed his movement, and in fact he suggests that "sensible pious Jews" have rejected the "partisan rabbis" and joined the Zionist movement.

The opera about Shabbtai Zvi is the only place in *Altneuland*—with one other exception[31]—in which Herzl refers to Oriental Jews. The Eurocentric character of Herzl's Zionism is, of course, no great surprise, and he was not the only one to suffer from a blind spot about the Orientals, whether Jews or Arabs. But his treatment of Sabbatianism was designed to contrast those backward Jews, whether of the Orient or elsewhere, who believed in miracles and were therefore swept up by false messianism, with an enlightened, modern movement based on technology. The Orient represented for Herzl the religious obscurantism and utopian thinking that Zionism had to oppose. The lack of any identifiable Oriental Jews in the *Altneuland* (as opposed to the presence of enlightened, pro-Zionist Arabs) suggests that Herzl proposed to ignore rather than modernize the real Jews of the Middle East.

EROTIC MESSIANISM AND THE ORIENT

In *Altneuland*, Shabbtai Zvi's finest moment comes when a young girl, who is his disciple, tries to defend him "in a grand aria" and is attacked by rabbis "in a great rage." The prophet then returns to save her, and she follows him after the rabbis ban him from Smyrna. At this point, Friedrich, the character who might be called Herzl's alter ego, stops following the opera when he spies the now-decrepit woman he was in love with twenty years earlier and as a result of whose betrayal he left Europe. The contrast between the manly, charismatic Shabbtai Zvi and the jilted Friedrich is clear: the European Jew cannot find his erotic fulfillment in Europe, for the woman of his initial dreams will turn into a middle-aged hag. Only by the end of the novel does Friedrich find true romantic fulfillment in Miriam, the daughter of the Jewish colony in the Orient.[32]

In his fictional opera about Shabbtai Zvi, Herzl never exploits the erotic possibilities of Sabbatianism. The young female disciple is described only as following Shabbtai and not as his romantic partner. In this chaste presentation, Herzl may, in fact, be suggesting his own repressed ambivalence about the erotic energies inherent in leading a great political movement. Yet Herzl's avoidance of explicit eroticism left him very much in the minority, for most of the writers about Shabbtai Zvi from our period focused disproportionate attention on the erotic and, not surprisingly, on Eros linked to the Orient.

One aspect of the Orient as imagined by Orientalists has almost invariably been its effeminate sensuality, personified, as Said demonstrates, in Flaubert's courtesan Kuchuk Hanem.[33] For Jewish Orientalists, the Sabbatian movement provided a rich opportunity for imagining an Oriental eroticism within the traditional Jewish world. This opportunity was a result of the stories that circulated already in the seventeenth century about Shabbtai Zvi's marriages, the first two unconsummated and the third to the mysterious Sarah, who some accounts claim was a Polish orphan of the Chmielnitski pogroms and who had pursued an adventurous and promiscuous life before marrying Shabbtai in Egypt. The figure of Sarah allowed authors to conflate the East of Europe with the Near East. Thus, for example, Kastein calls this "eccentric, erotic, and uncommonly vital creature" a "child of the East."[34] Kastein claims that the rabbinical response to Sarah's eroticism was similar to that of the Christian witch trials, but it never reached quite the same extreme: the Christians "hated eros and stifled the weird sensations provoked by witches by putting them to death. The Jewish rabbis and scholars were also afraid of eros, but they tried to circumvent it by sublimating its influence."[35] In any event, Shabbtai himself was never tempted by Sarah's seductions, and Kastein argues, quite implausibly, that he no more consummated this third marriage than he had the previous two. We recall that for Kastein the spirit of the Orient was ascetic, and Shabbtai, in his account, never gives in personally to the erotic. However, Sarah instigates orgies and has relations with Shabbtai's young followers. She also agitates for equality of women at Shabbtai's table and in the reading of the Torah. At her instigation and as a tactic for gaining power, Shabbtai adopts a protofeminist position, freeing women from the curse of Eve. As a result, says Kastein, women took an active part in the movement, "as sometimes happens in the case of revolutions when feminine instinct, added to the deliberations and motives of men, acts as a liberating and inciting factor."[36] Whether or not one wants to accept Kastein's dubious claim for the liberatory nature of "feminine instinct," his observation of the importance of women in the movement was highly perceptive and anticipates the groundbreaking work of Ada Rapoport-Albert.[37]

Other authors exploited the erotic possibilities of Shabbtai's marriages to the hilt. Israel Zangwill's 1898 anthology *Dreamers of the Ghetto* contains a long chapter entitled "The Turkish Messiah" among other fictional and factual tales of marginal Jews. Zangwill revels in Orientalist imagery throughout his tale:

> Obediently marrying . . . the maiden provided by his father, the young ascetic passionately denied himself to the passion ripened precociously by the Eastern sun and the marvelling Beth-Din released the virgin from her nominal husband. Prayer and self-mortification were the pleasures of his youth. The enchanting Jewesses of Smyrna, picturesque in baggy trousers and open-necked vests, had no seduction for him, though no muslin veil hid their piquant countenances as with the Turkish women, though no prescription silenced their sweet voices in the psalmody of the table, as among the sin-fearing congregations of the West.[38]

The Orient is the sun-drenched land of sensuality and liberation, and the Jewish women are seductive and available, unlike either the Muslims or the women of the Western Jewish communities. Shabbtai denies himself these pleasures, but his asceticism is itself a "passionate" denial of the passions. Sarah comes to free him from his self-abnegation: "She was clad in shimmering white Italian silk, which draped tightly about her bosom, showed her as some gleaming statue.... Her eyes had strange depths of passion, perfumes breathed from her skin.... Not thus came the maidens of Israel to wedlock, demure, spotless, spiritless, with shorn hair, priestesses of the ritual of the home."[39] There can be little doubt that Zangwill prefers this "Oriental" Jewess to the more conventional domestic "priestesses" of Western Jewry. Sarah declares to Shabbtai: "Thou hast kept thyself pure for me even as I have kept myself passionate for thee. Come, thou shalt make me pure and I will make thee passionate."[40]

Zangwill plays out Shabbtai's conversion to Islam as a struggle between the yin of his divinity and the yang of her worldliness. Shabbtai at first blames Sarah for his failure to embrace martyrdom: "Tis through thee that I have forfeited the divine grace.... Thou hast made me unfaithful to my bride the Law.... Woman, thou has polluted me! I have lost the divine spirit. It hath gone out from me; it will incarnate itself in another, in a nobler. Once I was Messiah, now I am man."[41] Then he reverses himself and embraces love as "the Kingdom" and his humanity as his true destiny. He is now prepared to become a Muslim, if only to live with Sarah: "I am a man, and thou a woman." But Sarah for her part declares that if Shabbtai is only a man, then her love for him is dead: "Nay, as a man, I love thee not. Thou art divine or naught."[42] Then, when he is taken to the sultan, she realizes that she has come to love him as a man and not only as Messiah. Zangwill produces this struggle between Shabbtai and Sarah with a great deal of ambiguity, neither allowing his characters to take a definitive position on the apostasy nor, it would seem, taking one himself.

Dreamers of the Ghetto was Zangwill's attempt to work out a Jewish identity on the margins by identifying with other heterodox Jews. It is also a surreptitious struggle with Christianity, as the poem on the frontispiece, entitled "Moses and Jesus," attests. Moses and Jesus are two Jews who "met by chance":

> *Then for the first time met their eyes, swift-linked*
> *In one strange, silent, piteous gaze, and dim*
> *With bitter tears of agonized despair.*

The encounter between Judaism and Christianity has no positive, definitive outcome, as it will in Zangwill's later, assimilationist play *The Melting Pot*;[43] instead, like Shabbtai Zvi's conversion to Islam, it is fraught with ambiguity and "agonized despair."

The very ambiguity of the ending of his Sabbatian chapter signals Zangwill's own ambivalence about whether a Jewish identity was even possible in the modern world. Within a few years, he was to become engaged to and marry a non-Jewish woman, an act that earned him the opprobrium of a number of his friends in Jewish and Zionist circles.[44] Perhaps Shabbtai Zvi's struggle between ascetic purity and Judaism on the one hand and erotic worldliness and apostasy on the other was a projection of Zangwill's own inner struggles. In this light, it is no surprise that he invested his account of Shabbtai Zvi with such melodramatic sensuality and romance, a tale of the passionate Orient far removed from the straitlaced Jews of late nineteenth-century England.

The intersection of eroticism, interfaith relations, and the Orient appears as well in Sholem Ash's 1908 Yiddish play *Shabbtai Zvi*. Ash's admittedly mediocre melodrama cannot be divorced from its author's preoccupation with Christianity, which, several decades later, would result in such controversial works as *Der Man fun Natseres*. Ash's Shabbtai Zvi is announced in phrases reminiscent of the Christian appropriation of the prophecy of Isaiah (7:14): "The voice of God came to me thus: 'A son is born to Mordecai in the city of Ismir in the East, near the sea. And I have called him Shabbtai Zevi.'"[45] The several references to Ismir as "the East" in the first act are revealing because the setting is supposed to be Jerusalem, relative to which Ismir would be in the West. It is, of course, the author and his audience who are in the West and for whom Ismir, Jerusalem, and indeed the whole drama of Sabbatianism all lie in the Orient.

But of course the Orient is also important for Ash as the site of Jesus's origins. His comparison of Shabbtai to Jesus in the opening act is reinforced later in the play by Shabbtai's claim that "I have torn the human from my heart and have become God" and Sarah's statement that Shabbtai is a "man-God," formulations that have no basis in Sabbatian theology, although they do appear in other nineteenth-century imaginative literature about Shabbtai Zvi.[46] For Ash, it seems, Sabbatianism was a seventeenth-century version of

Jewish Christianity, an episode in Jewish history that might perhaps make Jews more understanding of the Christian heresy. For if, as he suggests in his monumental novel of the life of Jesus, Judaism and Christianity differ only in whether one believes that the Messiah has already come, then the Sabbatian experience means that many Jews also once believed in a historical Messiah.

Ash's account of Shabbtai's failure is, however, theologically confusing. At one point, Shabbtai blames God for having sent him but then for having taken fright at how people considered him like a god and for retracting Shabbtai's divine powers. Much of the dialogue in the latter part of the play focuses the blame on Sarah, the erotic seductress who, as in Zangwill's story, represents sensual worldliness in opposition to Shabbtai's spirituality. Shabbtai's first two, rejected wives, significantly named Leah and Rachel, refer to Sarah as "the black queen," and Ash attributes to her the urge toward antinomianism. In one speech, she castigates the Torah as a set of prohibitions given by "foreign gods" and pleads with Shabbtai to choose her as a bride rather than the Torah, since she represents a Nietzschean mixture of "sin, death . . . repentance, resurrection, anger and reconciliation, loneliness and companionship, desire and negation."[47] It is Sarah who attracts followers to the movement by her eyes, her hair, and her passion, and she does so precisely because she is human, a "daughter of the Earth," but also the emissary of Satan. Despite her eastern European origins, Sarah is depicted as Oriental, promising Shabbtai a paradise made of Middle Eastern imagery, drawn in part from the language of the Song of Songs.[48] In the end, Shabbtai has been irrevocably contaminated by Sarah's sensuality, and he surrenders to his humanity by converting to Islam. The scene of his apostasy ends with the sultan promising him his most beautiful slave girls as wives. The Orient triumphs.

Like Zangwill, Ash ends his play in ambiguity. Where does he really stand on the choice between the Torah and Sarah as the Messiah's bride? Can Jewish messianism sustain the idea of a "man-God" without collapsing into either antinomian sensuality or ascetic spirituality? The play gives no definitive answers, but it certainly suggests how perilous the course is for those Jews who reject the strictures of the law for a more worldly (modern?) existence, represented, here as elsewhere, by the sensuous Orient. If, indeed, sensuality is a sign of modernity, then the Orient here is pressed into an unexpected role as the site of modern virtues.

The erotic implications of Shabbtai Zvi's biography were not discovered first by writers of the fin de siècle, and in fact these writers probably borrowed from earlier nineteenth-century models. S. Meschelssohn's *Sabbathey Zwy*, for example, published in 1856, demonstrates as much fascination with Shabbtai's asceticism in his first two marriages as with his later consummated marriage to the mysterious Sarah. Meschelssohn exaggerates Shabbtai's rejection of a first wife named Rachel by describing in exquisite detail Rachel's beauty and her attempts to seduce the celibate Messiah. One has the sense in this novel, as in others as well, that Shabbtai's initial celibacy and later presumed libertinism, as alien as both were to conventional Jewish marriage, exerted equally erotic attraction. And as we have also already seen in chapter 7, Leopold Sacher-Masoch's bizarre erotic biography of Shabbtai Zvi from 1884 exploits themes similar to Meschelssohn's.

The figure of Sarah, as a Jewish woman who, according to some accounts, was converted temporarily to Christianity, allowed writers to explore the relationship between Judaism and its Christian offspring. Some writers, such as Kastein, went so far as to claim that Christian millenarianism actually inspired the Sabbatian movement. For all the writers I have discussed, the Sabbatian episode could be exploited as a site for working out problems of Jewish identity in the modern world, and particularly the boundaries between Judaism and Christianity. And women repeatedly played a critical role in their works as the catalysts for transgressing those boundaries.

A final example of this complex of ideas that I should like to treat is Jacob Wassermann's *Die Juden von Zirndorf*, first published in 1897. Wassermann is often considered an assimilationist, a contention that has recently been challenged.[49] Although severely critical of both western and eastern European Jews, Wassermann extolled by contrast the Oriental Jew as "certain of himself, of the world, of humankind. . . . He is free, while they are slaves, he lives with his mothers, he rests and creates, while they are the eternally wandering unchangeables."[50] As Michael Brenner has pointed out, Wassermann, although not a Zionist, claimed hyperbolically that the lengthy prologue of his book, which is a fictional account of the impact of Sabbatianism on the Jews of Franconia, was "one of the most important causes of the emergence of the entire Zionist movement."[51]

Many of the themes that we have already encountered—eroticism, Jewish-Christian relations, and, more indirectly, the Orient—inform Wassermann's story. As in Isaac Bashevis Singer's 1935 novel *Satan in Goray*, the Jews, believing that the Messiah has come, throw off all legal restraints, abandon their religion, and indulge in wild sexual orgies, including lesbianism. Two women are at the center of the story: Zirle, who is modeled on the historical Sarah, except that she never actually marries Shabbtai Zvi, and Rachel, who conceives a child out of relations with a Christian seminarian. Zirle is said to be the Messiah's bride, but after Shabbtai Zvi's apostasy she vanishes forever. Her wild beauty attracts the son of an antisemitic pastor, named Wagenseil (after the anti-Jewish Christian Hebraist), who converts to Judaism and brings catastrophe upon the Jews.

Rachel, on the other hand, is the daughter of a materialistic usurer, described by Wassermann in terms indistinguishable from those of contemporary antisemites. Wassermann says of Rachel, "She could not be called beautiful but she had the opulent figure and superficial passionateness of the Jewess and there was in her eyes some dull sensuous gleam that drew the men to her."[32] Her Christian lover puts out a story that she has conceived her child as a virgin and that the child is destined to be the Messiah's bride, a kind of parody of Christianity. Thus, a certain dramatic tension is set up between Zirle and Rachel's child. As the Jews travel toward the East in response to Shabbtai's call, Rachel gives birth, but to a boy, which causes her opportunistic father to go insane.

Wassermann seems to be suggesting in this episode that the Jews are incapable of realizing their deepest desires, whether it be for sexual relations with Christians or for the coming of the Messiah: "The dark God of the Jews was not to be jested with; he stretched out his cruel hand till it stood like a wall cutting them off from the sweet and seductive prospects conjured up by an oriental imagination."[33] The messianic liberation of the European Jews, originating out of the Orient, falls victim to the cruel dictates of (Western?) Judaism, which has irrevocably distorted the character of the Jews.

Yet, anticipating Scholem, Wassermann suggests that Sabbatianism, the abortive movement of liberation from the East, formed the great watershed between the Middle Ages and modernity, serving, as in Carlebach's tale of the Dönmeh sect, as a model for the modern Jew:

And what came was always greater, freer and more perfect than what had gone before and the Jew, at first only a bondsman, fit to suffer the kicks of his angry lord, opened his eyes, discovered the weaknesses and guessed the secrets of his master.... Shabbtai became a Moslem, though some say but outwardly. The Jew became a civilized man, and again some say but outwardly.... This is certain: an actor or a true man, capable of beauty, yet ugly, lustful and ascetic, a charlatan or a gambler, a fanatic or a cowardly slave—the Jew is all these things.... The nature of a people is like the nature of an individual: its character is its fate.[54]

In his autobiography, *Mein Leben als Deutscher und Jude*, Wassermann, torn between his Jewish and German identities, describes his need to see the Jews as neither totally saintly nor totally materialistic but rather a human synthesis of all extremes. As the above passage suggests, underneath the modern Jew's "civilized" exterior lurk all the complexities of the Jew's real identity. Sabbatianism itself was the first movement of liberation that created this modern bifurcated identity. For Wassermann, writing *Die Juden von Zirndorf* was also act of personal liberation,[55] an attempt to reconcile his Jewish and German identities. Storytelling, which he calls "an Oriental instinct in my blood,"[56] functioned for him as his personal form of Sabbatian liberation, an attempt to reconnect with the Oriental Jews he so admired.

Wassermann's *Juden von Zirndorf* brings us back to Scholem. In the July 28, 1915, entry to his diary,[57] Scholem relates an intense discussion he had of Wassermann's novel with his friend Meta Jahr. *Die Juden von Zirndorf* is a book written not out of literary impulses but out of the "necessity of the soul" (*Seelennot*), and Scholem describes it and Herzl's life as "the two monuments, two myths of Jewish suffering from the nineties of the nineteenth century." Wassermann has provided a myth for the Western Jews; another will be needed for the Jews of the East.

Scholem does not clarify exactly what he found so "mythical" in Wassermann's novel, and it would perhaps be hasty to conclude that the long Sabbatian prologue was what particularly drew his interest. Yet his preoccupation with questions of Jewish national redemption, attested repeatedly in the diary entries from these years, as well as the early reference to Shabbtai Zvi mentioned above, suggests that Sabbatianism could not have been far from his mind. At the same time, Scholem was equally obsessed with longings for the Orient. Part of this longing came from Martin Buber's essay "Judaism and the Orient," which exercised a powerful early influence on the young Scholem. But it also stemmed from his disillusionment with Germany, fed in part by his revulsion at German war fever, and from his belief that personal salvation, like salvation for the Jews, lay in the East.[58] As he wrote on December 11, 1915, "It is clear that I would like to be away from here, but would I not like just as much to go to Arabia, Persia, China, the *Orient*? I have in me a great love for the Orient and believe that Eretz Israel can only enjoy its resurrection [*Auferstehung*] in conjunction with the rest of the Orient. But I also believe that while I wish to journey to the Orient, I wish to live in Eretz Israel. And this is the difference."[59] If one can draw conclusions from this passage, Scholem's early relationship to the Orient was marked by ambivalence: the Orient would be the site for Zionism to establish itself outside of Europe, but Eretz Israel would nevertheless be different. How, we might ask, did this difference play itself out in Scholem's historiography, especially his work on Sabbatianism? Can we identify an Orientalist dimension to his reading of Shabbtai Zvi?

On the face of it, the more obvious hallmarks of Orientalism that we have discovered in the fiction and popular histories about Sabbatianism are absent from Scholem's work. To take one example, he devoted relatively little attention to the erotic side of Shabbtai Zvi's biography, especially by contrast to the more popular writers.[60] Similarly, the role of women as early followers of Shabbtai Zvi, which we have seen in a number of accounts, failed to attract his interest. The Sabbatian movement remained for him largely a male affair. This one-sided focus corresponds to his more general position on the role of women in Jewish mysticism,[61] which he stated at the beginning of *Major Trends in Jewish Mysticism*: "The long history of Jewish mysticism shows no trace of feminine influence. . . . [Kabbalah], therefore, lacks the element of feminine emotion which has played so large a part in the development of non-Jewish mysticism, but it also remained comparatively free from the dangers entailed by the tendency toward hysterical extravagance which followed in the wake of this influence."[62] If the ostensibly effeminate qualities of "hysterical" emotionalism and "extravagance" are those commonly associated with the Orient, Scholem was seemingly determined to portray Jewish mysticism as "non-Oriental." Yet as Gil Anidjar has persuasively argued,[63] such overtly "anti-Orientalist" statements may well conceal a more subtle, quite possibly unconscious Orientalist agenda in the field of Kabbalistic historiography. Like others who wrote on Sabbatianism, Scholem focused on the curious bouts of passivity that Shabbtai Zvi exhibited, explaining them with a diagnosis of manic-depression. Yet how far is such modern clinical language from the less clinical "hysterical extravagance"? Isn't this passivity exactly the kind of "effeminacy" typically associated with the Orient? Similarly, Scholem associates the degeneracy of the later Frankist movement with its explicitly "feminine" theology, which may explain his surprising expressions of revulsion at this eighteenth-century by-product of Sabbatianism: one of the "most frightening phenomena in the whole of Jewish history: a religious leader who . . . was in all his actions a truly corrupt and degenerate individual."[64]

One might extend this analysis further. Scholem's interpretation of Sabbatianism as first and foremost a mystical movement has been accepted as virtually canonical. Yet as we have seen, it is possible to offer a political interpretation in which the Kabbalistic theology of the movement is no longer primary. According to the typical Orientalist view, the West is the realm of politics and reason, the East of impotent mysticism and emotionalism. By giving such weight to the mystical and virtually ignoring the political, Scholem perhaps unwittingly painted a portrait of Sabbatianism that was almost quintessentially Orientalist.

The obvious response to this suggestion is that for Scholem mysticism was anything but a pejorative and Sabbatianism itself was to be given pride of place in the dialectic of Jewish history. Yet my hypothesis that Scholem's reading of Sabbatianism may have involved Orientalist ambivalence can help solve one of the central tensions in his thought. As is well known, Scholem was politically active in the Brit Shalom in the 1920s. In his polemics against the Revisionists, he repeatedly labeled their extreme nationalism "latter-day Sabbatianism." He used almost identical language at the end of his life to describe the religious Zionists of the Gush Emunim.[65] How can one reconcile his positive historiographical estimation of Sabbatianism with this use of the term as a political pejorative?

The answer, it seems to me, lies in the ambivalence of the European Orientalist who is at once fascinated and repelled by the mysterious East.

Scholem famously called Zionism a "retreat back into history" and denied that it should have anything to do with apocalyptic messianism.[66] Zionism meant a turn to politics and not to mysticism. In this respect, for Scholem, Zionism was quintessentially a Western movement of political rationality and pragmatism, a "male" movement, if one wishes, as opposed to the "female" extravagance of the East. Despite his efforts to purge Jewish mysticism of the "feminine" element and Sabbatianism of its female side, his unease about their possible recurrence in Zionism demonstrates the anxiety of the European confronting the ambiguities of the Orient.

In this respect, despite the sophistication and erudition of his research on Sabbatianism, Scholem remained in the same Orientalist universe of discourse as the many popular works on Shabbtai Zvi that proliferated early in the century: the messianic movement out of the East became the site for projection of the struggles and anxieties of a generation living between tradition and modernity.

PART THREE

WEIMAR ANTINOMIANS

CHAPTER 10

Leo Strauss

The Philosopher as Weimar Jew

AT THE END OF THE introduction to *Persecution and the Art of Writing*, Leo Strauss suggests that the philosopher at all times, and not just in the Greek city, is in grave danger. He writes: "The understanding of this danger and of the various forms which it has taken, and which it may take, is the foremost task, and indeed the sole task, of the sociology of philosophy."[1] He seeks to show that philosophers, insofar as they teach the truth, always face the same danger as Socrates and therefore can protect themselves only by what he calls esoteric writing. Strauss's whole project in *Persecution and the Art of Writing* should be more properly termed the sociology of philosophy than philosophy itself. What he means by this term is something like Karl Mannheim's sociology of knowledge,[2] namely an understanding of the ideological function of ideas in a given social setting; only by understanding this function can one ferret out the true position of the philosopher beneath the explicit text.

Strauss claims that the status of philosophy in the medieval Islamic and especially the medieval Jewish world was fundamentally different from that of philosophy in the Christian sphere. While in Christianity philosophy in the form of theology was an official institutionalized discourse that fell under ecclesiastical supervision, Islamic and Jewish philosophy remained private endeavors, devoid of official status. In this respect, Islamic and Jewish philosophy was much closer to philosophy in ancient Greece than was medieval Christian scholasticism. According to Strauss, the private character of Greek philosophy, the fact that it did not enjoy governmental sponsorship, was what gave it the potential to be heretical with respect to conventional opinion and made it a dangerous occupation; this function, which Strauss holds is the true task of philosophy, was taken over by some of the Islamic and Jewish philosophers of the Middle Ages, and we must therefore turn to these philosophers if we are to discover what is, for Strauss, true philosophy in its medieval form.[3]

The purpose of my remarks here will be to apply Strauss's sociology of philosophy to Strauss himself and attempt to understand his thought in terms of its ideological function within its historical context. One of Strauss's favorite methodological statements, as is well known, is that we must understand a particular philosopher as he understood himself (a method he took from Spinoza's demand that we read the Bible according to the Bible).[4] Now, Strauss devoted much of his career to denouncing historicism, the attempt to understand the past within its own context. For Strauss, this "contextualizing" robbed the thought of great thinkers of its eternal truthfulness by making it "merely" the product of a particular set of historical circumstances. Yet the way Strauss understood himself gives us an opening to place his own thought in its historical setting. In the 1962 preface to the English-language edition of *Spinoza's Critique of Religion*, Strauss writes: "This study on Spinoza's *Theologico-Political Treatise* was written during the years 1925–28 in Germany. The author was a young Jew born and raised in Germany who found himself in the grip of the theologico-political predicament."[5] He goes on to spell out the political and theological context of Weimar Germany in which he wrote the work. The crisis of liberalism exemplified by Weimar led him to question the whole liberal political tradition and from this political critique to criticize the historical consciousness that lay behind liberalism. His rejection of historicism led him to theology and to an affirmation, or so he says in the preface, of Jewish Orthodoxy. Thus, the problem of the Jews in Germany seemed to Strauss emblematic of the crisis of liberalism, as indeed it seemed for many other Europeans. The failure of liberalism to solve the Jewish problem symbolized in an extreme way its failure generally and the need for political and religious alternatives.

Strauss therefore understood himself within the context of a particular generation, that of the Weimar Jews. Although generalizations about the mentality of a generation are always problematic, there are certain features of the thought of Weimar Jews against which Strauss's own philosophy resonates in harmony.[6] I should like to examine some elements of Strauss's thought against the background of those other Jewish intellectuals with whom he shared a common discourse, a common background, and ultimately a common fate. One key to unlocking the esoteric meaning of Strauss's thought is this intellectual context. I wish to show that, for Strauss, Jewish thought today constitutes, as it did in the Middle Ages, a mode of opposition to conventional opinion and that it preserves truth in a world dominated by the insidious philosophies of historicism and social science. If Western thought—or, read, Christian thought—has produced the sins of historicism, Jewish thought may provide an avenue back to truth.

The crisis of Weimar prompted many Jewish intellectuals to turn to radical political alternatives. Many of those who created the Frankfurt school of critical theory were Jews or half-Jews, such as Theodore Adorno, Max Horkheimer, Leo Lowenthal, and Herbert Marcuse.[7] Marxism also attracted such iconoclastic intellectuals as Walter Benjamin and Ernst Bloch. On the other side of the spectrum, the Jewish theologian Hans Joachim Schoeps developed a version of extreme German nationalism that made him believe that he could find common ground with the Nazis.[8]

For many Weimar Jews, and particularly intellectuals, Zionism represented the most fundamental alternative to the German liberalism in which the Jews had placed their hopes. Zionism was not simply one alternative among several, as it was for East European Jews, but rather the antithesis of their whole worldview. Few in the 1920s took the radical step of emigrating to Palestine, as did Gershom Scholem.[9] Zionism represented rather a theoretical challenge, so that even those, like Franz Rosenzweig, who rejected it felt compelled to grapple with it as they evolved their own philosophies.[10] Others like Martin Buber or Hannah Arendt saw in Zionism a utopian solution to the failure of modern politics; when Zionism took a pragmatic course, which was surely inevitable given its political and nationalistic character, these thinkers became disillusioned and critical.[11]

Strauss clearly shared this fascination with Zionism. In the preface to the book on Spinoza, he describes Zionism as the most authentic political response to the crisis of liberal emancipation. Strauss states that "[Zionism] procured a blessing for all Jews everywhere regardless of whether they admit it or not. It did not, however, solve the Jewish problem."[12] Zionism remained a partial political solution, a "profound modification of the Galut . . . but it is not the end of the Galut: in the religious sense and perhaps not only in the religious sense, the state of Israel is part of the Galut."[13] In other words, Zionism, for all its achievements, is not a utopian movement and has no bearing on traditional messianism, a position that Strauss shared with Gershom Scholem.[14]

Yet the failure of Zionism to fulfill messianic expectations was actually its virtue for Strauss, if we put his statements in the larger context of his political thought. He writes: "Finite, relative problems can be solved; infinite, absolute problems cannot be solved. In other words, human beings will never create a society which is free of contradictions. From every point of view, it looks as if the Jewish people were the chosen people in the sense, at least, that the Jewish problem is the most manifest symbol of the human problem as a social or political problem."[15] The inability of Zionism to solve the Jewish problem in an absolute sense is part and parcel, and indeed, the most symbolic expression, of the universal inability of politics to effect utopian solutions.

Strauss was not alone in seeing the problems of the Jews as emblematic for the human condition in general. Strauss may well have been influenced by Hermann Cohen (1842–1918) in this regard.[16] In his posthumously published *Religion of Reason Out of the Sources of Judaism*, Cohen argues that the Jewish condition of statelessness must become the messianic model for a unified mankind that will create a confederation of states. Moreover, Jewish suffering is a messianic sign to all mankind (it is possible that Cohen believed that the universal suffering brought about by World War I made the world receptive to the message of historical Jewish suffering).[17]

Similar notions can be found the writings of Strauss's contemporary

Hannah Arendt, whose fascination with the Greeks and pessimistic view of the modern state resembled Strauss's. As I argue in the next chapter at greater length, for Arendt the Jews represent what mankind might become, both negatively and positively. Arendt saw the Jewish refugees of the 1930s and '40s as metaphors for the dismal political life of our times: the inability of the modern state to tolerate human diversity leads to Auschwitz. The very reasons why the Jews attract hatred—their natural differences from other people—must become the basis for humanity. By teaching the world the importance of national diversity, the Jews will fulfill a mission "to achieve the establishment of mankind."[18] For Arendt as for Strauss, the Jewish experience was not a melancholy but isolated episode in the history of mankind; rather, it contained the seeds of the true philosophy, true for all time and for all peoples. In this way, both preserved idiosyncratic versions of the Jews as the chosen people.

Yet Strauss's radical opposition to a messianic politics distinguishes him from both Cohen and Arendt and, indeed, from all Jewish utopians who resort to the same figures of thought. His rejection of Zionism as a messianic movement corresponds to his iconoclastic reading of Plato as an antiutopian thinker. In his reading of al-Farabi's *Plato*, he writes: "We may say that Farabi's Plato eventually replaces the philosopher-king who rules openly in the virtuous city, by the secret kingship of the philosopher who, being 'a perfect man' . . . , lives privately as a member of an imperfect society which he tries to humanize within the realm of the possible."[19] Politics is not the realm in which to realize the absolute truths of philosophy; indeed, philosophy, as an endangered species, must be preserved from the interference of the political. Although this skepticism with respect to politics led some to consider Strauss a political conservative by the 1970s, it is no surprise that a philosopher who defined himself as a child of the Weimar Republic should be so suspicious of political movements that make messianic claims. Indeed, the above lines from the introduction to *Persecution and the Art of Writing* were based on Strauss's article "Farabi's *Plato*," published, significantly enough, in 1945.[20] Even though Strauss rarely makes explicit references to the political context in which he wrote, a reading "between the lines" demonstrates, I believe, the degree to which the twentieth-century crisis of politics determined Strauss's reading of ancient authors: no one writing as the Nazi regime came to its end could be sanguine about the perfectibility of the political realm.

One of the dominant characteristics of Weimar intellectuals, whether utopians like Arendt or antiutopians like Strauss, was opposition to conventional ideas and discovery of suppressed or forgotten ideas that might inspire contemporary thought. Frequently coming out of secular backgrounds, many thinkers were obsessed with finding their way back to remote historical traditions. Yet this return to tradition was possible not on the high road of "official" traditions but rather on the byways of heretical or subterranean movements. Consider the following examples: Ernst Bloch, who studied atheism and heretical movements within Christianity; Gershom Scholem, who restored Jewish mysticism and antinomian messianism to an important place in Jewish thought; Hans Joachim Schoeps, who searched for the Jewish roots of Christianity; and Hans Jonas, who wrote on Gnosticism as the precursor to contemporary existentialism.[21] All of these thinkers engaged in what I have elsewhere called counterhistory, the inversion of conventional wisdom and the explosion of unquestioned myths.[22]

Strauss's esoteric hermeneutics must be seen in the context of this counterhistorical approach. Philosophical truth lies not in what a philosopher explicitly says and certainly not in what the conventional interpreters say he said; instead, it is to be found by "reading between the lines," or by what Walter Benjamin, whose work is a kind of counterhistory of German literature, called "brushing history against the grain."[23] Like the apocalyptic writer who decodes old prophecies or the mystic who "uncovers one handbreadth while covering two," Strauss holds that the truth is never revealed and must be discovered by the reverse of the process with which it had been concealed.

It is in the details of the mainstream that one can find hints of the subterranean. According to Allan Bloom, Strauss said that "only by the closest attention to the surface could one get to the core; . . . the surface is the core."[24] By painstakingly searching through texts for details hitherto unnoticed one might find the esoteric truth. Strauss was not unique in this obsession with detail. Walter Benjamin developed a whole hermeneutics based on collecting seemingly trivial and unrelated details and constructing out of them an entirely unexpected edifice. Gershom Scholem's extraordinary studies of the Kabbalah were a result of similarly minute philology of dusty manuscripts. And it was Aby Warburg's favorite saying that "the beloved God lives in details." Only by attention to that which had previously been deemed unimportant or even heretical could this generation establish a creative relationship to the past.

With all of these Weimar intellectuals, Strauss shared a belief that the solution to modern dilemmas, or at least a better understanding of them, was available by studying old thinkers, by returning to old traditions, reinterpreted according to their esoteric truths. For Strauss, the Greeks in particular were the old thinkers who needed to be reinterpreted and made accessible to the modern sensibility. For Strauss as for these other Weimar iconoclasts, the return to tradition, as I have argued, was not to orthodox interpretations but rather to sources of heterodoxy, to radical readings of the ancients.

Here, however, a major question about Strauss himself arises: Was he as iconoclastic toward the Orthodox Jewish tradition as he was toward the orthodox tradition of Western philosophy? In the preface to the book on Spinoza, he argues that the solution to the theological problem of the Jew lies not in Zionism or in Spinoza's historicism but in *teshuva*, repentance or return to the Jewish community in a religious sense. Here Strauss is led to Rosenzweig, who also believed Zionism to be an inadequate solution to a problem beyond the realm of politics. But while Rosenzweig and Strauss agreed that the problem of Judaism lay beyond history, Strauss rejected Rosenzweig's subjective approach to the tradition. Rosenzweig's neo-Orthodoxy allowed for his own experience to dictate what aspects of the tradition he would adopt; in this way, his "new thinking" became tainted with historical relativism. Against Rosenzweig, Strauss argued that a return to Judaism meant a return to the Torah in its totality, not to some part of it. The Torah, he held, must be understood and accepted as it understood itself, that is, as absolutely true. Judaism is quintessentially antihistoricist because of this adherence to absolutes that are independent of history. Strauss's critique of Rosenzweig therefore led him to an affirmation of Orthodoxy as such, which he believed could withstand even the assault of Spinoza's critique of religion. In short, the preface to *Spinoza's Critique of Religion* gives us the distinct impression that we are dealing with a spiritual descendant of Samson Raphael Hirsch, a defender of Orthodoxy in the face of rationalist and existentialist alternatives. Certainly, Strauss's Orthodox upbringing and education might support such an interpretation.

What did Strauss mean by Jewish Orthodoxy? Once again, it is necessary to understand Strauss as he understood himself. Above all, Strauss was an esoteric writer, not only in the obvious sense that his writing is obscure and hard to penetrate but in the structural sense that his true position can be discerned only between the lines, by what he may say about others: the same method that he applies to al-Farabi or Maimonides must be applied to himself.

I would submit that what Strauss meant by a return to Orthodoxy was radically different from any conventional idea of Jewish Orthodoxy. In his essay "Literary Character of Maimonides' *Guide for the Perplexed*," he argues that Maimonides's *Guide* and his *Mishne Torah* are two thoroughly independent works, the first aimed at a small circle of cognoscenti (or what he calls in another essay, the "young men") and the second aimed at the *vulgus*.[25] The *Mishne Torah* is an orthodox work of *halakhah* or *fiqh*, to use the Arabic term that Strauss employs. Since the *Guide*, properly interpreted, is Maimonides's esoteric teachings of the secrets of the Bible, it must be a work with heterodox intent. It wishes to teach the identity of Greek philosophy and the secret wisdom of the Torah. In other words, the true Maimonides is the Maimonides of the *Guide* rather than the *Mishne Torah*, a Maimonides who taught secret truths that had heretical potential.

Now, if Strauss's interpretation of Maimonides reveals something of his own esoteric project, his call for a return to Orthodoxy in the preface must mean a return to the esoteric Maimonides and not to the Maimonides of the *Mishne Torah*. Orthodoxy for Strauss meant not *halakhah* but the secrets of the Torah in the Maimonidean sense (or in the sense that Strauss understood Maimonides). Like other Jewish intellectuals of his generation, Strauss could not envision a return to Jewish Orthodoxy as the Orthodox would define it; instead, he, like Scholem, Rosenzweig, and Martin Buber, needed to redefine Orthodoxy according to his own lights.

If I am correct, then the secrets of the Torah that constitute the truth of the Jewish tradition are for Strauss none other than the truths of Greek philosophy, quite possibly the esoteric meaning of Plato: from an esoteric point of view, Athens and Jerusalem are one and the same. Thus, Jewish philosophy becomes for Strauss not just one field in the history of philosophy but an avenue to truth, just as Zionism is emblematic of the true status of political action. The case of the Jews, Strauss's own existential context, is not a mere episode in history, as it might be to the historicist, but rather the *tabbur ha-olam*, "the navel of the world" or the symbolic center of history.

Strauss's attack on historicism has yet another dimension. Counterhistory is history that is *engagé*, that seeks a living connection between the historian and his sources, as opposed to arid antiquarianism or radical historicism. What one finds in many of those who searched for hidden traditions is a complex relationship between text and exegete, in which the commentator derives his own method from the sources he studies. For instance, Gershom Scholem stood in creative ambivalence to his mystical texts: although not a mystic, he saw in the mystical tradition a religious precursor to secular historical science.[26] The philosophical problems of the historian are identical to the theological problems of the mystic. Similarly, Franz Rosenzweig found the basis for his existentialist approach to the Jewish tradition in statements in the tradition itself. And Hans Jonas discovered Heideggerian phenomenology in ancient Gnosticism. In all these cases, the modern thinker becomes the latest incarnation of the tradition in which he works.

Strauss understood himself as the modern incarnation of the Greek, Islamic, and Jewish philosophers whose truths had to be hidden in esoteric form. He believed that the rise in modern historic consciousness came simultaneously with the interruption in the tradition of esotericism.[27] Since Strauss waged an unremitting war against historicism, it would appear that he believed himself to be the singlehanded reviver of the esoteric tradition. Moreover, because he rejected historical relativism, he considered the methods of Plato, al-Farabi, and Maimonides to be not historical relics but eternally true and, therefore, methods as appropriate to the modern philosopher as to his ancient or medieval predecessors. When Strauss speaks of writing or speaking to an audience of "young men," of those capable of understanding the esoteric truths, we immediately sense that he has in mind not only Socrates's disciples or Maimonides's adepts but his own circle of students. It is in the Straussian academy that the countertradition of philosophy that began with Plato and was inherited by Jews and Arabs in the Middle Ages found its proper modern home.[28]

For Strauss, the relationship of the true modern philosopher, and perhaps especially the Jewish intellectual, to the modern state is the same as the relationship of the ancient philosopher to the polis. True philosophy always stands in opposition to the established order and hides its dangerous truths in esoteric clothing. The Jewish intellectuals with whom I have grouped Strauss were all outsiders in one sense or another. Those thinkers who had particularly Jewish concerns, such as Rosenzweig and Scholem, typically came to Judaism from the outside, as assimilated Jews who could find only unconventional paths back to the tradition. Those who worked in other areas, such as Benjamin on German drama, Bloch on Christianity, or Strauss on ancient philosophy, also came to their fields as outsiders, as scholars outside the academic world. They belonged to the disciplines they studied but, by virtue of their unconventional ideas and unorthodox positions, remained foreigners.

This peculiar tension, which gave such creativity to the last generation of German Jews, became even more acute after Hitler came to power and those who could were forced to flee with the true Germany in their suitcases. Exile from Germany became the most acute expression of this alienated belonging. Small wonder that their personal experiences as Jews in a hostile world could become emblematic of their general philosophies. In this sense, it is no surprise that Strauss wrote the essay "Persecution and the Art of Writing" in 1941, for although he was already in the United States and therefore no longer in danger of direct persecution, his experience as a German Jew remained seminal for the rest of his career: like the twentieth-century German Jew, true philosophy could never have a secure home, for it must always teach a subversive form of truth.

It is therefore particularly ironic that so many of the best thinkers whose thought was originally heterodox have become the sources of new forms of orthodoxy. The disciples of Gershom Scholem's great challenge to Jewish historiography have become the academic establishment in Israel; Walter Benjamin is now the posthumous object of cult worship; Strauss himself is accused in the pages of the *New York Review of Books* of having fathered a generation of neoconservative intellectuals.[29] Indeed, divorced from the singular context of German Jewish culture on the eve of the Holocaust, much of this radical thought has assumed entirely different functions. And although Strauss wanted to believe that truth is eternal and independent of its origins, his own thought can best be understood as he himself understood it, as a lifelong project to solve the theologico-political dilemma of a Weimar Jew.

CHAPTER 11

Arendt in Jerusalem

Hannah Arendt on the Eichmann Trial

IT IS EXTRAORDINARY THAT MANY years after its publication, Hannah Arendt's *Eichmann in Jerusalem* remains as controversial as ever. As she herself points out in the postscript to the 1964 edition, the reception of the book and the well-orchestrated campaign against it assumed a life of their own quite apart from the actual contents of the book itself.[1] It is also remarkable that the issue that has involved the greatest debate and has brought down mountains of abuse on Arendt's head—the alleged cooperation of Jewish leaders in the destruction of the Jewish people—takes up no more than 9 pages out of the 312 in the book. Moreover, Arendt's position that the collaboration was almost universal and that without it far fewer Jews would have been killed is actually incidental to her argument, and she included it only because she believed that it was the most glaring omission to the "general picture" that the prosecution had tried to draw of the Holocaust. In fact, with this one undoubtedly controversial exception, Arendt tries to stick as closely to the trial itself and to refrain from dragging in extraneous issues (as she argues the prosecution did) in considering whether justice was done in Jerusalem.

Why, then, the controversy? Why did this book create more accusations and counteraccusations than any other book on the Holocaust? Up until now, it seemed as if the controversies over collaboration and the banality of evil were actually about those issues. Yet the persistent misreading of the book and particularly the misreading by such shrewd observers as Gershon Scholem suggest that something very different is at stake. In the final analysis, the book was attacked as much for what it did *not* do as for what it did. What it did not do was present a historical or political account of antisemitism, Nazism, the Holocaust, or the State of Israel. Because the book's intent was misunderstood, or perhaps because it did not directly address issues about which people had strong ideological opinions in a conventional way, it created the kind of unease and even anger that one often feels about things that cannot be conveniently categorized.

The fact of the matter is that the analytical substance of the book is *legal* and the real controversy over it should have evolved around the juridical theory that Arendt presents, particularly in the epilogue. For only by understanding these arguments can one begin to understand the book as a whole and particularly her position on the trial, a position that was much more positive than most of her critics assume. The book is really an investigation of whether our current concepts and practice of justice are adequate to dealing with the crime of genocide. In the pages that follow, I will try to examine some of Arendt's legal arguments in detail, reflect on the general legal theory behind them, and, finally, show their connection to historical and political principles that she develops elsewhere in her corpus of writings. One significant benefit of this close exegesis will be the recovery of Arendt's Jewish commitments, about which she was always far less ambivalent than her critics believed her to be.

The epilogue of *Eichmann in Jerusalem* addresses a number of legal objections to the trial. I will not discuss all of these or Arendt's treatment of them, since some are purely technical or have no general ramifications.[2] Two, however, are of general interest: the claim that the Jerusalem court had no legitimate jurisdiction to try Eichmann and that the charge against him (that he had committed crimes "against the Jewish people") was legally problematic, as was the Israeli law under which the charge was made. We shall see that Arendt's solutions to these two problems are actually contradictory but that the contradiction turns out to have fruitful consequences for understanding her thought.

The Jerusalem court invoked three principles of international law to justify Israel's trying Eichmann: passive personality, universal jurisdiction, and territoriality. The first says that the country of the victim may try a criminal even if the crime was committed in another country, as, of course, was the case with Eichmann. This would be akin to France demanding extradition of an American citizen who had killed a Frenchman in America. Arendt regards this doctrine as highly suspect because it has a strong political motive, that of the desire for revenge by the aggrieved party. Justice, she argues, does not seek vengeance for the victim but punishment of the guilty, which are two very different matters. Even if the victim does not wish to bring charges, the community prosecutes, because the crime undermines its stability and order. Hence, the country of the victim is not generally recognized as having a legitimate claim of jurisdiction, and Arendt concurs and dismisses this claim.

She also dismisses the second principle of universal jurisdiction. This is an old doctrine applied in cases such as piracy, where anyone who catches the pirate—considered *hostis humani generis* (an enemy of mankind)—can try him. It is clear that this principle cannot apply to Eichmann, who was acting not on the high seas but as a representative of a sovereign state. Moreover, Eichmann was not captured on the high seas, as it were, but was kidnapped from another country. It should be noted that this is the only feature of the case that Arendt regards as unprecedented, and she condones it as a non-precedent-setting act justified by the necessity of bringing Eichmann to justice.

The court advanced a third argument for jurisdiction—territoriality—and it is here that Arendt fully supports the legitimacy of the Eichmann trial. The principle of territoriality states that a criminal is judged in the place where he committed his crime. This was the principle invoked by the so-called successor trials following the war, which tried Nazis whose territorial purview was limited to a specific country, as opposed to the Nuremberg defendants, whose scope was truly international. Arendt argues that the reason Eichmann was not a defendant at Nuremberg was not that he was missing (Martin Borman, after all, was tried and convicted in absentia), but that his scope was not *essentially* international. He had to cross borders for an *accidental* reason, namely, that the Jews lived in more than one country and his function was to round up Jews: "It was the territorial dispersion of the Jews that made the crime against them an 'international' concern.... Once the Jews had a territory of their own, the State of Israel, they obviously had as much right to sit in judgment on the crimes committed against their people as the Poles had to judge crimes committed in Poland."³ On this basis, Arendt argues that the Eichmann trial was no more and no less legitimate than the other successor trials held all over Europe after the war.

Arendt's strenuous defense of the right of Israel to try Eichmann seems rather weak as I have presented it here. Even though the Jews *qua* Jews were Eichmann's only victims, he still committed his crimes on soil other than that which became the State of Israel. In what sense were his activities different in kind from those of "truly" international criminals such as Göring or Speer? Arendt herself recognizes these difficulties and responds by suggesting that the court should have redefined the territoriality principle:

> Israel could easily have claimed territorial jurisdiction if she had only explained that "territory" is a political and a legal concept and not merely a geographical term. It relates not so much, and not primarily, to a piece of land as to the space between individuals in a group whose members are bound to, and at the same time separated and protected from each other by all kinds of relationships, based on a common language, religion, a common history, customs, and laws. Such relationships become spatially manifest insofar as they themselves constitute the space wherein the different members of a group relate to and have intercourse with each other. No state of Israel would have come into being if the Jewish people had not created and maintained its own specific in-between space throughout the centuries of dispersion, that is prior to the seizure of its old territory.⁴

Arendt professes astonishment that the court failed to redefine territory on this basis, since the judges must have been aware of the special conditions that brought about the Jewish state. Yet this extraordinary statement actually conceals a radical redefinition of nationality that owes a great deal to Arendt's earlier writings on Jewish nationalism.

Arendt was certainly not alone in claiming that the Jews are a nation despite their lack of territory. She uses the notion of an international Jewish people in several of her essays criticizing Herzlian Zionism, written mainly in the 1940s. Herzl held that the Jewish people were a nation "held together by a common enemy." Arendt explicitly rejects this definition. Herzl bases his definition of the Jewish nation on antisemitism, and his political movement primarily on the search for a national territory. Arendt contrasts Herzl's view with that of Bernard Lazare, Herzl's French contemporary, whom she was largely responsible for rescuing from oblivion.[5] Lazare considered territory secondary and sought to build a national Jewish movement throughout the world allied with other revolutionary movements: "What he sought was not an escape from antisemitism but a mobilization of the people against its foes."[6] Regardless of whether one agrees with Arendt's praise for Lazare as a "conscious pariah" or considers him a hopeless utopian (although Herzl himself must have sounded as utopian in his day), Arendt's distinction between these two types of Zionism is crucial to her redefinition of the territoriality issue in the Eichmann trial. The Jews are a nation because of the nonterritorial "in-between space" created through the centuries of dispersion. The search for a territory does not negate this definition but remains secondary to it and can even become dangerous if that part of the nation that is territorially based should cut itself off from the rest of the nation. This nonterritorial nationalism, which resembles Simon Dubnow's position in some respects, is suspicious of national sovereignty, since the latter concept is necessarily rooted in the primacy and inviolability of territory. Indeed, Arendt's essays against political Zionism in the 1940s and her ardent support for the Ichud movement of Judah Magnes and Martin Buber, which opposed Jewish statehood, should be read in this light. A believer in the Jews as a nation and a strong advocate of the Yishuv, she argued nevertheless for the largely hopeless possibility of Arab-Jewish political confederation. Yet interestingly enough, it is on the basis of her nonterritorial definition of the Jewish people and on that basis alone that she justifies Israel's kidnapping, trial, and execution of Adolph Eichmann.

Arendt supports the court on its jurisdiction, albeit with her own arguments. But she comes to rather different conclusions on the second issue, the nature of the crime committed. Eichmann was charged under the Israeli law (1950) against Nazis and Nazi collaborators with "crimes against the Jewish people." Arendt rejects the legitimacy of this law. Just as she assails the doctrine of passive personality for the reason that criminal justice is not designed to satisfy the victims but to restore order to a community, so she argues that a crime is defined not by its victims but by the nature of the act committed. For instance, we would not charge a murderer who kills storekeepers with "crimes against storekeepers" but with murder. Hence, murder—regardless of the identity of the victim—requires punishment. The notion of "crimes against the Jewish people" confuses the nature of the crime with its victims.

It is this legal argument that lies at the heart of Arendt's persistent and even vituperative criticisms of Gideon Hausner, the Israeli prosecutor. Hausner, she claims, was more interested in establishing what he called the "general picture" of antisemitism and the Nazi extermination program than in trying the specific individual in the dock. Arendt accuses him of dragging extraneous issues into the case in order to show why the Jews were chosen as victims and to give a history of the Holocaust even when it had nothing to do with Eichmann's jurisdiction. While the court itself rejected this approach—and Arendt compliments the judges with almost lavish praise—the prosecution, guided by "the invisible hand" of the Israeli prime minister, David Ben Gurion, was more interested in the political and historical message of the trial than with the aims of justice. Yet the "show trial" aspect of the Eichmann case was no mere consequence of Ben Gurion's desire to teach young Israelis a lesson about the Holocaust; Arendt's argument implies that it was a necessary result of the law under which Eichmann was tried, a law dictated more by the political and historical background of the Jewish state than by the commonly accepted canons of justice.

If Hausner's approach was illegitimate because it had political rather than legal goals, it also failed because it did not discern that Eichmann's crime was entirely new and required a thoroughly innovative theory of law. Hausner assumed—as did most Jewish nationalists—that the Nazi holocaust was but one more pogrom, if on an unprecedented scale, in the long history of antisemitism. He therefore reviewed the history of antisemitism in an effort to establish Eichmann's motive, surely a legitimate part of any trial, especially with respect to sentencing. Yet what Hausner—and most other people, Arendt suggests—did not understand is that the crime of genocide can be carried out by bureaucrats who do not necessarily hate the people they send to death. Hence, the history of antisemitism may not really help in understanding Eichmann. Our legal system assumes that "intent to do wrong is necessary for commission of a crime." What seems to characterize totalitarian systems is that they invert all notions of right and wrong. So we are led to question how bureaucrats can be held responsible for their crimes, especially if it can be shown that they had no intent to do wrong.

This notion of genocide as a bureaucratic crime that may elude our legal axioms lies behind Arendt's much-debated phrase "the banality of evil." One may legitimately wonder whether this phrase really describes Eichmann, for the Eichmann Arendt saw in Jerusalem may have looked very different from the Eichmann in Berlin. But whether or not this new notion of evil applies to Eichmann, Arendt is not suggesting that since totalitarianism robs the individual of his autonomy, the "banality" of the criminal's intent exculpates his crime. Nothing could be farther from her intention. She argues strenuously that notions such as "collective guilt," in which all are innocent because all are equally guilty, are sophisms to avoid individual responsibility: "Guilt and innocence before the law are of an objective nature, and even if eighty million Germans had done as [Eichmann] did, this would not have been an excuse for [him]. . . . Let us assume, for the sake of argument, that it was nothing more than misfortune that made [Eichmann] a willing instrument in the organization of mass murder, there still remains the fact that [he] carried out and therefore actively supported a policy of mass murder."[7]

Whatever Eichmann's motivation—banal or demonic—what counts legally is that he committed the crime of genocide while the rest of us did not and would not necessarily do so in the same situation. Arendt holds no brief for the idea, which some have attributed to her, that "there is a little bit of Eichmann in all of us." Because she is resolutely not a determinist in her view of human nature, she believed that we can and should judge specific individuals for politically motivated crimes, even under totalitarian systems. The possible "banality" of Eichmann's evil, while interesting and provocative, has no legal consequences for her.

It is precisely this willingness and even compulsion to judge that made Arendt's book so distasteful to many readers, for just as she does not believe in the collective guilt of the Germans, neither does she believe in the collective innocence of the Jews. Again, specific individuals can and should be judged for their actions by those who were not in their place, for the law presumes that such judgment is not only possible but also essential if criminals are to be brought to justice. This is the theory that lies at the heart of her criticism of the Jewish leaders. It should be noted that she never says that *only* the Jews collaborated but, quite to the contrary, that "this chapter of the story . . . offers the most striking insight into the totality of moral collapse the Nazis caused in respectable European society."[8] On the other hand, the remarks sound almost as if she believes in the collective guilt of the Jewish leadership—undoubtably a consequence of her long-standing antipathy to the Jewish communal establishment—and she has been justly criticized for not distinguishing between the many types of leaders, some of whom were surely heroes by any standards.

But if individuals—whether Nazis or Jews—can be held legally accountable even if they had no intent to commit wrong, a radical revision of our legal concepts becomes necessary. This is exactly Arendt's position, and, quoting Yosal Rogat, she argues "'that a great crime offends nature, so that the very earth cries out for vengeance; that evil violates a natural harmony which only retribution can restore; that a wronged collectivity owes a duty to the moral order to punish the criminal. . . .' I think it is undeniable that it was precisely on the ground of these long-forgotten propositions that Eichmann was brought to justice to begin with and that they were, in fact, the supreme justification for the death penalty."[9] Not the criminal's motivation but the very nature of the crime is what is at stake. Against those who believe in some kind of universal conscience that would dictate right and wrong,[10] Arendt argues for standards drawn from nature, external, as it were, to human beings. The case of Eichmann shatters the assumption that the law is based on conscience, for the law under which he operated was clearly "illegal" in terms of common convention, yet there is scarcely any evidence that conscience compelled resistance to this law.

Against what I take to be this Kantian view of law, Arendt wants to return to the Platonic idea of deriving laws from nature, a notion she shares with Leo Strauss.[11] The affairs of men have a natural order dictated by certain immutable laws just as surely as the processes of nature. A crime like genocide violates this natural order, and it must be punished to set that order right. In fact, Arendt seems to hold that genocide is the archetypical case of a crime that could not be recognized by any other legal theory. Under our current legal doctrines, genocide is considered nothing but murder writ large. Arendt argues that genocide is a crime different in kind from any other and that it "is an attack upon human diversity as such, that is, upon a characteristic of the 'human status' without which the very words 'mankind' or 'humanity' would be devoid of meaning."[12] This is perhaps the closest one could come to a crime against the order of nature, namely, the natural condition of the human race.

What is so crucial about this theory in relation to the Eichmann trial is that it makes the existence of nations an essential and natural condition of humanity and therefore the desire to destroy the Jews not a crime against *that* nation ("crimes against the Jewish people") but a crime against humanity perpetrated "on the body of the Jewish people." The notion of "crimes against humanity" was first developed by the Charter of the Nuremberg Tribunal in order to make it possible for the tribunal to reach those Nazis whose crimes were against German citizens.[13] These criminals would normally be protected by the doctrine of national sovereignty. The charter also had a more general notion of crimes against humanity as crimes unrelated to the prosecution of war (crimes related to the latter are defined as "war crimes"). But the Nuremberg Tribunal generally avoided the radical consequences of this new crime by tying it to other charges that had more widespread acceptance in international law (crimes against peace and war crimes). Had the Jerusalem court based its case against Eichmann on the idea of crimes against humanity instead of crimes against the Jewish people, it would have had to forgo its claim of representing only the Jews and instead assert that it was acting in the name of all humanity. Aside from the technical issue that Israeli law did not include the crime of genocide as such, such a charge would have undermined the court's claim of jurisdiction, for, as Arendt points out, an international tribunal would be more appropriate to try such a crime.

Here we encounter what seems to be a contradiction in Arendt's discussion. On the one hand, she fully supports the Israeli's claim of territorial jurisdiction, although she gives an idiosyncratic definition of territory. On the other hand, she follows Karl Jaspers in advocating an international tribunal to try Eichmann based on the understanding of Eichmann's crime. I would argue that these conflicting arguments are rooted in Arendt's definition of humanity and human rights.

In *The Origins of Totalitarianism*, Arendt attacks the French Revolution for tying human rights to national sovereignty.[14] Although the French Enlightenment developed the idea of humanity as such, it immediately compromised it by making it impossible for a human being to enjoy these rights unless he was a member of a national polity. This situation became particularly evident after World War I, when special minority treaties were drafted to ensure the rights of minorities in the new states of eastern Europe under the assumption that they could not be protected by universal human rights. The undermining of human rights by national sovereignty became complete in the late 1930s, when masses of stateless people flooded various nations and, bereft of a government to protect them, discovered that their "human rights" were hardly worth the paper on which the Declaration of the Rights of Man was written. These refugees "could see that ... the abstract nakedness of being nothing but human was their greatest danger.... Not only did loss of national rights in all instances entail the loss of human rights; the restoration of human rights, as the recent example of the State of Israel proves, has been achieved so far only through the restoration of the establishment of national rights."[15] This statement is not, one should note, a condemnation of the State of Israel but rather a commentary on modern nationalism as such. For Arendt, the conjunction of national sovereignty and human rights actually robbed the concept of humanity of any meaning.

The subordination or even elimination of human rights is connected for Arendt with the modern utilitarian concept of law: "A conception of law which identifies what is right with the notion of what is good ... for the individual, the family, or the people, or the largest number, becomes inevitable once the absolute and transcendent measurements of religion or the law of nature have lost their authority."[16] As we have observed, it is precisely the concept of a law of nature, independent of any relative human standard, that Arendt wants to restore to our legal theories. Modern nationalism, virtually by definition, must be based on the subordination of general human rights to the law of corporate self-interest.

Arendt does not, however, oppose the existence of nations or argue for some kind of utopian cosmopolitanism. Her definition of humanity is inextricably linked to diversity rather than equality. Her critique of modern nationalism focuses on the tendency of nation-states to resent diversity: "[Nation-states] often insist on ethnic homogeneity [in order]... to eliminate as far as possible those natural and always-present differences and differentiations which by themselves arouse dumb hatred, mistrust, and discrimination because they indicate all too clearly those spheres where men cannot act and change at will."[17] Since the Greeks, these natural differences have been relegated to the private sphere: "Highly developed political life breeds a deep-rooted suspicion of this private sphere, a deep resentment against the disturbing miracle contained in the fact that each of us is made as he is—single, unique, unchangeable."[19] The political sphere finds it difficult to tolerate the "mere givenness" of human diversity and therefore falls back on an artificial notion of formal equality that obscures a fundamental human right: the right of human beings to differ naturally one from another. By developing a concept of diverse humanity divorced from nationalism—but not divorced from the "givenness" of national differences—Arendt hopes that it may be possible to restore diversity to the political arena.

This theory, argued somewhat enigmatically in *The Origins of Totalitarianism*, receives much fuller treatment in *The Human Condition*, where she maintains—perhaps unhistorically—that the Greek polis had such an idea of a political theory in which human dignity was the central premise. Modern political theory, whose origins she traces back to Plato, has inverted this hierarchy of public and private spheres and relegated diversity to the private.[18] The modern concept of "society," which Arendt regards as a disastrous invention for public life, elevated the concerns of the private sphere in the polis (economic survival) to the main principle of the political arena. It is the function of law to set the proper boundaries between the public and private spheres, to define the legitimate purview of the political.[19] Law is therefore a kind of prepolitical definition of political life. The utilitarian concept of law therefore defines the utilitarian teleology of modern political life and dictates the notion of formal equality. In her desire to return to an earlier system of natural law, Arendt suggests redefining the political sphere to guarantee the right of diversity.

Arendt does not advocate a return to the polis, which may well have served as no more than a fictionalized construct for her in any case. Instead, she has in mind some form of world government as advocated by her teacher Karl Jaspers, which would be composed not of sovereign states but of national groups that have given up their sovereignty.[20] Whatever exact political system she might have had in mind, the crucial aspect of this theory is the necessity of establishing the idea of humanity as such in the political realm.

We need not be detained by the obviously arguable aspects of Arendt's critique of the modern nation-state or her perhaps utopian alternative. Our task is to understand Arendt in Jerusalem, and what is crucial about this theory for our purposes is the role of the Jews. I believe that it has not been sufficiently noticed how, for Arendt, the Jewish people are the model for mankind as it should be. Such a proposition will certainly confound those who have always claimed to smell a self-hating Jew behind Arendt's writings. Yet it seems to me indisputable from her definition of the Jewish nation in *Eichmann in Jerusalem* that Arendt regards the Jews as proof that national sovereignty is not a *conditio sine qua non* for maintaining a national identity. The international character of the Jewish people, which of course provoked the anger of the antisemites, is for Arendt the concrete case of a nation without territorial nationalism. As such, the Jews represent what all mankind might become. This is what she means by her somewhat cryptic references in *The Origins of Totalitarianism* to the Jewish mission "to achieve the establishment of mankind."[21] The very reason why the Jews attracted hatred—their natural differences from other people—must become the basis for humanity. Indeed, it was primarily the Jews as stateless people who first exposed the hypocrisy of the Rights of Man and demanded a new notion of humanity. In the same light, the genocide of the Jews focused more acutely than any other event the need for a new concept of law based on human rights.

It should be clearly understood that this argument does not call for an end to nations, nor did Arendt ultimately condemn the Jews for wanting their own territory. To be sure, during the debates over Jewish statehood in the 1940s she came out against an exclusively Jewish state on the same grounds that she opposed all ethnic nationalism. In particular, she believed that the Zionist movement had been taken over by the Revisionist statist position, which she seems to have identified with imperialistic "tribal nationalism." This danger was already inherent in Herzl's politics. But these arguments were against the idea of a state and not against a Jewish territory. In fact, she seems to have regarded the Yishuv under the British Mandate as a political community with some utopian characteristics. Her argument was that since the day of the nation-state, and especially the small nation-state, was over, the Jews should not fall for an antiquated nationalism. She regarded the Zionism that made a sovereign state its *Endziel* as a dangerous throwback to the nineteenth century.[22]

Whether or not one agrees with Arendt's historical analysis of modern nationalism and the place of Zionism in it, one must recognize the importance of these ideas for her reaction to the Eichmann trial. By the time she came to Jerusalem in 1961, it is my impression that she had at least come to accept the State of Israel as a fact. Yet her argument that Eichmann should have been tried for crimes against humanity was based on her belief that the mission of the Jewish people was "to achieve the establishment of mankind," and she saw the trial as an ideal opportunity for this messianic task. Hence, whether conducted by an international tribunal or by an Israeli court deriving its jurisdiction from the extraterritorial nature of the Jewish nation, the Eichmann trial provided a test case for crimes "against the human status."

Arendt's unquestionably high expectations of the Jewish people are, surprisingly enough, linked to her evident belief in the chosenness of the Jewish people. To be sure, she criticizes what she takes to be the modern idea of Jewish chosenness, epitomized by Disraeli, which is nothing but racism pure and simple. But this denigrated notion is a result of separating the traditional tie between chosenness and messianism, which for Arendt means, once again, the "establishment of mankind."[23] Whether or not this definition of Jewish messianism bears any relation to historical reality, it is striking that Arendt finds her political ideal in an interpretation of Jewish tradition.

It is also striking that Arendt's Jewish commitment comes not only out of theoretical or historical speculations but out of her own experience. Practically the first essay she wrote upon arrival in the United States was "We Refugees" (January 1943), and there she first develops the notions of statelessness that were later to play such an important role in *The Origins of Totalitarianism*.[24] As a stateless person in France, she escaped the gas chambers only by the skin of her teeth. Undoubtedly, it was this experience that taught her to be skeptical about nation-states as protectors of human rights, and this skepticism surely played a significant role in her criticism of political Zionism. In "We Refugees," she elevates the refugee to the status of political prophet, and, significantly, she calls on the refugee to base his prophecy on his Jewish identity: "[The refugees] know that the outlawing of the Jewish people in Europe has been followed by the outlawing of most European nations. Refugees driven from country to country represent the vanguard of their peoples—if they keep their identity. For the first time, Jewish history is not separate but tied up with that of all nations. The comity of European peoples went to pieces when, and because, it allowed its weakest member to be excluded and persecuted."[25] Arendt's elevation of human diversity to a cardinal principle of natural law is reflected in and emerges from her own Jewish identity. This fact emerges with extraordinary clarity in her reply to Gershom Scholem's critique of the Eichmann book.[26] Scholem attacks her for lacking *ahavat yisrael* (love of Israel) in her treatment of the Jews during the Holocaust and goes on to imply that she lacks true Jewish commitment. She answers that, indeed, she does not love any collective people but only individuals. Yet on the other hand, "I have always regarded my Jewishness as one of the indisputable factual data of my life. . . . There is such a thing as basic gratitude for everything that is as it is; for what has been given and what was not, could not be, *made*."[27] For this latter reason alone, she says that she is more grieved by wrong done by her own people than wrong done by any other. Here, in brief, are the fundamental categories of her theoretical discussion expressed on a personal level: on the one hand, she rejects the idea of "love" of one's people, a sentiment she would no doubt identify with chauvinism and tribal nationalism. But on the other hand, she affirms the natural "givenness" of national identity. It seems to me that Arendt's political theory, whose legal manifestation we have found in her discussion of the Eichmann trial, is an abstraction of this profound personal commitment to Jewishness. The theory of the natural right of diversity is an urgent expression of her concern that Jews be allowed the right to be themselves. She holds that the system of the nation-states undermined this natural right even while seeming to uphold it and that Eichmann's crime of genocide was a consequence of this fundamentally flawed political order. Whether or not justice was done in Jerusalem becomes for her an implicit question of whether our notions of justice will assure a world safe for diversity, that is, a world safe for Jews as well as all other peoples.

CHAPTER 12

Gershom Scholem's "Ten Unhistorical Aphorisms on the Kabbalah"

Translation and Commentary

IN 1958, GERSHOM SCHOLEM PUBLISHED a series of ten aphoristic statements entitled "Zehn unhistorische Sätze über Kabbala."[1] Although later republished in the third volume of his collected German essays, *Judaica*,[2] these aphorisms have received little or no attention in the English-reading world, despite their considerable interest both for Scholem's own thought and as philosophical reflections on some fundamental issues in the Kabbalah.[3] The word *unhistorical* in the title immediately suggests Scholem's intention to take off the hat of historian and philologian that he wore in most of his writings and to look at his material from a different perspective. Since Scholem's primary achievements lay in the history and philology of the Kabbalah, his more philosophical and theological reflections have often been treated as occasional pieces, peripheral to his main contribution. I have argued elsewhere that an understanding of Scholem as a historian requires an examination of these writings and attention to his place in modern Jewish thought.[4] From the beginning of his career, when he planned to write a dissertation on the Kabbalah's philosophy of language, he was attracted to the Kabbalistic treatment of philosophical and theological issues that have contemporary resonance. While it would be a mistake to assert that he imposed these modern categories on his historical studies, they did influence the themes he chose to address and, in many instances, dictated the language in which he cast his writing.

One of the main characteristics of these aphorisms is just such an interplay between historical theses and modern philosophical language. Scholem boldly suggests parallels between modern schools of thought and the Kabbalah: dialectical materialism and the Lurianic Kabbalah, phenomenology and Moses Cordovero, Franz Kafka and the eighteenth-century Frankist Jonas Wehle. At the end of aphorism 4, he notes: "The conception of the Kabbalists as mystical materialists with a dialectical tendency would certainly be thoroughly unhistorical, yet anything but meaningless." At first blush, to impose modern categories on a historical subject would certainly seem unhistorical. Yet Scholem assumes that the philosophical issues treated by both the Kabbalah and modern philosophy are universal, even as they are addressed historically in different terms by different movements. The seemingly "unhistorical" procedure of these aphorisms is therefore philosophically meaningful: modern philosophy and the Kabbalah illuminate and explicate the same problems and can therefore shed light on each other. But it is also historically meaningful because it allows the modern sensibility to grasp a system of thought that appears initially alien and remote.

This telescoping of historical ideas by viewing them through modern prisms is not, however, a subject only for "unhistorical" aphorisms. It lies at the heart of one of the classic problems of all historical work: What changes do ideas necessarily undergo as they are refracted through the eyes of a historian whose categories of thought are historically different?[5] The very ability of the historian to reconstruct the past lies in his finding a common ground or common language between himself and his sources: if the past is utterly alien, it cannot be reconstructed. Hence, the historian must engage in a delicate balancing act between past and present, maintaining the bridge between them without collapsing one into the other. The fact that Scholem gives explicit consideration to this issue in these aphorisms does not mean that he ignored it in his historical work. On the contrary, one can find repeated instances where he consciously used modern categories to illuminate and explicate problems in the Kabbalah. Indeed, one of the keys to Scholem's success as a historian of the Kabbalah was in turning an ostensibly alien system of ideas into one with a contemporary resonance and urgency. Yet unlike Martin Buber, who also found striking parallels between modern thought and the Kabbalah, Scholem was largely able to maintain the distinction between them.

That Scholem chose to express these ideas in the form of aphorisms and in language that is much more opaque than his normal German style deserves some comment.[6] The tradition of aphoristic writing in German goes back to Lichtenberg in the eighteenth century and Feuerbach in the nineteenth. But it was Nietzsche who exploited the aphoristic form as a vehicle for his attack on systematic philosophy. What better way to destroy the idea of systems than by writing in a deliberately fragmentary and elusive style that hid as much as it revealed? The aphoristic style was particularly effective in conveying paradoxes, which also suited Nietzsche's antirationalist intent.

Nietzsche's influence can be detected in a variety of German writers in the twentieth century, and particularly starting in the 1920s. Theodor Adorno, Ernst Bloch, and Walter Benjamin, among others, all composed some of their best writing in aphorisms. Scholem was close to all of these German Jewish thinkers, although, as is well known, he was not at all sympathetic to their neo-Marxism. Yet it is quite likely that his own attempt at aphoristic writing may have owed much to their influence. In particular, Walter Benjamin's "Theses on the Philosophy of History,"[7] written in 1940, must have evoked in Scholem the desire to set down some of his ideas in the same style as that adopted by his deceased friend. Although the aphorisms presented below lack the literary flair of Benjamin's theses, it seems to me that Scholem was attempting to imitate Benjamin's late work.

An additional influence, which Scholem suggests in the tenth aphorism, is that of Franz Kafka. Scholem saw in Kafka's writings, and particularly in his parables, a modern form of Kabbalah.[8] Like Nietzsche's aphorisms, Kafka's parables are characterized by ironic twists and reversals. The expulsion from Paradise turns out to have been "a stroke of luck, for had we not been expelled, Paradise would have had to be destroyed." By making daring use of counterfactual conditionals, Kafka explored alternative interpretations of biblical and other classical stories, a procedure that might well be termed "midrashic." It was this ability to explode the conventional reading of well-known texts and reveal their secrets that must have reminded Scholem of the Kabbalah and made him see in Kafka a kind of neo-Kabbalist.

For Scholem's own purposes, the aphoristic style clearly held particular attraction. Although these aphorisms are "on" or "about" (*über*) Kabbalah, they are, in their own way, Kabbalistic in both style and content. In order to convey the parallels between the intellectual problems of the modern historian and those of the Kabbalists, Scholem adopts Kabbalistic formulations that he, of course, avoided in his more historical essays. The aphorism conveys a sense of mystery and impenetrability: opaqueness is almost part of its definition. The sense of secrets hidden behind the explicit text in an aphorism is thus reminiscent of the Kabbalah, for which truth is by nature secret (*sod*). Aphorisms mirror the Kabbalistic concept of esoteric truths. That which is hidden cannot be expressed without altering its meaning, and therefore the aphorism, which suggests more than it expresses, is a better vehicle for these reflections than direct exposition. Hence, Scholem's choice of aphorisms is itself proof of the relationship between the historian of the Kabbalah and his subject matter. Indeed, the very number of aphorisms— ten—hints at a Kabbalistic "subtext," for that is the number of *sefirot* (divine emanations). And just like the *sefirot* themselves, these aphorisms are at once discrete and seemingly unlinked to one another, yet at the same time unified by a common theme that is treated in each from a different angle. That theme, to which we have already alluded, is the fundamental tension or even paradox of communicating a truth that is, by definition, secret or hidden. What is the definition of a "secret" (*Geheimnis*)? On the one hand, it may be something that is known but deliberately hidden, or, it may be that which is essentially inaccessible (hidden by nature rather than by design). It is this latter sense of a secret that Scholem has in mind here. Kabbalistic truth is inaccessible because God is transcendent. Historical truth is inaccessible because the past cannot be known in the same way we know the perceptual world. Both Kabbalist and historian face the same problem of how to convey a truth that is hidden.

The subtle influence of the Kabbalah on Scholem as a historian becomes particularly apparent in deciphering the language of the aphorisms. Scholem writes in German but often thinks in the technical language of the Kabbalah (either Hebrew or Zoharic Aramaic). Thus, a correct understanding of the text requires sensitivity to the Kabbalistic language lurking behind it. For instance, in discussing the epistemology of the Kabbalah, he uses the term *Erkenntnis* (knowledge). Yet it becomes clear in the context that he has in mind the Kabbalah's understanding of knowledge in the form of the *sefirah* (divine emanation) called *hokhmah* (wisdom). One is thus faced with the problem of grasping both the philosophical vocabulary and its Kabbalistic background in reading the text. The function of the commentary to each aphorism will be in part to point out the Kabbalistic dimension concealed behind the text.

APHORISM 1

The philology of a mystical discipline such as the Kabbalah has something ironic about it. It concerns itself with a veil of fog that, as the history of the mystical tradition, envelops the body, the space of the thing itself, a fog, to be sure, that it brings forth from itself.

Does there remain visible to the philologian something of the law of the thing itself, or does the essential disappear precisely in this projection of the historical? The uncertainty in answering this question belongs to the nature of the philological enterprise itself, so the hope, from which this work lives, preserves something ironic, which cannot be separated from it. But doesn't this element of irony rather lie in the subject of the Kabbalah itself and not only in its history?

The Kabbalists claim that there is a tradition about truth that is transmissible [*tradierbar*]. An ironic claim, since this truth, with which we are concerned, is anything but transmissible. It can be known, but it cannot be passed on, and exactly that which can be passed on, it no longer contains. Genuine tradition remains hidden; only a fallen tradition stumbles upon [*verfällt auf*] an object, and only in its fallen state will it become visible in its greatness.

COMMENTARY

The "philologist" of this aphorism is equivalent to the "historian" of a mystical discipline, although Scholem often liked to call himself a philologist, by which he indicated the importance of establishing the textual and linguistic tradition of the Kabbalah as the key to its history. The problem suggested in the aphorism is, however, common to all the historical disciplines and is the question of what of the essence of the past remains accessible to the historian. History is concerned with the sources that have been produced by the past event, and the historian can reach that event only through the sources. To what extent, then, can such an indirect procedure yield knowledge of the truth?

But this is the very problem that also confronts the Kabbalist: the "element of irony resides rather in the subject of this Kabbalah itself and not only in its history." The truth of the Kabbalah is, by definition, a secret truth. It can be known, but not in the same sense that one "knows" the perceptual world. The very "hiddenness" of Kabbalistic truth, which is an essential part of its definition, makes it impossible to transmit, for any act of transmission or communication would immediately violate its secret character. Yet the very word Kabbalah means tradition, or that which has been handed down. The authenticity of Kabbalistic truth is based on the claim that the Kabbalist possesses an authentic tradition that has been handed down to him and that reveals the secrets of the Torah.[9] The Kabbalist is therefore caught in a tension between the secret nature of his truth and his claim that he has received it by a process that would violate that secret.

Yet on a deeper level, this problem of the accessibility of the source of a mystical tradition lies in Kabbalistic theology itself. The Kabbalah holds that the source of all creation is the hidden God, *ain sof* (the "Infinite"). The hidden God, by definition, cannot be known, yet the Kabbalah, through its theory of *sefirot*, attempts to comprehend something of this God. Thus, Kabbalistic theology is caught in the same tension between the knowability and hiddenness of its subject.

Scholem alludes to this last level in his metaphor of the "veil of fog" that surrounds the subject matter studied by the philologist. The fog is presumably the texts that are available to the scholar but that do not permit actual access to the truths that they describe. But exactly the same metaphor can be found in that passage in the Zohar which describes the first steps of creation within the *ain sof*: "In the beginning—when the will of the King began to take effect—he engraved signs into the heavenly sphere. Within the most hidden recess a dark flame issued from the mystery of the Infinite, like a fog forming in the unformed [*kutra' be-gulma*]."[10] In his translation of this passage into German,[11] Scholem rendered the "fog" as *Nebel,* the same term he uses in this aphorism. Thus, the epistemological problem of both historian and Kabbalist is represented by the metaphor that hints at the theological problem of knowing the hidden God.

On the other hand, the problem of the historian differs fundamentally from that of the Kabbalist. Although both confront truths that are inaccessible to ordinary sense perception, the secrecy of Kabbalistic truth is a result of the *transcendence* of God, while the historian deals with events that are part of the world. Historical truth is "secret" only in the sense that what lies beyond the temporal horizon of the historian is unknowable in the perceptual sense of the word, while Kabbalistic knowledge is secret because God is essentially absent. Thus, only by metaphorically conceiving of the past as somehow parallel to the hiddenness of God does the analogy between historian and Kabbalist make sense.

APHORISM 2

The publishing of the main works of the old Kabbalistic literature is the most important guarantee of their secrets. For we no longer see [the secrets], and when will we be able to address them? No Kabbalistic work was attacked on account of its popularizing tendencies, on account of its supposed betrayal of the secrets of the Torah, like the book *Emek ha-Melech* of Jacob Elchanan Bachrach of Frankfurt am Main, published in 1648. However, if one opens these pages today, it appears that our awareness of this betrayal of mysteries must have vanished. There is scarcely a less understandable book than this "Valley of the King." Are we once again dealing with that mystical-anarchistic politics, which better protects secrets by expressing them than by silence? And which among all the expressed worlds is more sunk in its mysterious expressibility than the world of the Lurianic Kabbalah?

COMMENTARY

In this aphorism, Scholem seemingly turns the conclusion of the previous aphorism on its head. Where in Aphorism 1, the greatness of a hidden tradition becomes visible only in a "fallen" or publicized state, the very public character of the Kabbalah in Aphorism 2 guarantees that the mysteries will remain hidden. Yet the paradoxical fact that publicizing a hidden tradition protects it better than hiding it must stem from the same epistemological principle Scholem develops in Aphorism 1: since the hidden truth cannot, by definition, be expressed, the more one attempts to express it, the more one leads one's audience away from the truth. Here, once again, the issue concerns the meaning of a secret. The German word *Geheimnis* is related to *Heim* (home), suggesting that a secret is that which is not public. The very act of publicizing a secret turns it into something it is not. Once a mystical truth is given public expression, it becomes divorced from the original insight that gave it birth. The reader "no longer sees" and cannot experience what the mystic himself experienced. In this aphorism and in the previous one, Scholem challenges the claim of Martin Buber and others that the reading of mystical texts can cause the reader himself to have a mystical experience.[12]

The issue of the public dissemination of Kabbalistic secrets became an acute one in the century following the Lurianic Kabbalah. While the Spanish Kabbalah of the thirteenth century remained largely an esoteric discipline limited to small circles of cognoscenti, the Lurianic Kabbalah was popularized by a number of writers, among them the author of *Emek ha-Melekh*.[13] Only today, in historical perspective, does it become apparent how misleading these popularizing texts are and how far from conveying the essential truth of Luria's teaching. But if such texts are misleading, then the historian, who is both temporally and temperamentally outside the small circle of Kabbalistic adepts, has a paradoxical relationship to the original truths: he is able to leapfrog over the popularizing texts and recover what contemporaries of Bacharach, who were much closer in time and spirit to Luria, could not understand. The very incomprehensibility of supposedly popular texts can be detected only by the historian, while those to whom the texts were directed lived under the "illusion" that they comprehended them. Because of his very distance from the material, the historian ironically has an insight into the Kabbalah that may be close to that of the original Kabbalists themselves.

Here, too, one may discern an echo of the Kabbalah itself behind the aphorism. Luria argued that the initial step in creation was the self-contraction of God and the creation of an empty space (*halal ha-panu'i*). The late eighteenth-century Hasidic master Nahman of Bratslav suggested that the empty space could be comprehended only through silence.[14] Public treatment of these mysteries or, for that matter, any verbal expression would therefore contradict their essence. If one accepts Nahman's mysticism of silence, then the Lurianic Kabbalah suffered a paradoxical fate: precisely that Kabbalistic system whose mysteries could be approached only through silence was the subject of a public campaign. The popularization of this quintessentially secret doctrine succeeded to the point where it became virtually the sole "public" Jewish theology of the seventeenth and eighteenth centuries. That this fate of the Lurianic Kabbalah was a case of "mystical-anarchistic politics" may be an allusion to the nihilistic outgrowth of Luria's system: the Sabbatian movement of the seventeenth century. For the very public campaign that spread Luria's teachings made possible, at least in Scholem's interpretation, the phenomenon of a mass messianic movement with an antinomian Kabbalistic theology.

APHORISM 3

The character of knowledge in the Kabbalah: the Torah is the medium through which all essences are known. The symbolism of the "shining mirror," which the Kabbalists carried over to the Torah, is revealing of it. The Torah is the medium in which knowledge is reflected, darkening as it brings with it the essence of tradition, and emanating into the pure realm of the "scriptural," but this is a teaching that cannot be applied. For what can be applied is only what is "oral," that is, that which can be transmitted. Knowledge is the emanation through which man seeks to penetrate from its medium to its source—remaining inescapably in the medium, since God himself is in fact the Torah and knowledge cannot proceed out [of it]. There is something infinitely despairing about the lack of an object of this highest knowledge, which is taught in the first pages of the book *Zohar*. The fundamental nature of this knowledge is revealed in the classical form of the question: knowledge is a question rooted in God to which no answer corresponds. The "who" is the final word of all theory, which, surprisingly enough, leads so far away from the "what" to which adheres its beginning.

COMMENTARY

The Kabbalistic background to this aphorism is perhaps more important than to any of the other aphorisms in the series. Many of the terms Scholem uses are translations of technical Kabbalistic terms related to the *sefirot* symbolism and can be understood only in that context. Knowledge is represented by the *sefirah hokhmah*, which is the highest *sefirah* that can be known. Beyond *hokhmah* lies the realm of the hidden God and his will (*keter*). The *sefirah tiferet* is designated as a "shining mirror" that stands in the middle of the system and transmits light from the *sefirot* above to the *sefirot* below. In Kabbalistic symbolism, *tiferet* also stands for the written Torah, while the *sefirah malkhut*, which mediates between the world of emanation and the lower worlds, is called the "oral Torah." The light from *ain sof* darkens as it emanates into the lower *sefirot* from *tiferet* to *malkhut* and, ultimately, into the lower worlds. This "knowledge" becomes "usable" only where it is "oral," meaning that it can be transmitted and understood in our world only where it has passed through the "refracting mirror," which is the Kabbalistic designation of *malkhut*.[15]

On the literal level, the Torah is regarded as the medium through which all knowledge from God is conveyed, but since God himself remains forever hidden and inaccessible, one can never attain the source of this knowledge. Here we have a restatement of the same issue raised in Aphorisms 1 and 2 of the hidden nature of the source of revelation. But on a symbolic, mystical level, the Torah is also the system of the *sefirot* as a whole, through which the light from *ain sof* emanates. This system can be known, but the source of the emanation—the hidden God—cannot. Yet the *sefirot* are not emanations *outside* of God; they are part of God's substance. Therefore, one who attains knowledge of the *sefirot* (the mystical Torah) attains direct knowledge of God. The ambiguous or equivocal nature of this knowledge is that it is both of God and not of God: it is knowledge up to the *sefirah hokhmah* but not of the hidden aspect of God. He who possesses the "highest knowledge" (viz. *hokhmah*) seemingly possesses everything, but also nothing at all. If our earlier analysis of the relationship of historical to Kabbalistic knowledge is correct, then might this aphorism also allude to the ambiguous nature of the historian's quest for the whole truth?

APHORISM 4

The materialistic language of the Lurianic Kabbalah, especially in its deduction of *tzimtzum* (the self-contraction of God), raises the question whether the symbolism, which is served by such images and speech, might not also be the thing itself. Such a materialistic aspect fundamentally accompanied the Kabbalah at the moment when the law of a living organism was introduced as a fundamental vision of its theosophy. It matters little if one now says that we are subject to this law because it is the law of the life of the Godhead itself, or if one only "transfers" it "as it were" also onto the Godhead. The effective circle of this law encompasses everything equally, no matter how one may turn it. It might be argued that the expressions of the Kabbalists about the *tzimtzum* are lacking in contradiction and are meaningful only if one treats them as having a material substrate, whether this is now the "*ain sof*" itself or his "light." The accusations against the heretical theologians of the Sabbatian Kabbalah, that they have misunderstood spiritual mysteries as materialistic, shows where things can end up when one attempts to think through the inner logic of the images. From the very beginning, a dialectical moment in this materialism accompanied the teaching of *tzimtzum* and the breaking of the vessels. The idea in Nathan of Gaza's Sabbatian Kabbalah according to which in *ain sof* itself there is a light "full of thought" set against a light "lacking in thought," yet the two emanate into each other, is but the most radical expression of this process of dialectical materialism exercised through God himself. The conception of the Kabbalists as mystical materialists of a dialectical tendency would be thoroughly unhistorical, yet anything but meaningless.

COMMENTARY

The problem of this aphorism is stated at the outset: Does a mystical, symbolic language merely "represent" its subject, or is the language an essential part of the "thing itself"? We shall see how Scholem returns to this issue of the theory of mystical language in later aphorisms. The specific problem of whether the Lurianic Kabbalah should be understood literally or metaphorically plagued all the disciples of Luria and continued to be a crucial issue in eighteenth-century Hasidic theology.[16] If Luria meant that God literally contracted himself, then there would be a place where there was no God—a heretical proposition! But if Luria meant such statements metaphorically, the whole system loses much of its originality and meaning.

If one can legitimately call those Kabbalists who understood the Lurianic theory of creation literally as "materialists," then it would be necessary to extend such unhistorical language and call them additionally "dialectical materialists." If God literally absented himself from the empty space he had created, creation would have a dialectical logic: the Becoming of the world would be the result of a movement of Being through Nothing.

Such thinking could lead to heretical positions, as it did in the radical thought of the Sabbatian theologians of the seventeenth century. By understanding the process of divine contraction literally, the Sabbatian theologian Nathan of Gaza had to posit two kinds of light within the *ain sof* itself: a light full of thought and a light devoid of thought.[17] The *ain sof* could not contain only a light full of thought, since "thought" is identified with one of the emanated *sefirot*. Such a light would be limited and would place limitations on the infinitude of the hidden God. The concept of a light devoid of thought was therefore necessary to preserve the unlimited character of the *ain sof*, but Nathan understood this light as the source of the "roots of evil" (*shorshei ha-dinim*). Thus, in Nathan's theology, the *ain sof* itself is caught in a dialectical conflict between two contradictory principles. The unknowable, hidden God loses both his unknowability and his inner harmony.

APHORISM 5

In the old Kabbalah's concept of the relationship between *ain sof* and Nothingness, there is expressed, in the final analysis, the same feeling of the dialectic of creation as later in the idea of *tzimtzum*. What then is the fundamental meaning of the separation between *ain sof* and the first *sefirah*? Just this, that the full essence of the hidden God, which remains transcendent to all knowledge (including the intuitive), in the primordial act of emanation, above all, in the pure turn to creation, becomes Nothing. This is that divine Nothingness, which in the perspective of its way must appear to the mystics necessarily as the last step of "becoming." But for the Kabbalists, there remains the consciousness of a last abyss, an abyss of the Will, which is represented as Nothingness. From this act onwards, in the abyss of the Will, everything, in fact, is already given. For God's turn toward creation is indeed creation itself, even if it is worked through for us only in endless gradations and processes. But within God, all of this is one unified act. In this sense, the principal distinction between *ain sof* and the first *sefirah* is certainly connected to the problematic of pantheism: it is greatly circumscribed in this distinction, and indeed came especially to clear consciousness with Moshe Cordovero, that the movement from *ain sof* to the first *sefirah*, the primordial act, represents an infinitely more significant step than all the subsequent steps combined. It is from this perspective that one must see the decisive rejection, by all Kabbalists from 1530 on, of the identification between the *ain sof* and *Nothingness [ayin]*. At work here appears to be a feeling that this thesis is endangered by identifying these two concepts: it lacks the dialectical moment in the concept of creation. It is this lack of a dialectic that makes this thesis helpless in the face of pantheism. Without transcendence, the Nothing penetrates into the Something. One could say that those Kabbalists of the early period who wanted to claim that the difference between *ain sof* and *ayin* was only a difference in name rather than in essence in doing so in fact struck from the cosmic drama the first act, which contains the dialectical exposition of the whole. Thus, that theory of identity contains its pantheistic expression: creation out of nothingness is only a cipher for the essential unity of all things with God. The [mystic's] "lived experience" [*Erlebnis*] can in fact never penetrate further than Nothingness, and it is out of this real ground of experience that the pantheistic identification of *ain sof* and Nothingness was so often written by the old Kabbalists. The mystic, who treats his experience undialectically, must end up in pantheism.

COMMENTARY

In this aphorism, Scholem enlarges upon the dialectical logic of the Kabbalah to which he alluded in Aphorism 4. The dialectics of the Kabbalah begin with the relationship between the *ain sof* and the first *sefirah*, frequently referred to as *ayin* (Nothingness).

Some of the early Kabbalists saw no essential difference between the first *sefirah* (sometimes also called the divine "will") and *ain sof* itself, while for the others the emanation of the "abyss of the will" (or Nothingness) was in fact the first act of creation. According to traditional monotheistic theology, the world was created by God *ex nihilo,* meaning that God and the world are fundamentally different. Such a theology is the very antithesis of pantheism. But those who conceived of God as identical to Nothingness radically reinterpreted *creatio ex nihilo* to mean that the world emanated directly out of God. This doctrine therefore bordered on pantheism, since it held that the world shared in the divine substance. On the other hand, those who held that Nothingness was an emanation of *ain sof* and not identical with it were able to maintain the absolute transcendence of the hidden God by erecting a dialectical barrier between him and all subsequent emanations. This second theory of the status of the divine Nothingness was therefore closer to the traditional antipathy to pantheism.

It was this antipantheistic understanding of Nothingness that took hold in the later Kabbalistic tradition and was given new expression in the sixteenth century. Moses Cordovero argued that all of subsequent emanation and creation was already contained in the movement from *ain sof* to the first *sefirah*. He posited an infinite number of dialectical steps in this first movement such that the "will" of God approaches but is never quite identical to the Infinite. In Isaac Luria's theory later in that century, the hidden God must first create an empty space—a Nothingness—in order to make a place for the world. This was the radical theory of *tzimtzum* or the self-contraction of God. Thus, centuries before Hegel, the Kabbalists understood the importance of a dialectical logic of creation. It was not so much that they anticipated Hegel as that the theological necessity of avoiding pantheism and maintaining God's transcendence led to dialectical thinking: "Without transcendence, Nothingness extends down into Somethingness." In this way, mystical and rational modes of thought converged in a remarkably similar logic.[18]

The mystical experiences of the early Kabbalists (of which we possess little direct information) could never yield knowledge of the hidden God, but only knowledge of a mystical Nothingness. The mystic who relies on his experience rather than on theoretical reflection might confuse *ain sof* with Nothingness, a mistake that the theoretical or theosophical Kabbalist presumably would never make. On what basis Scholem believes that experience might attain only a perception of Nothingness is unclear. But what may explain this passage is the word Scholem uses for experience: *Erlebnis*. We have here an allusion to his youthful polemic against Martin Buber's

Erlebnismystik, which Buber propounded until approximately 1917, when he began to evolve his dialogic philosophy of *Ich und Du*.[19] Buber's "mysticism of experience" led to a sense of unification with the cosmos, which could be understood as pantheism. Scholem not only rejected Buber's mystical philosophy but argued that Jewish mysticism was essentially different: it was not a mysticism of lived experience but rather a theosophy in which the individual identities of God and the mystic were maintained. As opposed to Buber's mysticism, and, indeed, to other historical mysticisms, Scholem insisted that there is little evidence of a pantheistic *unio mystica* in the Jewish sources.[20] The early confusion of *ain sof* with *ayin*, with its pantheistic and experiential overtones, was soon corrected in the mainstream of the Kabbalah.

APHORISM 6

The Kabbalists sought to give popular dissemination to deep mystical teachings. The reckoning for this foolhardy undertaking did not require a long wait. They desired a mystical transfiguration of the Jewish people [*Volk*] and Jewish life. Kabbalistic folklore is the answer from the folk—and one is forced to realize, not without a shudder, that the answer is also in accordance with it. However, that it even came actually as an answer is nevertheless noteworthy. Just as nature, Kabbalistically seen, is nothing but the shadow of the divine name, so one can also speak of the longer and longer shadow of the law that is cast over the way of life of the Jews. But the stony wall of the law becomes gradually more transparent in the Kabbalah, there breaks through a shimmer of that reality that surrounds and indicates it. The alchemy of the law, its transmutation into the transparent, is one of the deepest paradoxes of the Kabbalah, since there can't be anything fundamentally less transparent than this shimmer, this aura of the symbolic, which now becomes visible. But along with the ever-growing, if also ever more indistinct, transparency of the law, the shadows, which the law casts over Jewish life, dissolve. The end of this process must logically be Jewish "Reform": the shadowless, backgroundless, but no longer irrational, pure abstract humanity of the law as a vestige of its mystical decay.

COMMENTARY

The historical context of this aphorism is the process by which the Kabbalah, following the expulsion from Spain in 1492, gradually became accepted by most Jews to the point where it substantially influenced the course of Jewish history. One of Scholem's most famous, if not most controversial, theses was that the Lurianic Kabbalah, once popularized in the seventeenth century, became the impetus for the Sabbatian movement, which, in turn, so revolutionized the Jewish world that it laid the groundwork for the secularization of the eighteenth and nineteenth centuries.[21] Jewish secularization meant the dissolution of the authority of Jewish law, represented here by Reform Judaism, which rejected the *halakhah* as normative and prescriptive for daily life. Scholem, "logically speaking" (if not historically), claims that the roots of this abrogation of the law lay in the immanent dialectic of Jewish history and, specifically, in the Kabbalah.

The Kabbalah treated the law as symbolic, just as it treated nature as a "shadow of the divine name." One must follow the law not for its own sake or because it was commanded but for the sake of the divine secrets that it symbolizes. Where the rabbis had seen the law as a "hedge" protecting Jewish life (what Scholem calls here the "stony wall of the law"), the Kabbalists transmuted the law into transparency by rendering it symbolic. What made this procedure paradoxical is that the reality symbolized by the law is the divine mysteries. That which is revealed by this "alchemy of the law" is that which is most obscure and secret. Once again, the Kabbalist is involved in a paradox of revealing what is by definition hidden. If in Aphorism 2 Scholem argued that the very act of publicizing Kabbalistic secrets protected them, here he seems to suggest that dissemination of the Kabbalah subverted the very legal tradition that gave mysticism a social framework.

Although Scholem does not mention the Sabbatian movement in this passage, he surely has it in mind when he refers to the "mystical dissolution" of the law. The logical consequence of turning the law into a symbol was the antinomianism of the Sabbatians. From mystical antinomianism it was but a small dialectical step to the rational antinomianism of the Reformers: rationalism and irrationalism are not polar opposites but are instead intimately interconnected. In this way, the dialectical logic of the Kabbalah led to the dissolution of the very tradition of which it was an intimate part. Making a secret public transforms it into a force for destruction.

One cannot read this aphorism without noticing the ambivalent language that Scholem uses with respect to both the Kabbalah and the law. The popularization of Kabbalistic ideas gave birth to the demon of Sabbatianism. The Kabbalah created its opposite: Jewish Reform, for which the symbolic irrationality of the Kabbalah was anathema. Given his fundamental hostility to Reform Judaism, Scholem would surely have to regard the Kabbalah in an ambivalent light: the Kabbalah was ultimately responsible for the sterile rationalism of the nineteenth century. At the same time, the language he applies to the law is even more uneasy. The law is a "stony wall" that casts "ever-longer" shadows around the life of the Jews. This language comes close to the Enlightenment critique of medieval Judaism as enmired in obscurantist legalism. Indeed, Scholem elsewhere asserts that the *halakhah* is "a well-ordered house" in need of an "anarchic breeze" to give it vitality.[22] For Scholem, the Kabbalah was this anarchic breeze and it was due to the Kabbalah that the Jewish legal tradition did not become a sterile fossil. As opposed to the adherents of the Enlightenment, Scholem holds that it was the Kabbalah rather than modern rationalism that allowed light into this gloomy world. But it was a light that, in Sabbatianism, ignited into a fire that consumed traditional Judaism and left in its wake the sterile rationality of the nineteenth century.

APHORISM 7

As the actual misfortune of the Kabbalah (as with many nonindigenous forms of mysticism), one ought to consider the doctrine of emanation. The insights of the Kabbalah concern the structure of what exists. Nothing would be more disastrous than to confuse the connections of this structure with the doctrine of emanation. This confusion perverts its promising formulations in favor of the most comfortable and intellectually lazy of all theories. Cordovero would be much more at home as a phenomenologist than as a disciple of Plotinus. The attempt to construct the thought of the Kabbalists without the doctrine of emanation (and to think it through to the end) would have to pay the debt that a true disciple of Cordovero would incur, if one should ever exist. In the form of theosophical topography, which

Kabbalistic teachings have assumed in the literature, its objective content remains inaccessible. The conflict between mystical nominalism and its light symbolism in Kabbalistic writings derives from the irreconcilable tension between the Kabbalists' most significant intentions and their inability to help bring these to pure expression.

COMMENTARY

This is probably the most obscure of all the aphorisms. Scholem uses terms like *phenomenology* and *nominalism*, whose meanings are less than clear, even in the best of circumstances. The core idea of the aphorism is that the Neoplatonic theory of emanation, which is typically associated with the Kabbalah, is actually misleading. The Neoplatonists asserted that the emanations were outside of the One, the source of the emanations, while in the Kabbalah the *sefirot* are within God. The Kabbalah therefore attempted to describe activity within God himself that led to the creation of the world, while Neoplatonism did not account for how the process of emanation began in the first place. Because the Neoplatonic theory of emanation failed to confront this most difficult of questions, Scholem considers it "intellectually lazy." The Kabbalah, on the other hand, attempted to reconcile the tension between the One and the Many within the divine sphere itself. Moreover, the God of Neoplatonism was utterly impersonal, while the Kabbalah sought to preserve both the personal God of the Bible and the impersonal God of the philosophers by the relationship between the attributeless *ain sof* and the *sefirot*.[23]

The Kabbalah was therefore led to a dialectical theology that is notably absent in Neoplatonism. As we have seen in earlier aphorisms, lack of a dialectic leads to the danger of pantheism: without a dialectical moment—a moment of non-Being—the One would "swallow up" the Many. Indeed, the direct connection between the One and the Many in Neoplatonism would seem susceptible to the pantheistic interpretation it received from such medieval Jewish philosophers as Abraham ibn Ezra. The light symbolism of Neoplatonism conveys this sense of a direct emanation from the One to the Many, and it is probably because the Kabbalah adopted this symbolism from Neoplatonism that its emanationist theory has been mistaken for that of the Neoplatonists.

How this distinction between Neoplatonism and the Kabbalah can be connected to twentieth-century phenomenology is unclear. Husserl's phenomenology eschewed a discussion of Being or Essence in favor of individual beings or essences. Scholem claims that the Kabbalah was also concerned with the "structures of beings" (*Strukturen des Seienden*), a term that he borrowed from this school of philosophy. Yet what does it mean that the Kabbalah was concerned with individual essences rather than a universal Essence? Perhaps what he has in mind is that the dialectical theology of the Kabbalah established the principle of individuation within God himself, thus giving legitimacy to the essential distinctions between individuals in the lower worlds. This emphasis on singular individuals, based on the distinctions between the *sefirot*, was perhaps the result of the desire to avoid any pantheistic formulations. Where Neoplatonism failed to solve the problem of individuation and thus was threatened by pantheism, the Kabbalah postulated the movement from the impersonal One to the many attributes of the biblical God within the divine itself.

Similarly, the reference to "mystical nominalism" may be connected to the tendency in medieval nominalism to cast doubt on universal essences and to emphasize instead the singularity of individual beings. But more importantly, the Kabbalah might be called a school of "mystical nominalism" as a consequence of its notion that only names (or signs) signify essences, although, as opposed to the philosophical nominalism of William Ockham, the Kabbalah took the divine names to be essential attributes of God rather than merely subjective significations.[24]

In what sense, then, might Moses Cordovero be considered a "phenomenologist"? Although there are statements that look pantheistic in Cordovero's Kabbalah, as Joseph Ben Shlomo has shown, Cordovero was a fundamentally theistic thinker.[25] In order to preserve God's transcendence, Cordovero postulated an infinity of "divine wills" (the first *sefirah*) that approach the *ain sof* dialectically but never actually merge with it. With this theory, Cordovero gave the most rigorous expression to the dialectical relationship between the hidden God and his revealed attributes. Thus, if Neoplatonism had failed to hypothesize any movement within the One, Cordovero searched farther within the *ain sof* than any previous Kabbalist for the dialectical turn from the One to the Many.

Finally, the obscure final phrase of the aphorism concerning the "irreconcilable tension" between the "most important intentions" of the Kabbalists and their "inability to bring these to pure expression" is also deliberately evocative of phenomenology, which made "intentional acts" an important part of its thought. But what exactly Scholem may have had in mind here is unclear. In any event, the aphorism closes by pointing out a fundamental tension between the Kabbalah and phenomenology. Phenomenology claims to be able to make coherent and intelligible statements about the "structures of beings." But the Kabbalah, as we have repeatedly seen in these aphorisms, is trapped by the essential inexpressibility of its truths. Perhaps the adoption of Neoplatonic language to describe a theosophy radically different from Neoplatonism guaranteed that the Kabbalah would reach a linguistic dead end: it attempted to express an inexpressible truth in language that could only be misleading. If this is the case, then perhaps Neoplatonic language safeguarded the Kabbalah's essential secrets.

APHORISM 8

There is something in the Kabbalah like a transformative insight about which it remains doubtful if one might be able to signify it better than as magical or utopian. This insight discloses all worlds, even the secret of *ain sof* itself, to the place on which I stand. One need not deal with what is above and what is below, one need only (only!) see through the point where one stands oneself. For this transformative insight all worlds are, as one of the greatest Kabbalist has said, nothing but "names that are sketched on the paper of God's essence."

COMMENTARY

Scholem seems to be referring here to the Kabbalah's doctrine of microcosm-macrocosm. All the worlds, from upper to lower, are parallel: the *sefirot* are symbolically the body of God, which has the same anatomy as the human body. Thus, by examining oneself, one can arrive at the mysteries of the divine. From this point of view, the Kabbalah appears much closer to modern humanism as a philosophy than it does to traditional God-centered theology. To be sure, such a "humanistic" formulation of the Kabbalah would have been alien to the Kabbalists, for whom the focus was God rather than man. But it is surely a legitimate, if unhistorical, development of Kabbalistic thought: by turning Kabbalistic images upside down, man as the image of God becomes the measure of all things.

The relationship between the lower worlds and God can also be understood as the relationship between names (human language) and the Name (divine language). The Kabbalists regarded the name of God (or the names of God) as equivalent to God himself. Since all worlds proceed from God, the lower worlds may be thought of as linguistic derivations from the divine name. The relationship between human language and divine language, which is the subject of the next aphorism, makes it possible to comprehend the divine essence: since our language derives from God, we can grasp divine truths by examining our own language. Otherwise, God would remain irretrievably transcendent and unknowable.

Although a "theoretical" Kabbalist would not regard these insights as having "magical" properties,[26] there is a sense in which the interconnectedness of all worlds is "transforming." Because this world is a mirror of the world of emanations, the actions of human beings directly influence the divine realm. The mystical importance of human activity took on a specifically messianic or utopian dimension in the Kabbalah of Isaac Luria in the sixteenth century and ultimately led to the messianic activism of seventeenth-century Sabbatianism. Thus, the Kabbalah developed a mystical form of utopian humanism foreshadowing dialectically the secular utopian movements of a later era.

APHORISM 9

Totalities can be transmitted only esoterically. The name of God can be spoken to [*ansprechbar*] but not spoken [*aussprechbar*], since only what is fragmentary in the name of God can render it speakable [*sprechbar*]. The "true" language cannot be spoken, any more than the absolute concrete can be fulfilled.

COMMENTARY

This aphorism is a commentary on the relationship between divine and human language alluded to in the previous passage. The name of God is the source of all human language, but it is not itself meaningful in the sense that human language has meaning (that is, signifies something). The divine language acquires meaning (becomes "expressible") only as it is "translated" into human terms. But this act of translation communicates only part of the divine truth, since human language is necessarily fragmentary or limited, while God's language is infinite. Yet because human language has its source in the divine, it is not arbitrary; rather, it is the legitimate, if the only, vehicle we have for expressing ultimate truths. Thus, the Kabbalistic attempt to transmit divine mysteries is caught, once again, in a paradox: it uses human language to speak of that which is, by definition, inexpressible. But its enterprise is not doomed, because its language is guaranteed by the divine origin of language. Because language has this equivocal meaning, it is capable of communicating the divine truths, but not in a direct, unmediated fashion. The dialectical relationship between divine and human language requires that the divine (which Scholem here calls *Ganzheiten* or "totalities") be communicated "in an occult fashion." Only that which is cloaked in mystery can truly communicate a mystery; only when the linguistic form fits the theological content can language escape its merely human limitations and signify that which is infinite.

This aphorism is directed against the existentialist theology of Karl Barth and his Jewish interpreter Hans Joachim Schoeps. In a 1932 review of a work by Schoeps, Scholem wrote: "The word of God in its absolute symbolic fullness would be destructive if it were at the same time meaningful in an unmediated way. Nothing in historical time requires concretization more than the 'absolute concreteness' of the word of revelation."[27] The absolutely concrete word of God cannot be comprehended by human beings directly, as existentialists such as Barth, Schoeps, and Martin Buber thought. Instead, this word must undergo a process of mediation, of translation into human terms, which is the historical tradition. Thus, the commentator on the tradition rather than the ecstatic, who claims direct communication from God, is the true *homo religiosus*. In this sense, the historian, who deals with the sources of tradition, is a secular manifestation of the religious personality, for both translate the inexpressible truths of their subjects into the fragmentary language of human beings.

APHORISM 10

A hundred years before Kafka, in Prague, Jonas Wehle[28] (through the medium of his son-in-law Löw of Hönigsberg) wrote his never-published letters and writings, [which were] carefully collected from his Frankist disciples. He wrote for the last adepts of a Kabbalah transformed into heresy, a nihilistic messianism that sought to speak the language of Enlightenment. He is the first to have proposed (and answered affirmatively) the question whether Paradise had lost more than man himself as a result of the expulsion of humanity. This aspect of the question has until now been too quickly decided. Was it then a sympathy of souls a hundred years later that brought Kafka to profound communicating thoughts? Perhaps because we do not know what happened in Paradise, he posited for consideration why the good is "in a certain sense hopeless"—a consideration that truly seems to have sprung from a heretical Kabbalah, since it brought to unsurpassed expression the border between religion and nihilism. For that reason, his writings, which are a secularized expression of (what was unknown to him) a Kabbalistic world-feeling, have for some of today's readers some of the luster of the canonical, of perfection, which it destroys.

COMMENTARY

In a letter written in 1937 to Zalman Schocken in which he discusses his reasons for choosing to study the Kabbalah, Scholem anticipated almost verbatim what he says in this aphorism: "Many exciting thoughts had led me in the years 1916–18 . . . to intuitive affirmation of mystical theses that walked the fine line between religion and nihilism. I later [found in Kafka] the most perfect and unsurpassed expression of this fine line, an expression that, as a secular statement of the Kabbalistic world-feeling in a modern spirit, seemed to me to wrap Kafka's writings in the halo of the canonical."[29] For Scholem, Kafka expressed the conflict of the secular Jew still bound to his tradition: on the one hand, he believed deeply in the existence of "the Law," but, on the other, he regarded the Law as fundamentally inaccessible. The notion of the hiddenness of the source of revelation was surely Kabbalistic, but where the Kabbalists claimed to be able to penetrate these secrets, the secular Jew remained impotently paralyzed outside the first gate of the Law. Thus, Kafka represented the nihilistic (or antinomian) secular consequence inherent in the Kabbalah, a theme that Scholem developed in his historical studies of eighteenth-century Frankism.

The radical theology of the Frankists led to speculations in which the literal message of the Bible might be inverted altogether, such as the notion that Paradise had "lost more with the expulsion of man than had man himself." This type of inversion was already one of the characteristics of the way some of the Christian Gnostics of late antiquity read the Bible, and the similarity that Scholem pointed out between the Gnostics and the Frankists in terms of theology can therefore be found also in their similar biblical exegesis.[30] But Kafka, perhaps moved by some deep "kinship of souls," also employed such inversions in his parables on classical stories. These parables may be understood as Kafka's attempts to penetrate those religious texts by reading them, in Walter Benjamin's expression, "against the grain." For the secular Jew, as for the radical Kabbalist, the truth is now alien and hidden; the texts handed down by tradition do not reveal this truth if read literally. Only by reading the texts against their literal intent can the reader reveal what is hidden.

This interpretation of Kafka as a heretical neo-Kabbalist appears first in letters that Scholem wrote to Walter Benjamin in 1934 in response to Benjamin's essay on Kafka, published in the *Jüdische Rundschau*. Scholem took strong exception to Benjamin's denial of the theological element in Kafka, and particularly the theological problem of the inaccessible Law (*halakhah*), which Scholem held was the key to understanding Kafka's *Trial* and the parable "Before the Law." He wrote to Benjamin: "Kafka's world is the world of revelation, yet from that perspective in which revelation is reduced to its Nothingness [*Nichts*]."[31] The Kabbalistic overtones to this remark are evident in the word *Nothingness*, the divine abyss that stands between the mystic and comprehension of the hidden God. Unlike the Kabbalist, who claims to be able to penetrate, if only partially, the mystery of the *ayin*, Kafka remained confounded by the utterly incomprehensible nature of revelation. Here the paradox of comprehending the incomprehensible, which characterized the historical Kabbalah, as we have seen in these aphorisms, became fully apparent, as it could only from a secular viewpoint. No wonder, then, that Kafka ended up in an abyss of despair and regarded his writings as failures deserving only to be burnt.

A correct understanding of Kafka therefore required a correct understanding of theology. Here Scholem's polemic against Hans Joachim Schoeps, mentioned in the commentary on the previous aphorism, becomes relevant once again. In his essay on Kafka, Benjamin had mentioned Schoeps as one of those who incorrectly found in Kafka a position similar to his own theology. Scholem agrees with Benjamin, but for the reason that Schoeps's theology was wrong. It is the theological position that Scholem found in the Kabbalah and that he himself adopted that should be identified in Kafka: "The *unrealizability* [*Unvollziehbarkeit*] of that which is revealed is the point at which, in the most precise way, a *correctly* understood theology (as I, immersed in my Kabbalah, imagine it and as you can find it given rather responsible expression in that open letter against Schoeps, which you know) and the key to Kafka's world come together. Not, dear Walter, the absence [of this theology] in a preanimistic world, but its *unrealizability* is its problem."[32] Thus, the problem for theology is how to realize and comprehend in the finite world of human beings the infinite revelation of God. The realization of revelation in the medium of the historical tradition is necessarily inadequate and even paradoxical, as these aphorisms repeatedly assert. This was the problem for the Kabbalists, and it was also the problem, in its most acute form, for Kafka. Interestingly enough, Benjamin came to this conclusion himself several years later in a formulation that seemingly anticipates Aphorism 1: "Kafka's real genius was that . . . he sacrificed truth for the sake of clinging to its transmissibility, its haggadic element. Kafka's writings . . . do not modestly lie at the feet of the doctrine, as the Haggadah lies at the feet of the Halakhah. Though apparently reduced to submission, they unexpectedly raise a mighty paw against it. This is why, in regard to Kafka, we can no longer speak of wisdom. Only the products of its decay remain."[33]

For Scholem, the historian, the "products of decay," the tradition produced by vanished wisdom, were equally all that remained. The historian works in the deepest darkness, always striving like Kafka for some communication from the Castle, for some revelation from the mountain that was the site of the primordial revelation. As he wrote to Schocken: "For today's man, that mystical totality of systematic 'truth,' whose existence disappears especially when it is projected into historical time, can become visible in the purest way only in the legitimate discipline of commentary and in the singular mirror of philological criticism. Today, as at the very beginning, my work lives in this paradox, in the hope of a *true* communication from the mountain, of that most invisible, smallest fluctuation of history which causes truth to break forth from the illusions of 'development.'"[34] Like the Kabbalist, the historian works with the fragments left by tradition, but he nourishes the hope that through immersion in these fragments he too may have a revelation of the "secret" truth. Yet by the very nature of his enterprise, his experience of the past (and of God, if that is what he seeks) must be indirect and never immediate.

PART FOUR

HERETICAL POLITICS

CHAPTER 13

The Threat of Messianism

An Interview with Gershom Scholem (August 14, 1980)

ONE OF THE MOST DISTINGUISHED Jewish scholars of the twentieth century, Gershom Scholem almost singlehandedly created the field of academic study of Jewish mysticism. Yet his books on the arcane subject—*Major Trends in Jewish Mysticism, Sabbatai Sevi,* and *The Kabbalah and Its Symbolism* (to mention only a few)— won him a wide audience beyond the scholarly world. Scholem came to be recognized as one of the major spokesmen for Judaism in our time. Born in Berlin in 1897 and resident in Jerusalem from 1923 until his death in 1982, Scholem had a life and career that were singularly intertwined with the development of Zionist movement and the state of Israel. As professor of Jewish mysticism at the Hebrew University since 1925, Scholem was considered in Israel to be an authoritative voice on cultural and political affairs.

DAVID BIALE: In the English translation of your memoir, *From Berlin to Jerusalem,* you describe how, as a young German Jew from an assimilated family, you came to reject the German-Jewish milieu and adopt Zionism. In 1923, you left Germany and came to Palestine. How do you evaluate the development of the Zionist movement since that time? Did it fulfill the aspirations you had for it when you emigrated from Berlin to Jerusalem?

GERSHOM SCHOLEM: The people who came to Palestine between 1923 and 1933 had made up their minds that they wanted to live among Jews and not in a ghetto. They wanted to be free men and women and work for the renaissance of the Jewish people. These people—and I was one of them—regarded themselves as the *vanguard* of the Jewish people. In 1933 Hitler came to power and everything changed. Hitler proved that the Zionist analysis of the Jewish situation was right and the anti-Zionist analysis was wrong. But the majority of people who came after 1933 did not have the same idealistic convictions as those who had come before and they came because they had no choice. They were a different type of people; they did not come to create a new Jewish society but just to live in Israel because there was no other place for them to go.

After 1948, there came a major influx of Jews from Islamic countries who were also refugees. They also did not come with the conscious purpose of rebuilding something; very few of them were even Zionists. This affected the climate of the country and created the social problems we are now faced with. Some of these problems are not solvable in our generation. The Jewish state, which had to be created as a result of the historical crisis of our generation, now has to confront social problems that never existed before in Jewish history. For example, for the first time there is serious physical violence between Jews, including cases of rape. There has also emerged a Jewish underworld that was virtually unknown in Europe.

We now realize that there are two very different social groups among the Jewish people, the European or Ashkenazim and the Jews from Islamic countries. There has emerged a common stock of European Jews where there used to be German Jews and Romanian Jews; we all have the same grandparents and we have all experienced the Holocaust. But the Jews from the Arab countries have a very different background and often a different mentality.

The Zionist movement actually paid very little attention to the Oriental Jews. All the great Zionist leaders were from eastern Europe, and they imagined that Israel would be a state of European Jews. The Holocaust changed all that; all these Jews were massacred. As David Ben Gurion said: "Those Jews we hoped for are dead."

So Hitler changed the whole climate of the country. For me and my generation, this was quite a disappointment, although perhaps we should not have been disappointed. We never imagined what it would be like to have a state of over three million Jews. We thought of perhaps a million *halutzim* "pioneers," but instead, we have three million Jews trying to live in Israel and solve their social problems there.

DB: In the late 1920s and the early 1930s you were active in a political group called Brit Shalom that tried to bring about Jewish-Arab reconciliation. But you largely withdrew from such political activity after this period. What possibilities are there for peace between Jews and Arabs today?

GS: The 1920s were a period that philosophers of history call a "plastic hour of history." Then, perhaps, we could have made certain decisions that would have affected our relations with the Arabs. I'm not sure. Certainly, we made many mistakes, and our policy in the 1920s could have been wiser. But after Hitler, there was nothing to be done but to save as many Jews as possible.

In 1936, the Arabs revolted and tried to destroy us. From then on, the situation became much more serious. It was no accident that the 1948 War of Independence happened as it did. The riots of 1936 led to the White Paper of 1939, which effectively liquidated Jewish immigration. This led in turn to the policy of Ernest Bevin after World War II and thus to the War of Independence. The course of history was not completely determined, but it is hard to imagine how it could have changed after the events of 1936.

There was perhaps another such "plastic moment" after the 1967 War when we could have transformed the whole situation. David Ben Gurion suggested that we unilaterally return all the occupied territories with the exception of Jerusalem. No one can know what would have happened if we had done this, but I think there was much truth in his ideas. In August 1967, right after the Six-Day War, I signed a public letter of seven intellectuals opposing any annexation of the territories. That took some courage at the time. But who can say what would have happened if we had returned the territories? Now we have far less freedom to act. You see, we educated the Arabs about nationalism. It was our very existence that created Arab national consciousness. This is the particular dialectic of history, and I'm not sure that there is any escape from it.

DB: You sound very pessimistic about the current peace process [in the wake of the Camp David Accords of 1979 and the Peace Treaty with Egypt].

GS: Sadat is a very clever, first-rate politician. We don't have anyone like him. No one knows what will happen after he gets everything back. Will he rejoin the other Arab states? Still, the peace treaty was a worthwhile risk, and if it works, it will be a great thing. Even though no one in Israel knows whether to trust Sadat, you won't find anyone but a very small fringe opposed to the peace treaty. Even Begin, who would have opposed this treaty with all his strength if he had been in opposition, came to see that we had no choice but to take a chance. And now members of his own party call him a traitor.

DB: Is the settlement policy on the West Bank [begun under the previous Labor government and accelerated by Menachem Begin's government after 1977] harming peace prospects?

GS: I am totally opposed to what Begin and the Gush Emunim [the religious Zionist settlement movement] are doing on the West Bank. Still, it is not just Begin who is to blame for this situation. If the Labor Party had had the courage to evict those settlers from Hebron in 1968 when there were only a hundred of them, if they had dared to do it with force, we would not have this problem today. But Golda Meir and later Rabin sat back and did nothing.

DB: You have spent a large portion of your career studying the history of Jewish mysticism, and you have warned of the dangers that messianic expectations posed to the Zionist movement. Is the Zionist movement today threatened by messianism?

GS: The Jews have always had a fatal attraction to messianism. The Jewish involvement in communism, for instance, was definitely a consequence of Jewish messianism. Zionism is no exception. Today we have the Gush Emunim, which is definitely a messianic movement. They use biblical verses for political purposes. Whenever messianism is introduced into politics, it becomes a very dangerous business. It can only lead to disaster. It is, of course, possible that had these religious people moved into the

West Bank with, say, five thousand people directly after the Six-Day War, they might have succeeded. As I said, that was a plastic moment in history, and the Arabs were afraid we would drive them out. But now what they are doing is utter nonsense. It shows a total lack of political realism.

DB: Perhaps your best-known study of Jewish messianism is your book on Shabbtai Zvi, the leader of the abortive mass messianic movement of the seventeenth century. Is the Gush Emunim a modern-day version of the Sabbatian movement?

GS: Yes, they are like the Sabbatians. Like the Sabbatians, their messianic program can only lead to disaster. In the seventeenth century, of course, the failure of Sabbatianism had only spiritual consequences; it led to a breakdown of Jewish belief. Today, the consequences of such messianism are also political, and that is the great danger.

DB: Is Menahem Begin also a messianist?

GS: He was a messianist. But he is not a fool. He recognized the need for a pragmatic policy, and so he came to support the idea of a peace treaty. What he is doing on the West Bank is a regression to his previous beliefs.

DB: In a recent letter to Prime Minister Begin printed in *Haaretz*, the historian Jacob Talmon quoted the lessons of history in order to criticize Begin's autonomy scheme for the West Bank. Do you agree with Talmon that professors of history have something to teach politicians?

GS: I am very skeptical about that, although I know that Jacob Talmon thinks otherwise. Politics requires a sense of moderation, and I'm not sure that you can learn that from history. Take Bismarck, for example. He was a very conservative man, but he had the correct moderate instincts for studying history. In any event, history never repeats itself in exactly the same way. I doubt professors of history can teach such things to anyone. I have been a professor of history too long to believe that.

CHAPTER 14

Mysticism and Politics in Modern Israel

The Messianic Ideology of Abraham Isaac Ha-Cohen Kook

EVER SINCE HE GAVE SANCTION to the prophet Samuel to establish a monarchy for the Israelites, the Almighty has made it his business to interfere in the political life of his people. This divine nosiness—welcome or not—is believed by the Jews to lie at the heart of both their political triumphs and their unfortunately all-too-numerous disasters. Hence, it is only fitting that a volume on religion and nationalism should include at least one essay on a religious aspect of Jewish nationalism. If the Jews did not invent the intimate affair between religion and nationalism, they have at least kept it persistently alive for as long as anyone else.

This connection between religion and nationalism can be discerned even in those periods when the Jews had no state. The messianic desire to return political sovereignty to the Jews is the authentic premodern form of Jewish nationalism. Interestingly enough, one of the strongest impulses behind the great messianic movement of the seventeenth century, Sabbatianism, was not a pragmatic political ideology but ostensibly otherworldly mysticism: the Lurianic Kabbalah. This mystical theory—quite different from the passivity we typically associate with mysticism—argued that man's actions directly affect and are secular representations of cosmic history. Already by the seventeenth century, therefore, the connection between mystical religion and this worldly political nationalism was firmly established.

One might expect that the realization of the messianic dream in the modern creation of the State of Israel would similarly wed such ostensibly strange bedfellows. But the surprising fact about modern Zionism is its thoroughly secular character. Here is a militantly secular movement spurred on by a revolt against Jewish religion. Those religious supporters of Zionism—and they remained a minority of the religious world until after World War II—assiduously excluded messianic ideas from their Jewish nationalism. They saw Zionism as, at best, "the faint beginnings of the messianic era," and they conceived of their own role as defending the interests of a religious minority in a secular movement. Hence, they fought to establish religious schools and to safeguard the Sabbath. None of these activities—which were secular in form if religious in content—can be construed as a real attempt to unite religion with nationalism, or, more radically, to suggest that Zionism might be the flowering of the messianic times. If anything, it was the secular Zionists in both the socialist and right-wing nationalist camps who co-opted a secular brand of messianism into their Zionist ideologies. One of the greatest problems of the Orthodox religious Zionists of the last generation was to justify their collaboration with these secular Zionists, whose heresies seemed to pollute any redemptive potential in the return to Zion.

Since the Six-Day War of 1967, however, this religious silence has been broken by the rise of a militantly religious group who combine a nationalistic politics with a coherent messianic theory. This is the Gush Emunim—or "bloc of the faithful"—who have repeatedly set up illegal settlements in the occupied territories and who, if not a decisive force in Israeli politics, have become at least a very significant nuisance factor, capable of complicating the peace negotiations and of provoking heightened Arab hostility toward the Israeli occupation.

In the years following the Six-Day War, a new generation of Orthodox Jews who "did not know Joseph" grew to maturity. Estranged from the Diaspora origins of their parents, they did not understand the older generation's pragmatic approach to politics. Moreover, they were justifiably disgusted with the corruption of the religious parties, which is second to none in the Israeli political jungle. The Six-Day War and the challenge of the new territories represented to them an opportunity to demonstrate their political commitment independent of their parents. Too long scorned by the secular as emaciated "Yeshiva bochers," they could now prove that they were doing as much to fulfill the patriotic tasks of Zionism as their secular counterparts (witness, for example, the proud insistence by the Orthodox that they had absorbed the highest casualties of any group during the Yom Kippur War—surely a macabre way of proving one's involvement in society). Finally, the young Orthodox saw the new, postwar situation as an opportunity to put the corrupt past behind and forge a new, purified national consensus. It is no coincidence that a moral fervor pervades the Gush Emunim: they see themselves as a movement of national moral regeneration.

The vitalizing effect of the Six-Day War upon Orthodox youth born and raised in the Jewish state was surely connected with the results of the war: for the first time since the state was created, the biblical Land of Israel, and particularly the areas of Judah and Samaria, were in Jewish hands. The Yom Kippur War, since it accentuated pressures on Israel to relinquish the territories, heightened the feeling that the opportunity to settle and annex the land must be seized immediately. It is ironic indeed that the ideal of settlement of the land, so long the province of the socialist Zionists, has been appropriated under new slogans by the nationalist and religious Right.

In the case of Gush Emunim, the motivating force behind this annexationist drive is messianism. In the Ayatollah-like pronouncements of Rabbi Zvi Yehudah Kook, the acknowledged spiritual leader of Gush Emunim (as the head of the Merkaz ha-Rav yeshiva, where most Gush leaders were trained), we read that messianic days are upon us. Settlement of all the historic Land of Israel is the right and role of all Jews in the impending messianic drama. Because political conditions are ripe, yet may soon deteriorate, settlement and annexation are of the utmost urgency. Zvi Yehudah Kook combines shrewd political realism with urgent messianism.[1]

As important as Zvi Yehudah Kook's ideas are in the context of the current political situation, they are surely derivative and unoriginal. My interest here is to explore the source of these messianic notions and so to understand the ideological or, shall we say, theological connection between religion and nationalism in modern-day Israel. This search leads us from Zvi Yehudah to a much more original and influential thinker—his father, Abraham Isaac

Ha-Cohen Kook (1865–1935), one of the most unique religious thinkers associated with Zionism.[2] As chief rabbi of Palestine in the 1920s and 1930s, Rav Kook had a significant impact on the Zionist settlement during its formative years. Although not strictly associated with the religious Zionist parties (he was actually one of the organizers of the non-Zionist Aggudat Yisrael), he influenced the development of Orthodox Zionism. But he made a great impression on the nonreligious as well.

In recent years, quite a legend has grown up around Rav Kook. He has been appropriated by some secular and religious Jews as a paradigmatic "tolerant Orthodox rabbi" who sought to heal the. wounds of a divided nation.[3] Rav Kook argued that secular Zionists do God's dirty work without knowing it by settling the land; although they do not perform the *mitzvot*, they do fulfill the one commandment of settling the land, which, according to the midrash, is equal to all the others. This overarching nationalism allowed Rav Kook to accept all Jews as partners in the national enterprise. Moreover, his messianic theory contained a universalist component more amenable to liberal Jews than the palpable chauvinism of other Orthodox thinkers. Finally, as a personality, Rav Kook was remarkable for his tolerance and moral sensibility.

The legend of the liberal Rav Kook has recently even played a role in the polemics against Gush Emunim. In an article in *Shdemot* (the kibbutz movement quarterly) in winter 1975, Avraham Shapira tries to contrast the messianic statements of Zvi Yehuda Kook with those of his more illustrious father.[4] Shapira charges that the moral nationalism of Rav Kook has degenerated into an antinomian "Sabbatianism" in the hands of his son.

While by no means denying the positive impact of Rav Kook's personality, I believe that the connection between him and his son is more than genetic. Zvi Yehuda's political ideology can already be found in the writings of Rav Kook, although without the political urgency and concreteness of the contemporary situation. I do not claim that Rav Kook would necessarily have spoken like his son if he were alive today (clearly an unhistorical proposition), since his situation before the creation of the State of Israel generated a more abstract approach to political problems. Yet it should be no surprise that Rav Kook, as one of the few significant Orthodox thinkers close to modern Zionism who adopted messianic language, serves as a source for the new messianism. In fact, the Gush Emunim people quote him at least as much as do their opponents. I propose to examine briefly some of the messianic elements in Rav Kook's writings that could be appropriated by these messianic radicals today.

I have already mentioned that Rav Kook's tolerance and universalism are what prove so attractive to the non-Orthodox in search of an Orthodox model. Perhaps the most ingenious aspect of Rav Kook's thought is his solution to the classic problem of the religious Jew confronting the Zionist movement: How can this movement be messianic if its most active elements are secular? Kook argued against his anti-Zionist Orthodox colleagues that not only is there room for the secular in messianism, but they are, in fact, necessary. Using the medieval categories of form and matter, he writes that "the holy can be built only on the basis of the profane. The profane is the matter of the holy and the holy gives it form."[3] Both play necessary and balanced roles in the world. In the days of the Messiah, however, the profane paradoxically seems to increase. Rav Kook takes this idea from the Talmudic saying that "in the footsteps of the Messiah insolence [*hutzpah*] will increase." In the modern context, insolence clearly means secularism. In a striking passage in *Hazon ha-Geula* (*Vision of Redemption*) he compares the role of the secular to that of yeast in wine making:

> Just as it is impossible for wine to be made without yeast, so it is impossible for the world to exist without the wicked. Just as the yeast makes the wine and preserves it, so the crude inclinations of the wicked make possible the existence of all life. When the yeast disappears and the wine stands without it, it spoils and turns sour. The Exile has diluted the power of life of the nation, and our yeast has decreased considerably until there is danger that the nation will cease to exist for lack of coarseness, which is rooted in animality, land, and materiality. The Exile is a fragmented, diluted existence....
>
> But the demand for survival and the return of Israel to its land for survival is a necessary event; it creates its own yeast, namely the bearers of evil and insolence of the footsteps of the Messiah. And the end of the

process will be the precipitation of the yeast to the bottom of the barrel. But while it is still productive and is necessary to go together with the wine, it makes the wine hideous, and one's heart revolts at the sight of the fermentation. Only the thought of the future gives one peace and quiet.[6]

It is interesting the degree to which Rav Kook accepted the secular Zionist analysis of the need for Jewish territoriality. The very problem with the Exile is that it is too spiritual, too holy. While Rav Kook scarcely used economic language in his analysis, his belief that Jewish life is physically impossible in exile is not far from the views of Ber Borochov and other socialist Zionists.[7] Only a material, profane substrate can create the necessary conditions for the "footsteps of the Messiah." Similarly, for Borochov, only Jewish territoriality makes a socialist revolution possible for the Jews as for all other nations. For both, Zionism is a historical inevitability. Although both give man a central and active role in their respective versions of redemption, man's actions are still determined from the outset. The Marxist tension between free will and determinism that is so evident in Borochov's thought can be found equally, if unexpectedly, in Rav Kook's messianism. Parenthetically, it should be noted against the common belief that Jewish messianism was not always a passive doctrine. A long tradition, best articulated by Moses Maimonides and echoed by religious Zionists in the nineteenth century before Rav Kook, claims that messianic times will be brought about by Jewish political action and will not necessarily involve miracles. Rav Kook combined this "realistic" political messianism with his own brand of utopian, mystical messianism.[8]

Rav Kook was prepared to accept the secular as a temporary expedient without which the return to the land would be impossible. From a historical point of view, this theory explains why the days of the Messiah can come only after an age of secularism and assimilation. But far from genuine toleration of secular Judaism, Kook's view is Hegelian: God cunningly uses the wicked to further his own plan until they have fulfilled their purpose. Kook believed that national renewal will necessarily eradicate secularism; secular Zionists are fated to return to the Orthodox fold once they realize that they are actually fulfilling God's commandment in settling the land. This idea is the ideological basis for the remarkable openness of the Gush Emunim toward the secular community.

The notion of God's cunning use of the wicked goes back in the Jewish tradition to Maimonides, who saw Christianity and Islam as unwitting "road pavers" for the King Messiah. The Sabbatians at the end of the seventeenth century were the first to apply the idea to heretical Jews: the final stages of redemption will be accomplished by the paradoxical performance of commandments through the violation of them. This doctrine of the "holiness of sin" was originally developed to explain why the Messiah, Shabbtai Zvi, had to apostasize to Islam.

It is striking how close Rav Kook's ideas come to certain Sabbatian theories. Behind the above metaphor of the yeast we find a curious and radical Kabbalistic doctrine. While the Kabbalah traditionally argued that the *klippot* (shells of evil materiality) are maintained only by the divine sparks trapped within them, Rav Kook claims quite the opposite: the divine exists in history only by virtue of the profane and, indeed, can be redeemed only after the profane has strengthened itself. This doctrine closely resembles the Sabbatian argument that the Messiah's soul is part of the *klippot* themselves and that he must apostasize in order to redeem it.

Our suspicion is further strengthened by another metaphor Rav Kook used for the renewal of Israel, namely that of the seed that must rot in the ground before it can sprout and flourish: "And this rotting of the seed is analogous to what the divine light does in planting anew the vineyard in Israel in which the old values are forced to be renewed by the insolence that comes in the footsteps of the Messiah."[9] This image was evidently popular among the eighteenth-century Sabbatians to explain the dialectical process of redemption, at least as recounted in an eighteenth-century anti-Sabbatian text: "[The Sabbatians] say that the violation of the Torah has become its fulfillment, which they illustrate by the example of a grain of wheat that rots in the earth."[10] There is no way of knowing whether Kook was familiar with this Sabbatian metaphor, and I do not mean to portray him as a latter-day Sabbatian. Rather, the recurrence of this metaphor in his writing suggests that in order to justify the role of the secular within a religious framework, he came, perhaps even consciously, to a similar doctrine.

Far from advocating like the radical Sabbatians that Orthodox Jews break the law in order to bring redemption, Kook took an uncompromising position against backsliding within the Orthodox world itself. For instance, in one of his *responsa* he denounced Orthodox Jews who followed the Reform movement in abolishing the *mehitza* (the partition in synagogues between men and women), castigating them as "withered limbs of the nation."[11] If called upon, he could match unbridled language with the best of the Orthodox rabbinate. He was particularly concerned with preserving Orthodoxy in synagogues, since in this time, the days of the Messiah, the synagogue should approximate as closely as possible the Temple, which will soon be rebuilt. As if to underscore this belief, he sponsored study of the laws of sacrifice in his yeshivah.

Rav Kook was thus willing to allow heresies among the secular as part of God's plan of redemption, but he insisted that an Orthodox elite retain leadership in order to prevent materiality from entirely overpowering spirituality. There is a division of labor and a hierarchy in the Jewish world. The secular perform the function of settling the land and are superior to the Orthodox with respect to the "animal soul" (*nefesh*). The Orthodox provide spiritual leadership and are superior to the secular with respect to the "spiritual soul" (*ruach*).

What of the non-Jewish world and its relation to the messianic enterprise? Rav Kook's defenders have emphasized his universalism against the narrow particularism of contemporary messianists. Again, we find that his universalism is of a very special sort. In one of his essays, he asks whether Israel is the same as the rest of the nations except for an added increment of holiness, or if it is a different kind of people altogether. Originally, he argues, God wished merely to give Israel an added measure of holiness. But man had so degenerated that God had to purge the Jews of their profane humanity during the exile in Egypt and create a new creature, "Israelite from head to toe."[12] In another passage, he claims that Israel gained its divine nature not through being chosen by God but through "its racial character, physical and spiritual, which it did not take from chosenness, nor can any corruption of chosenness eradicate it."[13] One wonders how some Jews could become secular heretics if Israeli's holiness is inherited. The answer may be that since the secular fulfill a necessary role in modern Jewish history, their heresy is only apparent; once their messianic task is finished, they will revert to their true "holy" nature.

Such a "racial" concept of the Jewish people is not a mainstream tradition in Jewish history. Judaism, after all, is a religion that welcomes converts and was even, for a period of time during the Roman Empire, actively proselytizing. But ideas such as Rav Kook's have emerged from time to time, particularly in Kabbalistic doctrines. In the Middle Ages, it was Judah ha-Levi who gave them full articulation in his *Kuzari*: Jews inherit a certain prophetic soul that cannot be obtained by non-Jews even if they convert to Judaism.

Like Judah ha-Levi, Rav Kook also believed that the land of Israel possesses a special, intrinsic holiness parallel to the holiness of the Jewish people. Because of the uniqueness of the land of Israel, Israel's nationalism is necessarily superior to all other nationalisms. There are, to be sure, righteous and wise individuals among the nations, but as a collectivity only Israel possesses a divine soul. However—and here is where Rav Kook advocates universalism—through Israel's nationalism, all other nationalisms will derive holiness: "The nations are beginning to recognize that the basis of salvation will only be the holy value that carries the standard of God. The desire of Israel to be the living spirit of national renewal will give life to every national movement. And they will be redeemed forever through the redemption of the holy nation."[14]

Rav Kook and his followers believe that only when the Arabs recognize the divine right of the Jews to their land will they understand why Jewish nationalism also benefits their own nationalism. This belief is the theological counterpart to the secular Zionist conviction that the Arabs will learn modern politics and economic methods from the Zionists and will then recognize Zionism out of gratitude.

We have seen that Rav Kook's tolerance and universalism were direct products of his radical messianism. Both secular Jews and the non-Jewish nations play a positive and tolerated role in God's plan for redemption of the world. But Kook's belief in the superiority of the Orthodox and the biological holiness of the Jewish people are far indeed from the liberal politics of many of his proponents. Without the eschatological dimension, the liberal Rav Kook is perhaps more convincing. But given his goal of an Orthodox holy Israel leading the nations in the end of days, his tolerance and universalism assume different meanings.

The messianists from Gush Emunim have rightly found a spiritual grandfather (if Zvi Yehudah Kook is their spiritual father) in Rav Kook. Their moralistic emphasis on the unity of the Jewish nation, regardless of religious conviction, is the modern version of his tolerance of the secular. Their insistence on settlement of the land as the primary commandment (hence their campaign of settlements in the occupied territories, which has become their trademark) is borrowed directly from his doctrine of the holiness of the land and the importance of settling it as the precondition for the coming of the Messiah. Finally, Gush Emunim's blithe neglect of the Arabs in the occupied territories is the result not of moral callousness (as is no doubt the case with the right-wing secular nationalists) but of the peculiar optimistic universalism of Rav Kook. There is no doubt that the leaders of Gush Emunim believe that if Jews settle throughout the land of Israel, the groundwork will be laid for messianic peace with Israel's Arab neighbors.[15]

It is curious indeed that a religious thinker like the Rav Kook could become a model for two irreconcilably opposing positions. Both liberals and nationalist messianists use his thought as a source for ideologies to unite the Jewish nation. But such is frequently the fate of a suggestive thinker, and particularly a dialectical thinker (Hegel himself was blessed with spiritual sons on his right and on his left). It is a measure also of the great confusion in Jewish nationalism over the precise role of religion and religious identity in the modern state of Israel. If nationalism itself is a potent brew, the addition of mystical religion may indeed prove intoxicating and even fatal.

CHAPTER 15

The End of Enlightenment?

THE BIBLE HAD IT WRONG: the Jews are not "a people that dwells apart, not reckoned among the nations" (Num. 23:9). On the contrary, their history, especially at crucial turning points, is deeply, inextricably entwined with the fate of "the nations," even when they have seemed entirely small and marginal. The reunification of Spain in 1492 was causally bound to the expulsion of Jews (and Muslims) who refused to convert. The French Revolution's creation of the category of "citizen" meant that the Jews had to be emancipated. Conversely, the Nazi revolt against the democratic and egalitarian ideals of French republicanism necessarily entailed the reversal of Jewish emancipation, whether or not as a prelude to genocide. And finally, the defeat of Nazism led directly or indirectly to the defeat of antisemitism and to Jewish sovereignty.

The question facing us with the election of Donald J. Trump is twofold: 1) has an event of the magnitude of those just mentioned in fact taken place? and 2) does this event portend an epochal turning point in Jewish history? The tentative answer to both of these questions is yes. To be sure, the tea leaves are not yet dry enough to read, since, as Hegel taught us (and mixing the metaphors), the owl of Minerva flies only at dusk. Is the global—or at least European and US—turn to nativism and authoritarianism akin to the fascist and quasi-fascist regimes of the 1930s? There are certainly family resemblances: in both cases, the embrace of ethno-nationalism and the disdain for democratic norms have deep historical roots in the rejection of the rationalism of the Enlightenment and the politics of the French Revolution. It may well be that, like the Roman Empire, these new ethno-nationalist regimes will maintain the veneer of democracy while the real power will reside in those who reject the universal values of science and human rights. If we want to see a possible future, we need only look to Vladimir Putin's Russia, so admired by Donald Trump.

It is a truism, but one worth repeating, that modern Jews are all children of the Enlightenment, whether or not they endorse its precepts. Even ultra-Orthodox Jews are products of the Enlightenment, which serves primarily as a foil for their own equally modern antimodernism. And Jews of the Middle East and North Africa were also, willingly or not, products of the Enlightenment's colonialism project. The Enlightenment was not always an unmitigated blessing for the Jews, but their success in integrating into modern societies as a minority was predicated on the Enlightenment's promise to erase religious and ethnic barriers. This was a hard-won battle that took the better part of two centuries. We should not forget that even in the United States, arguably the most egalitarian of Western democracies, Jews did not win full acceptance until after World War II. In France, the forces of reaction were, if anything, stronger in the guise of clerical anti-Republicans in the Dreyfus Affair and the Vichy regime. There too, full Jewish integration came only after the Nazi genocide. One could multiply these two examples, but the point should be clear: the Enlightenment project did not end with the French Revolution but continued, contested, until recent times.

The famous phrase "dialectic of Enlightenment" suggests that revolts against Enlightenment are themselves the products of Enlightenment. We are witnessing today a new epoch in this dialectic in which countries such as Turkey, Poland, Hungary, and now the United States embrace antimodern, Völkisch, antiscientific, and antidemocratic ideologies in reaction to Enlightenment globalism. While the current form of globalism—multiculturalism, inclusion of minorities, universal human rights, erasure of national boundaries—is not the same as it was in the interwar period, the revolt against it looks eerily similar to the rise of European fascism.

What might this revolt portend for American Jews? If one can judge from exit polling, around one-quarter of the Jewish electorate voted for Trump, a number not inconsistent—give or take—with generic voting for Republican presidential candidates. For these voters, Trump no doubt represents nothing but a variant on Republicanism. These Jewish Trump supporters, many of them Orthodox, evidently do not fear that the Jews will be imperiled by his victory. If he does embody an anti-Enlightenment politics (one hesitates to call his incoherent tweets an "ideology"), these voters are apparently not concerned that a reversal of universal and rationalist values endangers the Jews. Their thinking must run like this: Jews are now part of the economic elite of America, the very elite Trump has installed in his cabinet (and some of the latter are Jews). In the global war, which they believe the West is fighting against Islam, the Jews are firmly part of the West (Israel plays a leading role in this drama, but more on that anon). So the Trump administration, far from being hostile to the Jews, is in fact their natural home. A perverse confirmation of this view can be found in neo-Nazi, antisemitic websites that criticize Trump for his many Jewish associates (including his daughter and son-in-law) and argue that "the only nationalism that Trump believes in is Jewish nationalism."

This right-wing Jewish embrace of Trump seems to be predicated on the idea that Jews no longer need the Enlightenment. As Stephen Bannon, Trump's court ideologue, states repeatedly, the "Judeo-Christian West" is at war with global Islam, thus discursively including the Jews in his nationalist camp. Bannon, of course, also allowed various antisemitic voices on Breitbart.com. We are thus presented with a regime that opposes "global capitalism," code for Jewish bankers (a position Bannon shares with more overt antisemites), but welcomes Jews as allies in the defense of "Western civilization." However, this version of Western civilization does not include the Enlightenment: it is at once reactionary in its throwback to medieval wars against Islam and authoritarian in its belief that democracy is too vapid to win this war of civilizations.

This brings us to Israel, which many of the supporters of Trumpism see as a natural ally. The same paradox we witness now can be found in the origins of Zionism: Theodor Herzl thought that European antisemites would make common cause with Zionism, since both wanted the Jews out of Europe. Yet it needs to be said, lest we forget, that Zionism was an Enlightenment project. Just as European nationalism in its more liberal manifestations was driven by the desire of ethnic groups for self-determination, so Zionism was a response to the inability of the Jews to realize the same desire within Europe. The success of Israeli democracy, with all of its faults, is a remarkable testimony to this Enlightenment legacy, especially since most of Israel's political elite did not come from democratic countries.

To be sure, Zionism ran quickly into Arab resistance to colonialism, but at least in its first decade and a half, the State of Israel defined itself as part of the anticolonial, nonaligned world. However, following the Six-Day War, as Israel's identity has more and more become hostage to the settlement enterprise, it has increasingly lost this anticolonial self-definition. With the virtual collapse of the two-state solution, Israel itself is headed in an anti-Enlightenment direction: undemocratic in its rule over millions of noncitizens and beholden to religious reactionaries in its domestic politics.

There is, therefore, a natural alliance between the most extreme elements in Israel, their American Jewish allies, and the Trumpists. For all of them—plus the nationalists of Russia, Britain, France, Denmark, the Netherlands, Austria, Poland, and Hungary—the Enlightenment is passé, a vestige of a false universalism and rationality that must now give way to nationalism based on the tyranny of ethnic majorities. Ironically, of course, the more Israel follows this tendency, the more it will resemble not so much Trump's America as the rest of the Middle East, which is determined, it seems, to eradicate the multireligious societies that were one of the positive legacies of colonialism.

As ascendant as all these anti-Enlightenment forces may be, they are not yet omnipotent. If only a quarter of the American Jews voted for Trump (as well as only 44 percent of Americans generally) and if consistent majorities in Israel favor a two-state solution, then resistance to ethno-nationalism is not impossible. Against all odds, most Jews have not abandoned the famous dictum of "earning like Episcopalians but voting like Puerto Ricans." They remain in their majorities committed to ideals of progressive inclusion and egalitarianism. The triumph of Trump has nevertheless demonstrated that

Jews, like millions of other people in endangered democracies, are willing to defend the Enlightenment. But no longer is it possible to take the Enlightenment's inevitable victory for granted.

We may be at a turning point in both world and Jewish history, but the direction in which history will turn remains up for grabs. We know from the 1930s that it is not necessary for totalitarian regimes to win electoral majorities in order to rule. The German communists liked to say after 1933: *Nach Hitler, uns!* They did end up in power, but only after twelve years and a world war that nearly destroyed Europe. Whether we face a similar catastrophe cannot yet be prophesied, but for Jews—as for all children of the Enlightenment—a clarion call to action has been sounded before the lights go out all over the civilized world.

EPILOGUE

By the Waters of San Francisco

A Partial Autobiography

AS THE PHILOSOPHER HEGEL TAUGHT us, the owl of Minerva only spreads its wings with the falling of dusk. So, too, my own personal and professional life choices have only begun to acquire coherent meaning as I look backward over the *longue durée*. Increasingly, it seems that the personal and professional cannot be easily disentangled and that both also owe much to the personal and professional choices of my parents, many of them before I was even born.

Jacob Bialoglowski was from Poland, a graduate of the socialist Zionist youth movement, Hashomer Hatzair, who came to the United States in 1928 to learn "scientific" agriculture in order to go to Palestine and join a kibbutz. His certificate from the British Mandate failed to arrive, so he accepted a fellowship to study for a PhD in fruit physiology, training that led to a professorship at UCLA.

Evelyn Karol was the daughter of immigrants from Zhitomir in Ukraine who, with masses of other Jews, came to the United States before World War I. They earned their living in the dish-decorating trade. Although they weathered unemployment during the Great Depression, they were able to send her, their oldest daughter, to Boston University, where she earned an

MA in mathematics and music, remarkable achievements for a woman at the end of the 1930s. Surprisingly adventurous, in 1940 she went west to California for a cousin's wedding and stayed, working first for the navy in San Diego and then as a teaching assistant in physics at UCLA. It was there, during the years of the war, that my parents met and married in 1945. I was born three and a half years later.

Their marriage was not an easy one, not least for reasons of ideology. My father was a fervent Zionist; my mother had never heard of this strange idea and remained skeptical about it throughout her life. In 1958, our family went to Israel for a year, with my father serving as an agricultural consultant to the young State of Israel for the UN Food and Agriculture Organization. He was offered a faculty position in Rehovot and wanted to stay; my mother would have none of it and insisted on returning to home and family in Los Angeles.

That year, when I was nine years old, was the best of my childhood. We lived in a basement apartment in Rehovot, conditions that my mother considered beneath their station as emissaries of the UN, not to mention a significant downgrading from her accustomed circumstances. After a brief, chaotic experience in the Rehovot public schools, I was moved to Kvutzat Schiller, a kibbutz on the outskirts of the town. It was a magical year, learning to plant a garden, work in the chicken coop, and peel cucumbers for the morning salad, in addition to baffling encounters with the language of the Bible (our first assignment was the instructions on how to build the Tabernacle, the importance of which my secular Hebraist father struggled to explain to me). I was also introduced to the fierce camaraderie of the kibbutz children's society when some now long-forgotten quarrel with one of my classmates led to the whole class ganging up on me. And through the Israeli scouts (the "Tzofim"), I encountered the children of Mizrahi immigrants, something utterly foreign to an Ashkenazi American Jew.

I knew nothing of Israel before we arrived, except that it held a place of honor and desire in my father's imagination. He had made his first trip there four years before and toured the land like an excited child. He renewed contact with friends and family he had only seen years before the Shoah. He wrote back his impressions: "It appears that the Jews have come here to stay." As we landed in the summer of 1958, I must have been infected by his enthusiasm. People were standing on the roof of the small terminal that was then the airport at Lod, waving to us as if we had come home. I somehow felt that we had.

Since we were allowed luxuries unknown to average Israelis, we had a car shipped from England, as well as an American-size refrigerator and canned peaches (at the time a great delicacy!). My father also had an "official" car with a driver. So we explored the country. We traveled to Kibbutz Mishmar Ha'emek, where Elisha, my father's cousin from Poland, set up a camp for us in the forest and cooked us a memorable onion omelet over an open fire. We hiked up Massada and camped in half-completed houses at Yotfata, with my father's former student, Dov Koller, standing watch all night against infiltrators from Jordan. Just as memorably, we visited the wooden shack of our housecleaner, Shoshana, in a *ma'abara*, one of the transit camps that immigrants were forced to live in until housing could be built. The children of the camp swarmed around my short, balding Polish father and yelled: "Ben-Gurion!" I had certainly never seen anything like this in Los Angeles.

By the end of year, I felt conflicted. I had imbibed my father's Zionism but also my mother's deep ambivalence (she refused to learn Hebrew and communicated with the shopkeepers in Yiddish). I, too, longed to return to the family house in Los Angeles, to my friends, my school, and the promise of one day getting a television. It was no doubt partly a result of this parental conflict that my own attitude toward Israel has been ambivalent.

And so began my adolescence. Since my father was a confirmed secularist, my Jewish upbringing was not in a synagogue but rather in the Labor Zionist group that my father founded with other would-be *halutzim* marooned in California. This group formed a kind of alternative community, celebrating holidays together and meeting for cultural and political discussions. I was sent briefly to Hebrew school, to which I reacted allergically and from which I contrived to be thrown out. My father could stomach membership in a synagogue only for a year, and, thus, we held my Bar Mitzvah at home. He and I studied Bialik together and also the book of Isaiah. My Bar Mitzvah speech was about the prophetic call for world peace, an appropriate theme in 1962, the year of the Cuban Missile Crisis.

The West Side of L.A. was a very Jewish area (although my immediate neighborhood was not). Antisemitism was nonexistent, but so, for that matter, was any kind of sense of Jewishness as a central component in one's identity. There was a general sense of Jewish difference, which, I remember, we felt in school in terms of an ostensibly "innate" intellectual superiority, a feeling that we consciously shared with our Japanese American schoolmates.

So Judaism played almost no role during the school year as I went from junior high to high school. Not so the summers. I was sent when I was thirteen, fourteen, and fifteen to the Brandeis Alonim Summer Camp outside of Los Angeles. There I experienced for the first time Judaism as an intellectual challenge, especially that first summer, when my counselor was Barry Kogon, who would later go on to teach medieval Jewish philosophy at Hebrew Union College. As important, though, were the singing, dancing, and intense group bonding of the camp, resembling in certain ways what I remembered of the kibbutz. And it was at the camp that I experienced the first awakening of Eros, otherwise dormant during the school year. There can be little doubt that these three summers, followed by several more during the first years of college at this camp and others, were instrumental in shaping my later intellectual and affective commitments.

The Brandeis Camp was founded by Shlomo Bardin, a charismatic but also dictatorial Russian Jew who had lived for a time in Palestine. Bardin created his own form of Judaism based on nostalgia for the Old Country (he came from a wealthy distilling family from the same region of Ukraine as my grandmother, who was from the other side of the tracks) and a pastiche of traditions, some real and others invented. Bardin's version of Judaism always seemed to me a little suspect, and I later became thoroughly disenchanted when I introduced him to my grandmother as his *Landsmann*, only to have him recreate the shtetl class structure by snubbing her. Despite these reservations, it was at the Brandeis Camp that I found a new kind of Jewish identity.

I graduated high school in February 1967 and took some classes that spring at UCLA. In May of that year the news was full of reports of escalating tensions in the Middle East. The fifth of June is engraved in my memory: since we were ten hours behind Israel, the word that war had broken out reached us when it was already almost a day old. At that point, the bulletins from Egypt proclaimed that its army had invaded Israel; reports from Israel were sketchy at best. My father had a grim expression on his face. His Hashomer Hatzair comrades had gone to Kibbutz Negba, and he feared a repeat of the battle there during the War of Independence. "I know these people," he said. "They will fight to the end." By the next day, it became clear that there was little reason to fear, as the details emerged of Israel's assault on the Egyptian army in Sinai. The effect of the war on Jews like myself in California was electrifying. There was enormous pride in Israel's victory and a sense of identification with a faraway country. Little did we realize how such a stunning victory might end up complicating Israel's future.

Nevertheless, when I went to university that autumn, Israel and Judaism were far from my mind. I spent my first year, 1967–68, at Harvard University, where California was treated as a foreign land. I found the atmosphere there stuffy and patrician, a far cry from the public school from which I graduated in Los Angeles. And that venerable institution had still not experienced the revolution of the '60s. I began to get reports from friends at UC Berkeley, where there was action on the streets and intellectual ferment on the campus. After much internal struggle, I decided to leave Harvard for Berkeley, a decision I never regretted. I met there a group of gifted and self-motivated students taking the same classes: European intellectual history, political theory, and Marxist philosophy. It seemed that what we were learning had urgent relevance for the tumultuous conflicts over the Vietnam War abroad and social revolution at home. My initial intention to study biochemistry fell by the wayside as I abandoned the laboratory for the library and the beakers for books.

My first year at Berkeley, 1968–69, was perhaps the most tumultuous in the university's history. There were strikes and demonstrations every semester. Some of these were against the Vietnam War, a conflict that consumed our attention virtually every day as we faced the possibility of being drafted and sent to fight. When, several years later, the government introduced a lottery system, I drew a low number, which made me eligible for the draft despite my student status. I had to fly to Los Angeles and take the physical exam for the draft. I had studied the regulations and procured a pair of glasses that were too strong for me. The technician examining my glasses asked if I was volunteering for the army, in which case he was prepared to lie for me. I declined the offer, he wrote down the prescription of my glasses, and I was excused from the army.

At the same time, with comrades from summer camp, I embraced Jewish student activism. We formed the Radical Jewish Union and published the *Jewish Radical*, the first Jewish student newspaper. Our earnest ideological debates were not without merit. Long before it was acceptable, we opposed the Occupation and called for a Palestinian state. We fashioned ourselves as socialist Zionists and fought the New Left over its rejection of Zionism as the "national liberation movement" of the Jewish people. Our Zionism was not the product of the Zionist or American Jewish establishment but instead the expression of a counterculture. Indeed, we also resisted the assimilationist culture of the American Jewish community by sitting in at the San Francisco Jewish Federation in favor of funding for Jewish education. And we demonstrated our contempt for the Jewish establishment by awarding a "Golden Calf" award to the Anti-Defamation League for honoring Ronald Reagan (then the governor of California).

In the midst of all this "action," I decided that it was time to return to Israel, to reconnect with my memories of a decade earlier and to reexamine my perhaps overly utopian image of the country. My Hebrew had virtually disappeared, with the fluency from the year I spent there suppressed by a couple of years of mind-numbing Hebrew school. So I began to study on my own and with my fellow activists. There was practically no Jewish studies on the Berkeley campus, so we taught ourselves, reading, among other things, Bialik's "Concealment and Revelation in Language."

In the summer of 1969, I spent two months as a volunteer on Kibbutz Lahav in the northern Negev. We awoke at 4:00 a.m. and cleared rocks from fields, a Sisyphean labor, since the plow would only bring up a bumper crop of them the next season. It was exhausting and exhilarating. And two months were not enough. The following spring of 1970, I returned for six months (since my draft deferment from the Vietnam War at that time required that I stay in school, a sympathetic professor, himself a former member of Kibbutz Beit Alfa, gave me "fake" units and was shocked when I actually read the books for the invented course of study).

When I landed, in April 1970, I joined a Hebrew University student group on the March to Jerusalem, an annual event that then, three years after the Six-Day War, wound triumphally through the West Bank around Beit El before ending in Jerusalem itself. It was a moment of political awakening.

The Palestinian villagers came out to watch us march joyfully through their villages. I suddenly realized from the expressions on their faces: they don't want us here. What was then billed as a "benign" occupation could not, I thought, remain benign. And I now had increasingly ambivalent feelings about the Israeli army, which had organized the march. The allergic reaction I had developed against militarism in America as a result of the Vietnam War now came to color how I felt about the role of the Israel's army in perpetuating the Occupation.

I returned to Kibbutz Lahav for three more months of volunteer labor. The kibbutz was quite leftist in its opinions and organized a group to join a demonstration against the Occupation in Tel Aviv. I went along for the ride. It was another political awakening. I was already something of a veteran of street demonstrations in Berkeley (during People's Park in 1969, one person was killed, another was blinded, and many were injured, including the brother of a friend). But I wasn't prepared for the violence of the thugs from Betar who set upon us.

After my second stint at Lahav, I enrolled in the intensive Hebrew program at Ulpan Akiva in Netanya. My two stays in Israel had now reawakened my dormant Hebrew. I had planned to spend the months of July and August at the ulpan, but my Hebrew was now good enough that I qualified for the highest class, which was only one month long. The month of August was now free, a fortuitous circumstance that led to the most momentous development for my future life. A girl three years my junior, Navah Haber-Shaim, was in my class at the ulpan, and she planned to spend the period afterward at Kibbutz Kfar Ruppin in the Beit She'an Valley, where the Korati family was to be her adoptive family when she enlisted in the army. She volunteered to take me along.

Beforehand, though, another story with future implications. During the month of the ulpan, Navah and I traveled to Jerusalem for a Shabbat. We spent an evening with Aran Patinkin, who had just organized a controversial letter of high school seniors protesting the government's failed policy in the War of Attrition with Egypt and expressing severe doubts about serving in the Israeli army. I felt an immediate connection with my thoughts about the Vietnam War. Next, Navah proposed, but then dismissed as "probably tiresome," a visit to some "elderly family friends" in Jerusalem. I later discovered that these elderly friends were Gershom and Fania Scholem. I was furious: at that very moment, I was working my way with growing excitement through Scholem's *Major Trends in Jewish Mysticism*. It would take me another five years to meet the great historian of Jewish mysticism and to tie my academic fate to his.

After the ulpan, I traveled to Kfar Ruppin. It was the last full month of shelling by the PLO from across the Jordan River, before King Hussein destroyed the PLO bases there in "Black September." As I descended from the bus in the oppressive August heat, I felt as if I had entered an inferno both because of the temperature (well over 40 degrees Centigrade) and because of the ever-present threat of shelling. I found my way to the Korati apartment, where I met their daughter Rachel. Without knowing it at the time, I had just met my soul mate.

In our family mythology, we met *under* the bed, because my third night there, a shelling from across the Jordan came so close that we didn't dare run to the nearby shelter. Rachel just ordered us to slide under a bed that served as a couch and hope for the best. The next day we found holes in the exterior walls made by fragments of a mortar shell. But as exciting—and nerve-wracking—as those mortar shells may have been, the real excitement lay in the increasingly long breakfasts and lunches in the kibbutz dining hall as Rachel and I discovered our shared fascination, albeit from a secular point of view, with the Jewish literary tradition. She was part of a circle of kibbutz high school students (she had just graduated and was studying for the matriculation exams that summer) who had studied with such luminaries as Adin Steinsalz, Ehud Luz, and Chaim Druckman (Druckman was later to perform our wedding—we were ignorant at the time of his right-wing, settler views, which became public later when he was among the cofounders of Gush Emunim and the Tehiyah Party). Our backgrounds were so different and yet in some ways the same.

Rachel and I began to correspond, first once a week but soon daily. Over the next nearly two years, we exchanged 258 letters.[1] At first, the letters were ideological and intellectual: Israel, kibbutz, Franz Rosenzweig, Hasidism, and so forth. It took some eight months before we finally declared our romantic intentions, in writing rather than in person. The letters, reread fifty years later are, by turns, philosophical and playful, poetic and prosaic, idealistic and uncertain, pensive and erotic. They are, in a way, a remarkable window into a certain period of the twentieth century—the early 1970s—and into the passionate souls of two young Jews, one American and the other Israeli.

I returned from Israel in September 1970 to begin my senior year in Berkeley. I was now coming closer to a decision to marry my Jewish activism with my academic career. That year, I wrote an honors thesis on Micha Yosef Berdichevsky, whose struggle over the question "Are we the last Jews or the first Hebrews?" seemed to echo my own questions about my Jewish future. Indeed, even though I didn't know it at the time, my fascination with Berdichevsky set a certain narrative that would inform much of my future academic work and my ideological commitments. Berdichevsky belonged to the radical secularist wing of cultural Zionism and rejected the more moderate position of Ahad Ha'am. He searched for hidden sources of vitality in Jewish history against the "official" religion of Judaism in what I would later call counterhistory. I would also define my own Zionism as cultural rather than political and as oppositional, that is, as an ideology of radical revolt against prevailing establishments and orthodoxies. Zionism meant for me the renewal of Judaism, whether in Israel or America. And as the introduction to this book shows, my historical work, like Berdichevsky's, has focused on debunking myths and searching for subterranean themes in Jewish history.

After completing my thesis on Berdichevsky, I was accepted to graduate school at Berkeley and earned an MA with a focus on Jewish history, a subject not formally taught there. If I wanted to study Jewish history seriously, I needed to get some in-depth text work under my belt, and a year as a visiting graduate student at the Hebrew University seemed the best way to do so. Besides, Rachel was there, and it was time to confirm that our futures really were going to be together.

It was an eventful year. In August 1972, I joined a student group that was the first to cross the Allenby Bridge to visit Jordan. At a time when Petra was a mythic place for Israelis, I explored the site and returned to the kibbutz to give a slide lecture on the "Red Rock." On Yom Kippur of that year, Rachel and I were deeply immersed in our exploration of Judaism. We fasted and went from one synagogue to another in the midst of a ferocious *hamsin*. As soon as we broke the fast at the home of friends, I became seriously ill and did not recover for six weeks. I never got a real diagnosis of what was wrong, but I concluded that if there was a higher power, he was giving me a message: "Don't follow my laws." I have not fasted since, and our family tradition is to take a hike in the Northern California redwoods instead of attending synagogue.

I'm not sure how much I actually studied that academic year of 1972–73. Rachel was in the army at a Nachal outpost overlooking the Dead Sea. I was there a lot, and when I wasn't there I would impersonate an Israeli soldier and call her through the army's telephone system (much better than the civilian system in those pre–cell phone days). In March of 1973, we married on the kibbutz and then left in May for a month in Europe before working at a Habonim summer camp for eleventh graders in the Catskill Mountains.

Before we left, though, we had to resolve the question of where to continue our studies: she for a BA and me for a PhD. We were both accepted to Brandeis University, and she won a prestigious undergraduate fellowship meant for foreign students. Our course seemed set when Brandeis suddenly withdrew the offer: they had learned that we were married, and the fellowship required the recipient to live in the dormitories, which had no arrangements for married students. So we had to go to Plan B, which was UCLA, close to my parents. But more to the point: to work with Amos Funkenstein, then barely known as a historian both of the Jews and of medieval intellectual history. I had audited some lectures of Funkenstein's a few years earlier and had been deeply impressed. But if it hadn't been for Brandeis's benighted policy, I might never have had the experience of studying with one of the greatest minds in the field of Jewish studies, an experience that shaped everything in my subsequent career.

We began our studies at the end of September 1973. Yom Kippur that year fell on a Saturday, about a week after the beginning of the fall semester. I can still remember waking up to a hot morning, turning on the news, and hearing of the outbreak of war. We thought that it might be over as quickly as the Six-Day War, but, then, as the days lengthened into weeks, it became evident that something much worse was taking place. Four young men from Rachel's kibbutz, all of whom I knew, lost their lives. We debated returning to Israel to volunteer and decided that since we had just started university, we could not afford to do so. To this day, I wonder whether we made the right decision.

I had come to UCLA with the intention of focusing on modern Jewish history, but Funkenstein was teaching a seminar on medieval biblical exegesis, far from anything I knew about. I immersed myself in the strange world of Abraham ibn Ezra and learned how radical some medieval Jews could be. I felt my mind expanding and changing at a furious pace. I told Rachel that she had to come hear the seminar. Only a college freshman, she came to listen and ended up the best of any of us in the class (she later earned an MA in Jewish history and wrote the pioneering book *Women and Jewish Law*).

That was the beginning, for both of us, of an extraordinary apprenticeship with Funkenstein. Unhappy at home, he was in his office at all hours of the day or night. If we passed by, he invited us in to study a text: biblical, rabbinic, medieval, or modern. Afterward, he insisted on taking us to dinner. His seminars followed the Socratic method: he'd pose a question, we would all struggle to figure out the answer, and, after an hour or so he'd give us his interpretation, which was invariably something we had never thought of. It was exhilarating, as if we were observing a brilliant mind thinking.

When it came time to decide on a topic for a dissertation, I wanted to return to the modern period. My work as an undergraduate at Berkeley on Berdichevsky set me thinking about a study of various radical philosophers of Jewish history, with Gershom Scholem as the last chapter. It so happened that the great Israeli historian Jacob Katz was visiting UCLA that term and I was taking a seminar with him. I shared my idea with Katz and could see immediately that he wasn't really interested. I went to Funkenstein and reported on my conversation with Katz. He suggested: "Why don't you make the last chapter on Scholem the subject and through Scholem talk about the other people who interest you." When I returned to Katz, his eyes lit up and he said, "No one in Jerusalem would dare write it, but they'll all read it."

And so it was that Gershom Scholem, who was still very much alive, became the subject of my dissertation. Katz generously paved the way to Professor Scholem with an introduction. I went to Jerusalem for four months to do research and set an appointment with the great man. "How will you come?" he asked me on the telephone. "I suppose by bus," I said. "That's good," he replied. "Taxis are very expensive in Jerusalem."

I met with him twice, the first time for four hours and the second for about two. In truth, the content was less important than the experience. Most of what he said could be gleaned from things I had already found in print (a long biographical interview by Muki Tsur had just appeared, anticipating Scholem's two memoirs). He was clearly pleased that a student wanted to write about him. On his eightieth birthday, he was interviewed on Israeli television and proudly waved my dissertation at the camera, saying: "You see, in California, they are writing about me."

My study of Scholem as a historian and philosopher, published in 1979, was the first book-length study of this figure, who is now recognized as one of the greatest thinkers—and not just Jewish thinkers—of the twentieth century. The book had personal meaning for me as well. Scholem's embrace of an idiosyncratic Zionism matched my own attraction to a countercultural vision of Jewish national renewal. So too his autodidact's immersion in Hebrew sources provided an inspiration for my own studies. But probably most important of all was the mystery of a secular Jewish thinker who sought to unlock the door to the most recondite sources of the Jewish religion. Here was a model worth emulating of how a historian far from Orthodoxy might find meaning in the mystical tradition without himself becoming a mystic. This dialectic between religion and secularism—"the fine line between religion and nihilism"—is one that has run through all of my work, as well as my thinking, in the forty years since.

The years have involved peregrinations from California to upstate New York, to Israel, and back to California, by the waters of San Francisco, where we now have lived happily for the past three and a half decades. Unlike Scholem's, my course did not bring me ultimately to Zion but rather to a very different life in a diaspora he could never have imagined in the Berlin of the early twentieth century. But his biography, which is the last book I have written, thus closing the circle with my first book, continues to speak to me as well, as I try to integrate the various sides of my own life: as a historian, a secular Jew, and an American born in the middle of the twentieth century.

My father's secular Zionism, much of which I inherited, now appears like a naive and utopian belief, which has foundered on the shores of rampant capitalism, ultra-Orthodoxy, and ethno-nationalism. But I am still unwilling to relinquish the shards of that belief. I find myself at times in a lonely position, as a secular Jew at home in both Israel and the United States but also at home in neither. And so it is that the dialectics between the State of Israel and the diaspora, between a Jewish and an American identity, and between religion and secularism continue to inform my life and work, as they have since the beginning.

Notes

Introduction

1. Gershom Scholem, *Luah Ha-Aretz* (Tel Aviv: Schocken Books, 1944–45), translated into English as "Reflections on Modern Jewish Studies," in Gershom Scholem, *On the Possibility of Mysticism in Our Time*, ed. Avraham Shapira, trans. Jonathan Chipman (Philadelphia: Jewish Publication Society, 1997), 51–71.

2. David Biale, *Gershom Scholem: Kabbalah and Counter-history* (Cambridge, MA: Harvard University Press, 1979).

3. Scholem's 1937 birthday letter to Salman Schocken, in Biale, *Gershom Scholem*, 215–16.

4. Leo Baeck, *The Essence of Judaism* (New York: Schocken Books, 1961). Baeck was writing against Adolf von Harnack, *Das Wesen des Christentums* (Leipzig: Hinrichs, 1900). It is important to note that Baeck rejected the idea of that Judaism had a single "essence."

5. BT Eruvin 13:b. Here and throughout this book, translations are my own unless otherwise specified.

6. See Leora Batnitzky, *How Judaism Became a Religion* (Princeton, NJ: Princeton University Press, 2011).

7. See my preface to *Cultures of the Jews: A New History* (New York: Schocken Books, 2002).

8. Peter Berger, *The Heretical Imperative* (Garden City, NY: Anchor Press, 1979).

9. See Menachem Kellner, *Dogma in Medieval Jewish Thought: From Maimonides to Abravanel* (New York: Oxford University Press, 1986).

10. See my *Not in the Heavens: The Tradition of Jewish Secular Thought* (Princeton, NJ: Princeton University Press, 2011).

11. David Biale, *Power and Powerlessness in Jewish History* (New York: Schocken Books, 1986), *Eros and the Jews* (Berkeley: University of California Press, 1997), *Blood and Belief: The Circulation of a Symbol between Jews and Christians* (Berkeley: University of California Press, 2007), and *Not in the Heavens*.

12. Karl Löwith, *Meaning in History* (Chicago: University of Chicago Press, 1949), 2.

13. I am using the term *synoptic* in its original etymological sense of a "view of the whole" rather than of paraphrase. For an analysis of the latter, see Martin Jay, "Two Cheers for Paraphrase: The Confessions of a Synoptic Intellectual Historian," in his *Fin de Siècle Socialism and Other Essays* (New York: Routledge, 1988), 52–63. Jay points out the dangers of an external, totalizing "gaze" but defends the role of the historian against the assault of deconstructionist literary critics.

14. Martin Jay, *Downcast Eyes: The Denigration of Vision in Twentieth-Century French Thought* (Berkeley: University of California Press, 1993), 18.

15. Biale, *Not in the Heavens*.

16. Walter Benjamin, "Theses on the Philosophy of History," in *Illuminations*, ed. Hannah Arendt (New York: Schocken Books, 1969), 257.

17. Yosef Hayim Yerushalmi, *Zakhor: Jewish History and Jewish Memory* (Seattle: University of Washington Press, 1982), chap. 4.

18. Benjamin, "Theses," 255.

Chapter 1

1. See the list of possibilities in Norman Walker, "A New Interpretation of the Divine Name 'Shaddai,'" *Zeitschrift für die Alttestamentliche Wissenschaft* 72 (1960): 64. The main nineteenth-century interpretations were "my destroyer" (Franz and Stade), "my rain-giver" (Robertson Smith), "my demon" (Nöldeke), and "mountain" (see below). For more recent bibliography, see below and Klaus Koch, "Saddaj: Zur Verhältnis zwischen israelitischer Monolatrie und nordwestsemitischem Polytheismus," *Vetus Testamentum* 26 (1976): 299–332 (esp. 308).

2. Friedrich Delitsch, *Prolegomena eines neuen hebräisch-aramäischen Wörterbuch zum Alten Testament* (Leipzig: J. C. Hinrichs, 1886), 95–97, and *Assyrisches Wörterbuch* (Leipzig: J. C. Hinrichs, 1894–96), 642–43; William F. Albright, "The Names Shaddai and Abram," *Journal of Biblical Literature* 54 (1935): 180–93.

3. P. Dhorme, "L'emploi metaphorique des noms de parties du corps Akkadien," *Revue Biblique* 31 (1922): 230–31.

4. Frank Moore Cross, "Yahweh and the God of the Patriarchs," *Harvard Theological Review* 55 (1962): 244–50, and *Canaanite Myth and Hebrew Epic* (Cambridge, MA: Harvard University Press, 1973), 52–60; Lloyd Bailey, "Israelite 'El Shadday and Amorite Bel Shade," *Journal of Biblical Literature* 87 (1968): 434–38; Jean Ouellette, "More on 'El Shadday and Bel Shade," *Journal of Biblical Literature* 88 (1969): 470–71; E. L. Abel, "Nature of the Patriarchal God 'El Sadday,'" *Numen* 20 (1973): 49–59.

5. The classic essays on the "god of the fathers" are by Albrecht Alt, "Der Gott der Väter"

(1929), translated in his *Essays on Old Testament History and Religion* (London: Oxford University Press, 1966), 3–77, and Julius Lewy, "Les textes paleo-assyriens et l'Ancien Testament," *Revue de l'Histoire des Religions* 110 (1934): 50ff.

7. Manfred Weippert, "Erwägungen zur Etymologie des Gottesnamens 'El Shaddaj,'" *Zeitschrift der Deutschen Morgenlandischen Gesellschaft* 111 (1961): 42; see also Norman Walker, "A New Interpretation of the Divine Name 'Shaddai,'" *Zeitschrift für die Alttestamentliche Wissenschaft* 72 (1960): 64–65. Walker departs from the mountain-versus-plain argument by suggesting that the name derives from one of Marduk's names meaning "the omniscient." He believes that this derivation is justified on contextual grounds from Gen. 17:1. Such an interpretation stretches the imagination, since, as I show below, the El Shaddai passages are most closely associated with fertility blessings, not divine omniscience.

7. E. A. Speiser, *Genesis* (Garden City, NY: Doubleday, 1964), 124.

8. Weippert ("Erwägungen zur Etymologie," 56) assumes that this theology was taken from the cult of the "god of the fathers," which, similarly, had no specific geographical location.

9. The only Old Testament critic to have attempted such a contextual analysis is Koch, "Saddaj," 299–332, esp. 309. But as I shall argue below, Koch fails to discern the actual meanings of the name in the exilic and postexilic (Isaiah-Job) tradition and in the Genesis tradition. He does not see that two traditions are at work with very different interpretations. Moreover, his dating of the Priestly materials is postexilic, which leads him to some conclusions quite at variance with those presented here.

10. On the dating of the Testament of Jacob, see B. Vawter, "The Canaanite Background to Gen. 49," *Catholic Biblical Quarterly* 17 (1955): 1–18; on the Balaam oracles, see W. F. Albright, "Balaam," in *Encyclopedia Judaica* (Jerusalem: Keter, 1972), vol. 4, cols. 120–23, and "The Oracles of Balaam," *Journal of Biblical Literature* 63 (1944): 207–33; on Psalm 68, see W. F. Albright, "A Catalogue of Early Hebrew Lyric Poems (Psalm 68)," *Hebrew Union College Annual* 23 (1950–51): 1–39.

11. Martin Noth, *Die israelitischen Personennamen in Rahmen der Gemeinsemitischen Namengebung* (Stuttgart: W. Kohlhammer, 1928), 130–31, and Albright, "Names Shaddai and Abram," 188n55.

12. The dating of Job is, of course, still hotly debated. I am in agreement with the mainstream of opinion, represented by Albright, that Job stems from the sixth or fifth centuries. See his "Some Canaanite-Phoenician Sources of Hebrew Wisdom," *Vetus Testamentum*, suppl. 3 (1960): 14. See also M. H. Segal, "Parallels in the Book of Job" [in Hebrew], *Tarbiz* 20 (1950): 35–40, where he argues for the priority of Deutero-Isaiah over Job. A strong counterargument has been made by M. H. Pope, *Job* (Garden City, NY: Doubleday, 1965), xxxiii–xxxiv. For the probable postexilic date of Ruth, see Sellin-Fohrer, *Introduction to the Old Testament* (Nashville, TN: Abingdon, 1968), 249–52 and the bibliography there.

13. See the Greek, Samaritan, and Syriac translations. The Masoretic has *ve-et*, which is contextually less convincing than *ve-el*.

14. In Job, Shaddai appears sixteen times out of thirty-one in parallel with El. See Koch,

"Saddaj," 307. On these occurrences, Pope comments (*Job*, 44–45): "The use of the word el along with Shaddai as the designation of the deity has all the earmarks of authentic early terminology."

15. F. M. Cross, *Canaanite Myth and Hebrew Epic* (Cambridge, MA: Harvard University Press, 1973), 52–60.

16. Cross, *Canaanite Myth*, 58.

17. Koch, "Saddaj," 309–16.

18. The duplicate line (1:20, 21) in which Shaddai appears in Ruth reads either "For Shaddai has embittered me" or "Shaddai has done evil to me." Significantly, one verse of Job (27:2) has almost the same reading as Ruth 1:20: "Shaddai has embittered my soul."

19. Koch, "Saddaj," 323.

20. Albright, "Names Shaddai and Abram," 187.

21. My colleague Saul Levin was kind enough to point out the similarity with Ezek. 13:18. The main difficulty in deriving Shaddai from *shadayim* is the doubling of the *dalet*. Albright solves this problem by assuming that the doubling already occurred in Akkadian ("mountain" to "mountaineer"). I do not have a suitable solution to this problem in Hebrew. Would the doubling have made a poetic derivation from *shadayim* or *shod* impossible for a biblical author? Is the strengthening of the consonant a later Masoretic invention or a feature of the original Hebrew? My guess is that the doubled *dalet*, whatever its origins or true meaning, did not interfere with the poetic associations of the two traditions of El Shaddai.

22. Albright suggests that Shaddai could not have been derived directly from the Semitic roots for "breast" because of the suffix. Hence, he was led to his "mountaineer" interpretation. The argument is based, however, not on philology but on phonetic association, which could easily ignore the problematic suffix even if Albright could not ("Names Shaddai and Abraham," 184).

23. Such an argument was made by I. Zoller, "Il nome divino Sadday," *Rivista degli Studi Orientali* 13, no. 1 (1931): 73–75. See Albright, "Names Shaddai and Abram," 184.

24. Cross, *Canaanite Myth*, 56.

25. I thank my colleague Gerald Kadish for drawing this possibility to my attention.

26. Both Cross and Koch, among those writing on Shaddai, adopt this assumption, although they both admit that the Priestly tradition is based on earlier sources. Nevertheless, the acceptance of this dating leads to conclusions inconsistent with the fertility contexts in which we find El Shaddai in Genesis.

27. Gen. 48:3, "El Shaddai appeared to me at Luz in the country of Canaan," refers to Gen. 35, which is, in turn, cast in the same language as Gen. 17. Hence, the author of Gen. 48, even if he wrote after the other patriarchal El Shaddai traditions were written down, reveals his debt to them.

28. For a discussion of some of the interpretations and a possible solution, see Speiser, *Genesis*, 365–66n10.

29. On the Priestly theology, see Walter Brueggemann, "The Kerygma of the Priestly

Writers," *Zeitschrift für die Alttestamentliche Wissenschaft* 84 (1972): 397–413, and Koch, "Saddaj," 316–32.

30. It may be possible to interpret another of the circumcision stories (Exod. 4:24–26) in this light. Moses's sin may have consisted in not offering the proper sacrifice (his son's foreskin) in gratitude for his wife's fertility. It may well be that the enigmatic *hatan damim* (bridegroom of blood) should rather be read as *hoten damim* (father-in-law of blood), suggesting that the deity is, quite literally, the "godfather" in the birth of (male?) children.

31. It might be argued that the law of the *sotah* in Num. 5 is also evidence of God's role in reproduction. The text seems to suggest that if the woman has committed adultery, the "Water of Bitterness" that she drinks will induce a miscarriage. Here God seems to abort pregnancy instead of promote it.

32. Phyllis Trible has collected a variety of sources attesting to female imagery applied to God in the Bible. See "God, Nature of, in the OT," in *Interpreter's Dictionary of the Bible*, suppl. vol. (Nashville, TN: Abingdon, 1976), 368–69.

33. Raphael Patai, *The Hebrew Goddess* (New York: Ktav Publishing House, 1967), 29–52.

34. Patai, *Hebrew Goddess*, 59–60; W. F. Albright, *The Archaeology of Palestine and the Bible* (New York: Fleming H. Revell, 1932), 110.

35. Patai, *Hebrew Goddess*, 35, and William Reed, *The Asherah in the Old Testament* (Fort Worth: Texas Christian University Press, 1949), 80–81, 87.

36. Zeev Meshel, *Kuntillet 'Ajrud. A Religious Centre from the Time of the Judaean Monarchy on the Border of Sinai*, catalog no. 175 (Jerusalem: Israel Museum, 1978). Meshel convincingly dates the texts to the period after Jehoshaphat. However, this reading of the text is not universally accepted. On Asherah generally in Israelite religion and with some alternative readings of this inscription, see Ronald Hendel, "Israel among the Nations," in *Cultures of the Jews*, ed. David Biale (New York: Schocken Books, 2002), 1:56–58.

37. Cyrus Gordon, *Ugaritic Literature* (Rome: Pontificium Institutum Biblicum, 1949), 75, Text 128, paras. 25–28.

38. The first is a refrain in Text 52 (Gordon, *Ugaritic Literature*, 59–62). The second (52:28) is debatable. Gordon translates "fields," but Vawter ("Canaanite Background") translates "breasts." Raham probably stands for Anat (Gordon, *Ugaritic Literature*, 57).

39. Cross, *Canaanite Myth*, 55–56n44.

40. Genesis Rabba 8.1. See also Rashi and Ibn Ezra on Gen. 1:27.

41. This is the translation suggested by U. Cassuto in *The Goddess Anath: Canaanite Epics in the Patriarchal Age* (Jerusalem: Magnes Press, Hebrew University, 1971), 84–85, 108.

42. Clement of Alexandria, *Paidagogos* 1.6, in Elaine Pagels, *The Gnostic Gospels* (New York: Random House, 1979), 67. On the androgynous themes in orthodox and Gnostic Christianity, see Pagels, *Gnostic Gospels*, 48–69, and W. A. Meeks, "The Image of the Androgyne: Some Uses of a Symbol in Earliest Christianity," *History of Religions* 13 (1974): 165–208.

43. Gershom Scholem, *Major Trends in Jewish Mysticism* (New York: Schocken Books, 1961), 229, and *Elements of the Kabbalah and Its Symbolism* [in Hebrew] (Jerusalem: Mossad

Bialik, 1976), 259–307. See further Moshe Idel, *Kabbalah and Eros* (New Haven, CT: Yale University Press, 2005).

Chapter 2

1. For the Bible, see Susan Niditch, *Underdogs and Tricksters: A Prelude to Biblical Folklore* (San Francisco: Harper and Row, 1987).

2. For a discussion of Korah in the Bible, see *Anchor Bible: Numbers 1–20*, ed. Baruch Levine (New York: Doubleday, 1993), 405–32; Jonathan Magonet, "The Korah Rebellion," *Journal for the Study of the Old Testament* 24 (1982): 3–25.

3. For a recent discussion of how the Korah story might be read in light of biblical politics, see Michael Walzer, *In God's Shadow: Politics in the Hebrew Bible* (New Haven, CT: Yale University Press, 2012), 127, 180.

4. Ps. 42, 44–49, 84, 85, 87, 88.

5. See David C. Mitchell, "'God Will Redeem My Soul from Sheol': The Psalms of the Sons of Korah," *Journal for the Study of the Old Testament* 30, no. 3 (2006): 365–84.

6. Numbers Rabba 18.3.

7. See Louis Ginzberg, *Legends of the Jews* (New York: Simon and Schuster, 1956), 3:104.

8. Pirke de-Rabbi Eliezer, Jonah.

9. Numbers Rabba 18.8.

10. Numbers Rabba 18.7 and 18.8.

11. b. Hagigah 14b–15a. On this central text, see Yehuda Liebes, *Hata'o shel Elisha* (Jerusalem: Akadamon, 1990), and Alon Goshen-Gottstein, *The Sinner and the Amnesiac: The Rabbinic Invention of Elisha Ben Abuya and Eleazar Ben Arach* (Stanford, CA: Stanford University Press, 2000). See, further, chapter 8 below.

12. b. Sanhedrin 11a. Yalkut Shimoni, para. Korah #752.

13. See Michael Walzer, Menachem Lorberbaum, and Noam J. Zohar, *The Jewish Political Tradition* (New Haven, CT: Yale University Press, 2000), vol. 1, chap. 7.

14. b. Baba Metzia 59b.

15. Jeffrey Rubenstein, *Talmudic Stories* (Baltimore: Johns Hopkins University Press, 1999), 34–63.

16. Pirkei Avot 5:17.

17. Cyprian, Letter 67.3, quoted in *Ancient Christian Commentary on Scripture: Exodus, Leviticus, Numbers, Deuteronomy* (Downers Grove, IL: InterVarsity Press, 2001), 230. Emphasis added.

18. Numbers Rabba 18.2.

19. Numbers Rabba 18.2.

20. b. Sukkah 23a–b.

21. b. Yoma 73b.

22. Yalkut Shimoni, Korah, #752.

23. Numbers Rabba 18.2.

24. Midrash on Ps. 1:15.

25. b. Sanhedrin 110a.

26. Sifre Numbers 99–100, b. Shabbat 87a. See further my *Eros and the Jews* (Berkeley: University of California Press, 1997), 33–34, and Naomi Koltun-Fromm, *Hermeneutics of Holiness: Ancient Jewish and Christian Notions of Sexuality and Religious Community* (New York: Oxford University Press, 2010).

27. b. Sanhedrin 109b.

28. b. Sanhedrin, 109b–110a.

29. For the role of hair in the Bible, see Susan Niditch, *My Brother Esau Is a Hairy Man: Hair and Identity in Ancient Israel* (New York: Oxford University Press, 2008). More generally on women's hair, see Howard Eilberg-Schwartz and Wendy Doniger, eds., *Off With Her Head! The Denial of Women's Identity in Myth, Religion and Culture* (Berkeley: University of California Press, 1995).

30. b. Sanhedrin 110a.

31. Numbers Rabba, 18.4.

32. b. Sanhedrin 110a.

33. Hadith Sahih-Muslim, Book 1: 256.

34. Esther Rabba 7.5. See also Ecclesiastes Rabba 1.18 and Pirke de-Rabbi Elizer, Haman.

35. See Tanhuma, *Yelammedenu* 9, which deals with the way God tests both the wealthy and the poor.

36. Tanhuma, *Yelammedenu* 9.

37. Num. 16:32.

38. Cassiodorus, *Exposition on the Psalms* 105.16–17.

39. Sura 29:35.

40. Sura 28:75–85.

41. For this source and those following, see Roberto Tottoli, "Korah," in *Encyclopedia of the Qu'ran* (London: Taylor and Francis, 2005), and D. B. Macdonald, "Karu," in *Encyclopedia Islamicus: A Bibliography of Books, Articles and Reviews on Islam and the Modern World* (Leiden: Brill, 2007), 4:673.

42. Shmuel Feiner, *The Origins of Jewish Secularization in Eighteenth-Century Europe*, trans. Chaya Naor (Philadelphia: University of Pennsylvania Press, 2010).

43. Feiner, *Origins of Jewish Secularization*, 225–26. The context for this accusation was a split in the Ashkenazi community in Amsterdam in the late 1790s between an "old" and a "new" community. The latter were fully Orthodox in practice but, under the influence of the French Revolution, sought freedom from rabbinic dictates.

44. W. Gunther Plaut, "Some Unanswered Questions about Korah," *CCAR Journal*, October 1969, 75–78.

45. Andrew Garb and Larry Ceplair, "Korach's Question Still Deserves an Answer," *Journal of Reform Judaism* 35, no. 1 (1988): 15–22. See also the interesting note of Robert J. Milch, "Korah's Revolt," *Commentary* 69, no. 2 (1980): 52–56.

46. Meshulam Feibush Heller, *Yosher Divre Emet* (Munkatsh, Hungary: Kahane, 1905), #30.

47. Yehudah Arye Alter, *El Sefat Emet* (Kiryat Gat, Israel: Alumot, 2016), par. Korah.
48. Menachem Leiner, *Me ha-Shiloah* (Austria: A. Della Torre, 1860), par. Korah.
49. *The Interpreter's Bible* (New York: Abingdon-Cokesbury Press, 1952), 2:221–22.

Chapter 3

1. Amos Funkenstein, "Anti-Jewish Propaganda: Pagan, Medieval and Modern," *Jerusalem Quarterly* 19 (Spring 1981): 56–72, and, later, *Perceptions of Jewish History* (Berkeley: University of California Press, 1993), 36–40, 169–201.

2. He first used the term in "Anti-Jewish Propaganda," following my own extensive, but somewhat different, development of the concept of counterhistory in *Gershom Scholem: Kabbalah and Counter-history* (Cambridge, MA: Harvard University Press, 1979). My own use of the term came out of extensive conversations with Funkenstein, since my work was originally written as a dissertation under his direction. For his treatment of "counterhistory" in *Perceptions of Jewish History*, see 36–49.

3. Funkenstein, *Perceptions of Jewish History*, 36.

4. See the published book of Amos Funkenstein's doctoral dissertation, *Heilsplan und natürliche Entwicklung: Gegenwartsbestimmung im Geschichtsdenken des Mittlalters* (Munich: Nymphenberger, 1965). For his later treatment of apocalypticism, see *Perceptions of Jewish History*, 70–87.

5. Erich Gruen, "The Use and Abuse of the Exodus Story," in his *Heritage and Hellenism* (Berkeley: University of California Press, 1998), 41–72. Some similar arguments, also explicitly reacting to Funkenstein but from the point of view of Egyptology, can be found in Jan Assmann, *Moses the Egyptian: The Memory of Egypt in Western Monotheism* (Cambridge, MA: Harvard University Press, 1997).

6. See the comprehensive study of Samuel Krauss, *Das Leben Jesu nach jüdischen Quellen* (Berlin: S. Calvary, 1902).

7. Quoted in Krauss, *Leben Jesu*, 236.

8. b. Shabbat 104b.

9. Morton Smith, *Jesus the Magician* (San Francisco: Harper and Row, 1978).

10. Mishna Ta'anit 3:8.

11. In the case of Haman, none of the trees would agree to serve to hang him, except, in one version, a thornbush. See Esther Rabba 9:2. A variant version (Targum Sheni to Esther 9:7) has a cedar, since this was the tree Haman planned to use for Mordecai.

12. b. Sanhedrin 43a holds that Jesus was executed by a Jewish court according to Jewish law and procedures.

13. See b. Sanhedrin 107b.

14. See his lecture "Passivity as the Characteristic of the Diaspora Jews: Myth and Reality" [in Hebrew], Tel Aviv University School of Historical Studies, 1982. I am indebted to this lecture for my subsequent *Power and Powerlessness in Jewish History* (New York: Schocken Books, 1986).

15. I have used the three variant versions (Constantinople, Jellinek, and Bodlein manu-

scripts) in Yehudah Even-Shmuel, *Midrashei Ge'ulah* (Jerusalem: Mosad Bialik, 1954), 379–85 (Even-Shmuel's text on 56–88 is generally regarded as a reworking without good textual foundation); the commentary and French translation of the Bodleian manuscript by Israel Levi, "L'apocalypse de Zorobabel et le roi de Perse Siroes," *Revue des Etudes Juives* 68 (1914): 129–60, 69 (1919): 108–21, and 71 (1920): 57–65; and "Sefer Zerubbabel," translation and notes of Martha Himmelfarb, in *Rabbinic Fantasies*, ed. David Stern and Mark J. Mirsky (New Haven, CT: Yale University Press, 1990), 67–90.

16. Funkenstein, *Perceptions of Jewish History*, 79–80.

17. Funkenstein, *Perceptions of Jewish History*, 73.

18. Levi, "Apocalypse de Zorobabel." Some of these events have been discussed most recently by Elliot Horowitz, "'The Vengeance of the Jews Was Stronger Than Their Avarice': Modern Historians and the Persian Conquest of Jerusalem in 614," *Jewish Social Studies* 4, no. 2 (Winter 1998): 1–39.

19. David Berger, "Three Typological Themes in Early Jewish Messianism: Messiah Son of Joseph, Rabbinic Calculations, and the Figure of Armilus," *AJS Review* 10, no. 2 (Fall 1985): 141–64.

20. See Wilhelm Bousset, *The Antichrist Legend: A Chapter in Christian and Jewish Folklore*, trans. A. H. Keane (London: Hutchinson, 1896), and, more recently, Bernard McGinn, *Antichrist: Two Thousand Years of Human Fascination with Evil* (New York: Columbia University Press, 2000).

21. See the chart of features in McGinn, *Antichrist*, 72–73, and Bousset, *Antichrist Legend*, 156–57.

22. Bousset, *Antichrist Legend*, passim, and McGinn, *Antichrist*, 109–11.

23. See McGinn, *Antichrist*, 59–61.

24. The term *bet ha-toref* does not appear in earlier rabbinic literature in this form. Instead, one of the technical terms for vagina is the feminine form, *bet ha-torpa* (See m. Niddah 8:1, b. Shabbat 64b, and b. Berakhot 24a—with the exception of the mishnaic attestation, all the other appearances of this term are Babylonian). The play on words in the *Sefer Zerubavel* is based on one of the other meanings of the root *trf*, namely, "idol" (as in the biblical *terafim*). A *bet terafim* is therefore a house of idolatry. By using the unattested masculine singular, our author may well be intentionally creating a word association between idols and vaginas.

25. As Martha Himmelfarb notes in "Sefer Zerubbabel," the Talmudic text (b. Sanhedrin 98a) that describes the bandaged Messiah sitting at the gates of Rome does not refer to the Isaiah suffering servant tradition as proof text. The suffering servant tradition is invoked in a Jewish messianic context much more consistently in *Pesikta Rabbati* (Piska 36), a text that was probably written in Palestine in the seventh century shortly after the *Sefer Zerubavel* and that may also have been directly influenced by Christian sources.

26. When he sees this Messiah figure, Zerubavel says, according to some manuscripts, *va-tivar bi hamati* ("and my anger burned within me"; in other versions, *hamato* or "his anger"). Without any textual warrant or explanation, Even-Shmuel renders here *va-tivar bi*

tshukatai ("and my lust burned within me"). Although this eroticizing of the text may not be justified textually, Even-Shmuel put his finger on what seems to me an erotic undertone in the encounter between the prophet and the Messiah.

27. See Sanhedrin 94a, Berakhot 28b, and further Even-Shmuel, *Midrashei Ge'ulah*, 75n.

28. See Martha Himmelfarb's discussion in *Rabbinic Fantasies*, 69. On the role of women in Sabbatianism, see Ada Rapoport-Albert, *Women and the Messianic Heresy of Sabbatai Zevi* (Oxford: Littman Library, 2011).

29. b Sukka 52a. See Joseph Klausner's still very useful discussion in *The Messianic Idea in Israel*, trans. W. F. Stinespring (New York: Macmillan, 1955), 483–501, and, more recently, Joseph Heinemann, "The Messiah of Ephraim and the Premature Exodus of the Tribe of Ephraism," *Harvard Theological Review* 68 (1975): 450–61, and Berger, "Three Typological Themes," 143–48.

30. David Flusser has suggested that the author of the *Sefer Zerubavel* may have drawn some of these motifs from a first-century Jewish pseudepigraphon, the *Oracles of Hystaspes*, which may have been based on a Zoroastrian text. Flusser argues that this text also served as a source for the Christian book of Revelation. See "Hystaspes and John of Patmos," in David Flusser, *Judaism and the Origins of Christianity* (Jerusalem: Magnes Press, 1988), 390–453 (I thank Israel Knohl for this reference). But our author might have used the book of Revelation itself, although it speaks of two prophets who die and are resurrected, rather than one (see Rev. 11).

31. Vasiliki Limberis, *Divine Heiress: The Virgin Mary and the Creation of Christian Constantinopole* (London: Routledge, 1994). I thank Daniel Boyarin for this reference.

32. Himmelfarb, *Rabbinic Fantasies*, 69. See also Levi, "Apocalypse de Zorobabel," [vol. 71 (1920)], 60, and Ernst Kitzinger, "The Cult of Images in the Age before Iconoclasm," *Dumbarton Oaks Papers* 8 (1954): 110–12. I wish to thank my colleague Jim Skedros for providing me with additional information on the iconography of Mary in sixth- and seventh-century Byzantium. While working on this essay, by accident I came across a particularly fine example of an icon of the Virgin on a wool tapestry from sixth-century Egypt in the Cleveland Museum of Art.

33. Moritz Steinschneider, "Apocalypsen mit polemischer Tendenz," *Zeitschrift der deutschen morganlandischen Gesellschaft* 28 (1876): 360.

Chapter 4

The outlines of Ibn Ezra's exegetical theory were developed in part in a seminar with Professor Amos Funkenstein in the fall of 1973. I am grateful to Prof. Funkenstein for many valuable suggestions and criticisms.

1. The first modern commentator on Ibn Ezra was Baruch Spinoza, *Theological-Political Treatise*, trans. Samuel Shirley (Indianapolis, IN: Hackett, 2001), chap. 8. See also Richard Simon, *Histoire critique du vieux Testament* (Amsterdam: Daniel Elzevir, 1680), introduction, 35 and 49. For modern critics, see Isaac Husik, "Maimonides and Spinoza on the Interpretation of the Bible," supplement, *Journal of the American Oriental Society*, no. 1

(September 1935): 22–40; Asher Vizer, "Ibn Ezra k'parshan," *Sinai* 62 (1967): 113–26; and D. Rosen, "Die Religionphilosophie Abraham Ibn Ezra's," *Monatsschrift für Geschichte und Wissenschaft des Judentums* 42 (1898): 17–33 et passim and 43 (1899): 22–31 et passim. More recently, see Irene Lancaster, *Deconstructing the Bible: Abraham Ibn Ezra's Introduction to the Torah* (London: RoutledgeCurzon, 2003).

2. For Spinoza's exegetical method and its basis in his natural science, see the *Theological-Political Treatise*, particularly chap. 3. See further my *Not in the Heavens: the Tradition of Jewish Secular Thought* (Princeton, NJ: Princeton University Press, 2011), chap. 2. For the relation of Spinoza to seventeenth-century biblical criticism, see Klaus Scholder, *Ursprünge and Probleme der Bibelkritik in 17 Jahrhundert* (Munich: Kaiser, 1966). See also Leo Strauss, *Spinoza's Critique of Religion* (New York: Schocken Books, 1965). Despite Strauss's effort to show the connections between Spinoza's critique of religion and his exegesis, he exaggerates his case. For Spinoza, imagination (the source of revelation) has a legitimate epistemological status; its ideas may be confused, but they are not categorically false. Hence, revelation is a vague reflection of philosophic truth. To fully understand Spinoza's exegesis on the background of his philosophy, one would have to do what Strauss largely ignored: a careful study of Spinoza's *Ethics* together with the *Theological-Political Treatise*.

3. All references to Ibn Ezra's commentaries are given according to the relevant biblical verse. The *Mehokekei Yehudah* (Bnei Brak, Israel: Horev, 1961) edition was used for the commentary on the Pentateuch. Unless otherwise noted, the references are to the long recension. The Shiloa edition of the *Mikraot Gedolot* references (Tel Aviv: Pardes, 1969) was the source for the commentaries on the remaining books of the Bible.

4. For instance, "Og's bed" seems to refer to a historical artifact known to a later author, most likely no earlier than King David, who conquered Rabbat Ammon, where the bed was on display. Ibn Ezra does not comment on Deut. 3:11, where the passage appears, and leaves it to us to draw our own conclusions. The "secret of the twelve" so often discussed in the Ibn Ezra literature is indeed obscure. It does not seem to refer to Deut. 1:1–5, where the problem seems to be the expression "across the Jordan," implying that the introduction to Deuteronomy was written by someone who had already crossed the Jordan. Nor does it refer to the last twelve verses in Deuteronomy, since he explicitly says that Joshua wrote the passage (an accepted interpolation): here there is no need for a secret. Neither could it have been the "twelve stones" referred to in Deut. 2, since Ibn Ezra there explicitly endorses the opinion of Sa'adia Gaon (itself a rare occurrence) that the stones simply contained a number of commandments of warning.

5. Simon, *Histoire critique,* 49; Michael Friedländer, *Essays on the Writings of Ibn Ezra* (London: Trübner, 1877), 60. (Friedländer's book is the only in-depth study of Ibn Ezra before Lancaster's *Deconstructing the Bible*, but it bears the bias of a hagiography. It is an indispensable source of references for the philosophical allusions in Ibn Ezra's commentaries.) See also the commentary *Mehokekei Yehudah*, by Yehudah Leib, which directly addresses Spinoza in defense of Ibn Ezra (Deut. 1:1–5). Spinoza's view is found in his *Theological-Political Treatise*: "Aben Ezra, a man of enlightened intelligence and no small learning who

was the first to treat of this opinion (that Moses was not the author of the Pentateuch), dared not express his meaning openly" (120–21).

6. Ibn Ezra argued that Job was translated from Aramaic into Hebrew. He also claimed that there were two authors of Isaiah, using the historical argument that Cyrus came during the Babylonian exile and that the author of chapter 40 onwards must have lived during the Exile, unlike the author of the first thirty-nine chapters, who clearly lived before. The argument is couched in veiled language.

7. Perhaps Isaac ben Suleiman or Isaac Israeli, whose Neoplatonism resembles Ibn Ezra's and may have been one of his sources. See A. Altmann and S. M. Stern, *Isaac Israeli* (London: Oxford University Press, 1958).

8. Ibn Ezra was familiar both with Sa'adia's commentaries on the Bible and with his *Book of Beliefs and Opinions*, trans. S. Rosenblatt (New Haven, CT: Yale University Press, 1948), to which he refers explicitly in Eccl. 7:3.

9. Introduction to the Pentateuch, Part 1.

10. In Part 3 of the Introduction, Ibn Ezra rejects "the way of darkness and murkiness." While Friedländer believes this may refer to Christian or Kabbalistic exegesis (*Essays*, 121), there is no evidence in the commentaries that Ibn Ezra was aware of Kabbalistic exegesis, which began seriously in Spain in the thirteenth century with Nachmanides. There is likewise no legitimate cause to believe that he refers to the Christians in his example of "uncircumcised of the flesh." I would suggest that he is alluding to all systems of excessive allegorization. His rejection of midrash in Part 4 on the grounds that "there is no end to midrash" and his list of midrashim surrounding Creation suggest that it was Ibn Ezra whom Nachmanides later criticized in his commentary to Gen. 1.1 ("men of little faith").

11. Introduction, Part 3.

12. Introduction, Part 4 and Part 5. He quotes a rabbinical source for support that the literal meaning has priority over midrash.

13. Hidden beneath Ibn Ezra's criticism of Sa'adia is, of course, his own preconception about God: that he works through natural bodies as mediators.

14. The doctrine that "the Torah speaks the language of human beings" has a long history in the Jewish literature. In Talmudic sources it is associated with the name of Rabbi Ishmael (cf. b. Sanhedrin 61b, b. Yebamot 71a). Ishmael's traditional opponent, Rabbi Akiva (2nd century), was known to derive law from every word repetition in the Bible. Biblical Hebrew commonly combines present-tense verbs (technically nouns) with future-tense (technically imperfect) verbs. Akiva would interpret such doublings as referring, for example, to "this world and the world to come," thus expanding the scope of the law in question. In response, Ishmael argued that "the Torah speaks in the language of men" and that one should not derive law from common linguistic devices. In his own way, Ishmael's position corresponds to the literalist attack on allegory, only he is criticizing the *midrash halakha* (legal hermeneutics). The dictum underwent a shift from a legal to an exegetical principle in the Middle Ages. On Ishmael's method, see Azzan Yadin, *Scripture as Logos: Rabbi Ishmael and the Origins of Midrash* (Philadelphia: University of Pennsylvania Press, 2004). Sa'adia Gaon

(*Book of Beliefs and Opinions* 2.3) himself implicitly used the doctrine. He argues that anthropomorphic expressions are unavoidable because precise vocabulary would preclude any discussion of God. Linguistic ambiguity is a necessity of every language, but reason can show how to deduce the precise meaning from the ambiguous usage. However, Sa'adia's argument is circular: in order to reconcile a passage with the dictates of reason, the philosopher applies a rational preconception to biblical language in order to reveal the precise philosophical meaning of the verse. Allegory rests on a prior philosophical position. Sa'adia sees the Bible as a philosophical treatise and thus considerably limits the use of the Ishmaelian dictum. Following Ibn Ezra, Maimonides's *Guide for the Perplexed* 1.33 (Chicago: University of Chicago Press, 1963), 70–72, employed the dictum to emphasize that the Bible is a book of the masses. For Maimonides, one of the rigorous exponents of the *theologia negativa*, anthropomorphisms have even less place than they do for Ibn Ezra. But since the ceremonial commandments are historically relativized for Maimonides, the status of the Bible is lowered: it is a pedagogical and not a philosophical book. Where philosophy is unambiguous, offensive biblical expressions can be explained by "the Bible speaks the language of human beings."

15. 1 Sam. 15:29.
16. Exod. 32:14.
17. Gen. 1:26; Gen. 11:5; Gen. 35:13.
18. Ps. 104:31.
19. Gen. 1:16.
20. The major exception to this is the essential name of God YHVH, whose formulation is unique in and of itself.
21. Exod. 20:1.
22. Listed in Gen. 1:26.
23. Abraham Ibn Ezra, *Yesod ha'Morah* (Frankfurt: n.p., 1840), 3.
24. Introduction to the Pentateuch, pt. 3.
25. Introduction to the Pentateuch, pt. 3.
26. Ibn Ezra draws an analogy between the heart, which is both corporeal and noncorporeal, and the angels as mediators between God and the world.
27. Ps. 2:2.
28. See his doctrine of natural law in Ibn Ezra, *Yesod ha'Morah*, 8: "The commandments that are primary and do not depend on space or time or any other thing . . . were known to the faculty of reason [*shikul ha'da'at*] before Moses gave the Torah."
29. Exod. 28:6 (the description of the ephod) is another passage that refers to knowledge of foreign science.
30. No attempt will be made here to trace Ibn Ezra's sources, although such a study is lacking. His cosmology is a mixture of Neoplatonic and Aristotelian elements, assimilated from Arabic sources. I am indebted to Joshua Lipton for the suggestion that Ibn Ezra's knowledge of Aristotle may have come in part from Abu Ma'shar, whom Ibn Ezra quotes in his astrological treatises.
31. The intelligence associated with governance of the constellations is *Shaddai*. Fried-

lander misinterprets *Shaddai* as the power to subdue nature. Ibn Ezra means that *Shaddai* is the force of regularity in the universe. Gen. 17:1, Exod. 6:3.

32. Exod. 3:16.
33. Ps. 19:3.
34. Exod. 3:15.
35. Gen. 1:14.
36. Exod. 3:16.
37. Eccl. 1:9; *Yesod ha'Morah*, 20.
38. The problem of how a finite number of forms can generate an infinite number of individuals was already solved by Aristotle. Each form is appropriate to a range of combinations of the four elements, but within that range there are an infinite number of combinations or variations. Matter, for Aristotle, was the principle of individuation, since it imposed the individual accidents upon actualized forms. I am indebted to Prof. Funkenstein for this reference.
39. The *general* (*klal*) refers not to God but to the laws that govern the universe.
40. Ps. 19:2, emphasis added.
41. Gen. 1:14–16 refers to Sam. 17.
42. Gen. 1:14.
43. *Yesod ha'Morah*, 20.
44. Exod. 33:21, Exod. 3:16, and Exod. 6:3 are various repetitions of this principle.
45. Introduction to Ecclesiastes.
46. Exod. 20:3, Deut. 31:16. The similarity of these ideas to those of Judah Ha'levi is perhaps no coincidence. By all accounts Ibn Ezra knew Judah Ha'levi, and there is even an improbable story that they were related. Cf. Rosen, "Religionphilosophie Abraham Ibn Ezra's," 21; Vizer, "Ibn Ezra k'parshan," 113–14. Ibn Ezra mentions Ha'levi by name in the commentaries on Exod. 20:1 and Deut. 14:22.
47. Exod. 3:16, Gen. 17:1.
48. *Yesod ha'Morah*, 8.
49. Hos. 6:2.
50. Eccl. 23:25.
51. Eccl. 7:3.
52. Eccl. 7:13.
53. Eccl. 23:25.
54. Exod. 3:15; *Yesod ha'Morah*, 20.
55. Isa. 20:3, Deut. 13:2, Isa. 8:18. In general, the relation of miracles to prophecy is fuzzy, since even false prophets were known to perform miracles. See the commentary on Balaam.
56. Exod. 3:16. The essential name (YHVH) is also an attribute name. An essential name that can only stand for itself, it denotes a unique individual (a proper name is a good example), and it cannot be pluralized, conjugated, indicated with a definite article, or placed in a construct with another noun. An attribute name can stand for an individual but also for

other individuals (e.g., the name of an occupation). Only YHVH can paradoxically be an essential and an attribute name because it is the essence and motive force of the world.

57. Exod. 6:3.

58. Exod. 33:22. Ibn Ezra argues for a miracle by coincidence: the inhabitants of a wicked city are told by a prophet that they will die if they do not pray to God for mercy. They leave their city to pray, and while they are outside, a river rises and destroys the city. This argument by coincidence is really not what he means by the intervention of God, although it indicates his discomfort with special providence.

59. In Exod. 23, he claims that if one follows the Bible, then one has no need for doctors. The correct orientation of the body—through proper diet and obedience to the commandments—can influence the relation of the upper soul to God.

60. Gen. 1:26, Exod. 23.

61. Exod. 23, Gen. 1:1. The essential name of God (cf. note 55) indicates that if God's name is in the angel, so is his essence.

62. Introduction to Ecclesiastes.

63. Ps. 2:4. These ideas bear a remarkable resemblance to those in Spinoza's *Ethics*, especially Part I. See also Num. 20:8 and 22:28.

Chapter 5

1. See Kay R. Jamison, *Touched with Fire: Manic-Depressive Illness and the Artistic Temperament* (New York: Basic Books, 1993). For a dissent, see Albert Rothenberg, *Creativity and Madness: New Findings and Old Stereotypes* (Baltimore: Johns Hopkins University Press, 1990).

2. On depression and creativity, see James Masterson, *The Search for the Real Self: Unmasking the Personality Disorders of Our Age* (New York: Free Press, 1988), chap. 12.

3. Hasidism, virtually by definition, is a sociological phenomenon of a sect of followers (*hasidim*) around a leader (*zaddik* or *rebbe*). While such charismatic sects can be found in the Jewish world outside of Hasidism, particularly among North African Jews, Hasidic theology evolved to an important extent as a theory to explain the sociological phenomenon. With the death of the Rebbe of Lubavitch in 1994 and the lack of a successor, another sect of Hasidism is beginning to experiment with following a dead zaddik. On the other hand, the lack of a dynastic successor following the death of Nahman was the rule rather than the exception in the early days of Hasidism. Only in Habad or Lubavitch Hasidism did the dynastic principle become established following the death of the sect's founder in 1812. Other Hasidic sects then followed suit by becoming dynastic. See Moshe Rosman, *Founder of Hasidism: A Quest for the Historical Ba'al Shem Tov* (Berkeley: University of California Press, 1996), chap. 12, and also David Biale et al., *Hasidism: A New History* (Princeton, NJ: Princeton University Press, 2018).

4. *Sefer Hayyei Muharan* II, 1.6 (Jerusalem: Keren de-Hasidei Breslav, 1975), quoted and translated in Arthur Green, *Tormented Master: A Life of Rabbi Nahman of Bratslav* (New

York: Schocken Books, 1981), 170. I am using Green's method of dividing the *Hayyei Muharan* into chapters. See *Tormented Master*, 375–76.

5. See Martin Buber, *The Origin and Meaning of Hasidism* (New York: Schocken Books, 1960) and *Die Geschichten des Rabbi Nachman* (Frankfurt: Rücker and Loening, 1906).

6. Jacob Becker, *R. Nahman mi-Bratslav: Mehkar Psikhoanaliti* (Jerusalem: De'ah, 1928).

7. Joseph Weiss, *Mehkarim be-Hassidut Breslav* (Jerusalem: Mossad Bialik, 1974), esp. 163–65.

8. Green, *Tormented Master*. See also Mendel Piekarz, *Hasidut Breslav* (Jerusalem: Mossad Bialik, 1972), 42.

9. *Likkutei Muharan* (Jerusalem: Hasidei Breslav, 1969), vol. 2, chap. 24. Partially translated in Green, *Tormented Master*, 164.

10. *Hayyei Muharan* II, 1.7. Slightly emended translation from Green, *Tormented Master*, 170.

11. *Likkutei Muharan* 2.24.

12. Nahman was not the only Hasidic thinker to develop the idea of "brokenness." The second Habad rebbe, Dov Ber, whose father, Sheur Zalman of Liadi, died in 1812, also held that communion with God required negation of the material self and heartbreak. See Rosman, *Founder of Hasidism*, 193

13. *Likkutei Muharan* 1.72.

14. For Nahman's views on sexuality as well as their connection with other Hasidic attitudes, see Green, *Tormented Master*, and my *Eros and the Jews* (New York: Basic Books, 1992), chap. 6.

15. *Sihot ha-Ran*, nos. 41–42. See also no. 231.

16. See especially Weiss, "Ha-Kushiya be-Torat R. Nahman," in *Mehkarim*, 109–49. The classic text dealing with God's transcendence and the paradox of a God who fills all worlds but is simultaneously absent from all worlds is *Likkutei Muharan*, vol. 2, chap. 64. See further Green, *Tormented Master*, Excursus I.

17. Masterson, *Search*, esp. 59–89.

18. See *Diagnostic and Statistical Manual of Mental Disorders (DSM-III-R)*, 3rd rev. ed. (Washington, DC: American Psychiatric Assocation, 1987), 230–32.

19. *Hayyei Muharan* II, 10.5.

20. *Sihot ha-Ran*, no. 43.

21. *Hayyei Muharan* II, 10.5.

22. Gershom Scholem, *Major Trends in Jewish Mysticism*, 3rd ed. (New York: Schocken, 1961), 340–41.

Chapter 6

1. See Immanuel Wolf's programmatic essay "Über den Begriff einer Wissenschaft des Judentums," *Zeitschrift für die Wissenschaft des Judentums*, translated in *Ideas of Jewish. History*, ed. Michael Meyer (New York: Behrman House, 1974), 143–55.

2. See particularly Eduard Gans's third address to the Verein as translated in Zalman

Shazar, *Ore Dorot* (Jerusalem: Mossad Bialik, 1971), 377–88, where he argues that whatever consciousness cannot comprehend has no reality. Following Hegel, he suggested that whatever is not rationally comprehensible is not real. As a presumed product of the imagination, the Kabbalah could appear to Wissenschaft as illusory and without any "real" existence in Jewish history.

3. See Franz Josef Molitor, *Die Philosophie der Geschichte oder über die Tradition*, 2 vols. (Münster: Theissing, 1834–57).

4. On Rapoport, see Isaac Barzilay, *Shlomo Yehudah Rapoport (Shir) and His Contemporaries* (Ramat Gan, Israel: Bar Ilan University Press, 1969), 86, 88. For Miesis, see his *Kinat ha-Emet*, 2nd ed. (Lemberg, Austria: M. Wolf, 1897). For general discussions of Haskalah attacks on the Kabbalah, see Fischel Lachover, "Revealed and Hidden in the Doctrines of Nachman Krochmal" [in Hebrew], *Keneset* 6 (1941): 298–99, and Gershom Scholem, "Die Erforschung der Kabbala von Reuchin bis zur Gegenwart," in *Judaica III: Studien zur jüdischen Mystik* (Frankfort: Suhrkamp, 1973), 247–63.

5. See S. D. Luzzato, *Viku'ah al Hokhmat ha-Kabbalah* (Goritzia: n.p., 1852).

6. On Milzahgi, see Gershom Scholem, *Judaica III*, 260–61, and Lachover, "Revealed and Hidden," 299–300. For Joel, see his *Die Religionsphilosophie des Sohar und ihr Verhältnis zur allgemeinen jüdischen Theologie* (Leipzig: O. L. Fritzsche, 1849).

7. Lachover, in "Revealed and Hidden," 296–341, was the first to point out Krochmal's unusually positive attitude toward the Kabbalah. Lachover did not, however fully follow up his observation and identify the precise status of irrationalism in Krochmal's philosophy. This essay attempts to complete the task Lachover began.

8. For Krochmal's biography, see Simon Rawidowicz's introduction to *Kitve Nachman Krochmal*, 2nd ed. (Waltham, MA: Ararat, 1961), 17–98. For a more recent study, see Jay M. Harris, *Nachman Krochmal: Guiding the Perplexed of the Modern Age* (New York: NYU Press, 1991).

9. *Moreh Nevukhei Ha-Zeman*, in Rawidowicz, *Kitve Nachman Krochmal*, 30; Lachover, "Revealed and Hidden," 300ff.; Eliezer Schweid, "Nachman Krochmal's Philosophy and Its Relationship to the Philosophy of Maimonides, the Kabbalah and Modern Philosophy" [in Hebrew], *Iyyun* 20, no. 1 (1969): 29–59.

10. On the question of the influence of German Idealism on Krochmal there is an extensive literature. The main issue is that of Hegel's influence. Zunz, who was the first to publish Krochmal's *Guide* in 1851, claimed that Krochmal had discovered Hegel late in his life and had been profoundly influenced by him. See Leopold Zunz, *Gesammelte Schriften* (Berlin: L. Gerschel, 1875–76), 2:155–56. The most extensive attempt to prove Krochmal's association with Hegelianism was by J. L. Landau, *Nachman Krochmal, ein Hegelianer* (Berlin: S. Calvary, 1904). Landau was subjected to a devastating attack by Simon Rawidowicz in "War Nachman Krochmal Hegelianer?," *Hebrew Union College Annual* 5 (1928): 435–582, English translation in Simon Rawidowicz, *Studies in Jewish Thought* (Philadelphia: Jewish Publication Society, 1974), 350–87, and in *Kitve Nachman Krochmal*, 160–201. Rawidowicz noted the influence of other Idealists such as Fichte and Herder and of the Italian philos-

opher of history Vico. More recently Jacob Taubes attempted to revive the Hegelian argument by claiming that "what Hegel did to Christianity [in historicizing it], Krochmal did to Judaism." See Jacob Taubes, "Krochmal and Modern Historicism," *Judaism* 12, no. 2 (1963): 150–65. I agree with Taubes that Hegel was not the main Idealist influence on Krochmal, but also that the structure of Krochmal's historicist arguments was so similar to Hegel's that one may speak of Krochmal's Hegelian interpretation of the history of Spirit quite apart from the question of actual influence.

11. Krochmal, *Moreh Nevukhei Ha-Zeman*, chap. 15. Scholem's relationship to Krochmal was, at best, highly ambivalent. Scholem unquestionably saw many of the Gnostic and Neoplatonic features in the Kabbalah that Krochmal had been the first to point out. But Scholem did not see the history of the Kabbalah as the history of Jewish philosophy. The Kabbalah, for him, had a distinct history and legitimacy of its own. One might argue that he took many of Krochmal's partially negative value judgments about the Kabbalah—such as its Gnostic "degeneration"—and turned them on their head. For a fuller discussion of Scholem's relationship to Krochmal, see my *Gershom Scholem: Kabbalah and Counterhistory* (Cambridge, MA: Harvard University Press, 1979), 114, 134, 198.

12. Krochmal took his arguments on the connections between Kabbalah, Gnosticism, and Neoplatonism from August Neander, *Genetische Entwicklung der vornehmsten gnostischen Systeme* (Berlin: Dümmler, 1818), esp. 1–22, "Einleitung: Elemente der Gnosis in Philo." Neander's study may also have been Hegel's source when the latter wrote "Die Kabbalistische Philosophie, gnostische Theologie beschäftigen sich alle mit diesen Vorstellung, die auch Philo hatte," in *Werke* (Berlin: Ducker und Humblot, 1832–87), 19:26. On Krochmal's metaphysics, see Julius Guttman, "Rabbi Nachman Krochmal" [in Hebrew], *Keneset* 6 (1941): 259–87, and his *Philosophies of Judaism* (New York: Schocken Books, 1973), 365–91.

13. Krochmal, *Moreh Nevukhei Ha-Zeman*, chap. L. The other maladies are superstition and excessive externalization of worship (ritualization).

14. Krochmal, *Moreh Nevukhei Ha-Zeman*, 271.

15. See Scholem's famous essay of 1937, "Mitzvah Ha-Ba'ah Ba'averah," translated as "Redemption through Sin" in his *Messianic Idea in Judaism and Other Essays on Jewish Spirituality* (New York: Schocken Books, 1971), esp. 129–33.

16. A similar historicization of *Netsach Yisrael* can be found in the sixteenth-century philosopher the Maharal from Prague, in his *Netsach Yisrael* (Jerusalem: Mekhon Yerushalayim, 1997). One might compare Krochmal's notion of Absolute Spirit as a guarantor of history to Hermann Cohen's revision of Kant in which God becomes the guarantor of the eternity of a world in which ethics is possible.

17. On the problematics of Krochmal's philosophy of history, see Nathan Rotenstreich, "Krochmal's Concept of History" [in Hebrew], *Zion* 7 (1942): 29–47, and his "Absolute and Change in the Thought of Krochmal" [in Hebrew], *Keneset* 6 (1941): 333–45.

18. Krochmal, *Moreh Nevukhei Ha-Zeman*, 112.

19. Gershom Scholem, *Major Trends in Jewish Mysticism*, 3rd ed. (New York: Schocken Books, 1961), 84.

20. Scholem, *Major Trends*, 258. Krochmal distinguishes between two types of Kabbalistic scholarship, that of the "literalists" (*pashtanim*) and that of the Kabbalists. The former, presumably including Yehudah Aryeh Mi-Modena and Jacob Emden, argued from an immanent exegesis of the Kabbalistic texts that they were written later than the texts themselves purported. The Kabbalists believe the claims of the texts to antiquity. Krochmal himself sides with the literalists. His use of this term seems to have been taken from Abraham Ibn Ezra, whom he treats extensively in the *Moreh Nevukhei Ha-Zeman*. Ibn Ezra defined his literalist exegesis of the Bible as just such an immanent method and used it to prove, for instance, that there are two authors of the book of Isaiah, a conclusion Krochmal adopted. Krochmal must have seen through Ibn Ezra's methodology the connection between a literal exegesis and historical criticism. On Ibn Ezra's exegetical theory and its implications, see chapter 4 above.

21. Lachover, "Revealed and Hidden," 308.

22. Krochmal, *Moreh Nevukhei Ha-Zeman*, 30.

23. Krochmal, *Moreh Nevukhei Ha-Zeman*, 30.

24. In his Hebrew-German lexicon of Krochmal's philosophic vocabulary (*Kitve Nachman Krochmal*, 211–18), Rawidowicz uses Kantian terms: *tz'iur* is *Vorstellung*, *musagim sikhliyim* are *Verstandesbegriffe*, and *musagim tevuniyim* (or *musagei binah*) are *Vernunftbegriffe*.

25. On Krochmal's view of idol worship, see *Moreh Nevukhei Ha-Zeman*, 29. While the Talmud (BT Hullin) considered worshipping the "spirit of the mountain" (*gada dehar*) to constitute a more serious form of idolatry than worship of the mountain itself, Krochmal turned this interpretation upside down and argued that it proves that even idolators worship a "spirit."

26. Krochmal, *Moreh Nevukhei Ha-Zeman*, 38.

27. Krochmal, *Moreh Nevukhei Ha-Zeman*, 271: "patah be-sekhel."

28. Krochmal, *Moreh Nevukhei Ha-Zeman*, chap. 15. Note the similarity with *sefarim hitzoniyim*, the term for extracanonical books of the Hebrew Bible.

29. Krochmal, *Moreh Nevukhei Ha-Zeman*, 13. See also 242, where Krochmal distinguishes between *limud hitzoni* (external study) and *limud penimi* (internal study).

30. For Kant, imagination occupied a problematic intermediary position between sensory images and rational concepts, seemingly similar to the status of the understanding (*verstand*). See *Kritik der reinen Vernunft*, 2nd ed. (Riga, Latvia: Hartknoch, 1787), 103, and W. H. Walsh, "Immanuel Kant," in *Encyclopedia of Philosophy* (New York: Macmillan, 1967), 4:312–13.

31. Krochmal, *Moreh Nevukhei Ha-Zeman*, 12.

32. Krochmal, *Moreh Nevukhei Ha-Zeman*, 35.

33. Krochmal, *Moreh Nevukhei Ha-Zeman*, 140 and 142–43.

34. Krochmal, *Moreh Nevukhei Ha-Zeman*, 142–43. Taubes quotes a similar passage from 255 in *Judaism*, 160: "It was not necessary and perhaps not ever within the range of the possible for the ancients to remove all dross of the strange stories in the Talmud and it remained as it was until the depth of the last days, the time in which we live, when the

enlightened believer will understand well that according to its character and condition, the damage of hiding is greater perhaps than would have been the damage of making it public in former days."

35. Taubes was the first to point out Krochmal's use of this eschatological term.

36. For an attempt to show that Krochmal had an open-ended theory of cycles, see Ismar Schorsch, "Philosophy of History of Nachman Krochmal," *Judaism* 10 (1961): 237–45. For the counterview that Krochmal intended only three cycles, see Taubes, *Judaism*. While my argument suggests support of Taubes's position that the subordination of Jewish history to the cyclical laws of history ends with historical science, there is also evidence that Krochmal did not view this as a foregone conclusion. In chapter 1 of the *Moreh Nevukhei Ha-Zeman*, he hints that the three maladies of religion might be bringing about a new materialism. As a result of superstition, mysticism, and ritualization of religion, the enlightened have come to despise matters of the Spirit, thus perhaps signaling the new beginning of a spiritual decline. If one examines carefully the dialectical way in which spiritualism declined into materialism in earlier periods, as Krochmal presents it in chap. 7 (pp. 35–36), it becomes clear that he feared a similar development in his time. Historical science was the correct method to avert this disaster, but Krochmal was evidently uncertain about whether it would succeed.

Chapter 7

1. The most comprehensive study of the *Ghettogeschichten* is Wilhelm Stoffers, *Juden und Ghetto in der deutschen Literatur bis zum Ausgang des Weltkrieges*, Deutsche Quellen und Studien 12 (Graz, Austria: H. Stiasnys Söhne, 1939). There is evidence of Nazi influence in Stoffer's work. See also Mary Lynn Martin, "Karl Emil Franzos: His Views on Jewry as Reflected in His Writings on the Ghetto" (PhD diss., University of Wisconsin, Madison, 1969), esp. chap. 1, and M. Schiffmann, "Die deutsche Ghettogeschichten" (PhD diss., Vienna, 1924).

2. On the history of the ghetto, see Daniel B. Schwartz, *Ghetto: The History of a Word* (Cambridge, MA: Harvard University Press, 2019).

3. Henry Wassermann, "Jews, Bürgertum and bürgerliche Gesellschaft in a Liberal Era" [in Hebrew] (PhD diss., Jerusalem, 1978).

4. See, for example, Leopold Kompert's *Zwischen Ruinen* (Berlin: Otto Janke, 1875), Karl Emil Franzos, *Die Juden von Barnow* (Stuttgart, Germany: Bonz, 1894), and *Judith Trachtenberg* (Breslau, Germany: Trewendt, 1894), to mention only three.

5. Most biographies of Sacher-Masoch are characterized by extreme partisanship and are therefore less than reliable. See C. F. Schlichtegroll, *Sacher-Masoch und der Masochismus* (Dresden: Dohrn, 1901), James Cleugh, *The Marquis and the Chevalier* (New York: Melrose, 1951), and Richard Federman, *Sacher-Masoch oder die Selbstvernichtung* (Graz, Austria: Stiasny, 1961). More recently, see John K. Noyes, *Mastery of Submission: Inventions of Masochism* (Ithaca, NY: Cornell University Press, 1997); Gilles Deleuze, "De Sacher-Masoch au masochisme," *Multitudes* 25, no. 2 (2006): 19–30, and, more extensively, Gilles Deleuze, *Presentation de Sacher-Masoch* (Paris: Editions de Minuit, 1967). Most lexicons put Sacher-

Masoch's death in 1895, but Cleugh suggests that this was a result of rumors to conceal the fact that he was hospitalized in an insane asylum.

6. Leopold von Sacher-Masoch, "Die jüdischen Sekten in Galizien," *Deutsche Revue* 1, no. 3 (1889): 40–49. He calls the Zaddik "Liebmann," which may well be a corruption of Friedmann, the family name of the Sadagora Hasidic dynasty. If the visit was, in fact, in 1857, Sacher-Masoch would have seen Abraham, the son of Israel of Ruzhin (the founder of the sect) and Israel's successor in Sadagora after 1851.

7. Most of the early Jewish enlighteners treated Hasidism with undisguised contempt, and it was only at the very end of the nineteenth century and the early twentieth that writers such as M. Y. Berdichevsky, Y. L. Peretz, and Martin Buber began to find positive sides to Hasidism. See David Biale et al., *Hasidism: A New History* (Princeton, NJ: Princeton University Press, 2018), ch. 21.

8. The pamphlet was published in Leipzig in 1885.

9. Sacher-Masoch's contribution to *Auf der Höhe* was a lengthy story, "Die Frau von Soldan," in which the noble Soldan family is portrayed as international (the children speak Polish, Russian, German, French, and English). The story is not about Jews, however, so that Sacher-Masoch's philosemitism would have to be derived from elsewhere.

10. These memoranda have been published by Raphael Mahler in his *Hasidut ve-Haskala be-Galizia u-be-Polin* (Merhaviya, Israel: Kibbutz Ha-meuhad, 1961), 117–20, 436, 438, 449, 462.

11. Sacher-Masoch, "Pintschew und Mintschew," in *Judengeschichten* (Leipzig: J. F. Hartknoch, 1878), 83. The Esterka legend, which dates from the reign of King Kasimir in the fourteenth century, has both Polish and Jewish variants. See Chone Shmeruk, "Contacts between Polish and Yiddish Literature: The Story of Esterka and King Kasimir of Poland" [in Hebrew], in his *Sifrut Yidish be-Polin* (Jerusalem: Magnes, 1981), 205–79.

12. Sacher-Masoch, "Pintschew und Mintschew," 85.

13. Haim Schwarzmann, *Studies in Jewish and World Folklore* (Berlin: de Gruyter, 1968), index, s.v. "poretz."

14. Leopold von Sacher-Masoch, "Der Prostek," in *Ausgewählte Ghettogeschichten* (Leipzig: n.p., 1918), 88.

15. Schwarzmann, *Studies,* 1:264–66, 477; Ignatz Bernstein, *Jüdische Sprichwörter und Redensarten* (Hildesheim, Germany: G. Olms, 1969), 281–82.

16. In the story "Madame Leopard," in Leopold von Sacher-Masoch, *Contes juifs* (Paris: Quantin, 1888), 106n 2.

17. See Pawel Maciejko, *The Mixed Multitude: Jacob Frank and the Frankist Movement, 1755–1816* (Philadelphia: University of Pennsylvania Press, 2011).

18. Sacher-Masoch knew Frank's biography and even wrote a story based on it entitled "Der Prophet von Offenbach," *Frankfurter Zeitung,* (January 24, 1889). I thank Israel Bartal for this reference and for his assistance with my questions on Frankism.

19. De la Croix was the only author to give Miriam as the name of Shabbtai Zvi's third wife (all other sources either give no name or call her Sarah). Since Sacher-Masoch also calls

her Miriam, he may have consulted de la Croix. However, Beer gives both Sarah and Miriam, and so we need look no further for Sacher-Masoch's sources, since in all other respects he either copies or paraphrases Beer.

20. The Jews of Lemberg petitioned the Austrian government for the right to form a Jewish regiment to fight against the Polish rebels. See *Toldot Yehudei Lvov,* part 1, 239, in *Entsyklopedia shel Galuyot* (Jerusalem: Hevrat Entsyklopedia shel Galuyot, 1956), vol. 4.

21. Leopold von Sacher-Masoch, "Des Dalles des roten Pfeffermann," in *Ausgewählte Ghettogeschichten,* 285–95.

22. Sacher-Masoch, *Contes juifs,* 11–20.

23. Sacher-Masoch, *Ausgewählte Ghettogeschichten,* 3–18.

24. Leopold von Sacher-Masoch, *Liebesgeschichten aus verschiedenen Jahrhunderten* (Leipzig: Ernst Julius Günther, 1874), 130.

25. Richard Krafft-Ebing, *Psychopathia Sexualis* (Stuttgart: Enke, 1903), English translation based on 12th ed. (New York: Bell, 1965), 103–71.

26. Cleugh, *Marquis and the Chevalier,* and Deleuze, *Presentation de Sacher-Masoch,* 13–134.

27. It is interesting that while Western writers frequently portrayed Jewish women as "semitic," eastern European Jewish writers sometimes took non-Jewish models when they portrayed Jewish girls. For example, Rochelle in Sholem Alechem's *Stempenyu* is fair with blonde hair.

28. See my "Eros and Enlightenment," in *Eros and the Jews* (Berkeley: University of California Press, 1997), chap. 7.

29. Some of the exceptions are "Der Ilui," where a yeshiva student abandons Judaism in order to marry a Christian, and "Rabbi Abdon," where the enlightened son rejects an arranged marriage in favor of a poor girl whom he loves.

30. That Sacher-Masoch made no real differentiation between the women of his various "ethnic" stories is evident in the introduction to *Die grausame Frauen* (Dresden: H. R. Dohrn, 1901): 'There is a certain female type which has claimed me unceasingly since my youth. It is a woman with sphinx eyes which lust cruelly, a woman with a tiger's body who is worshipped by men even though she tortures and degrades them. This woman is always the same, whether in biblical clothing as she severs the head of Holofernes; whether under the sparkling armour of the bohemian Amazons who break their seducers on the wheel; or whether a Sultaness dressed in furs who has her lovers drowned in the waves of the Bosporus."

31. Leopold Sacher-Masoch, *Neue Ghettogeschichten* (Leipzig: Hartknoch, 1881), 35–39. A similar statement can be found in "Pintschew und Mintschew," where Esterka is described as "saucy and supple as the Jewish girls seldom are" (81).

32. Sacher-Masoch, *Neue Ghettogeschichten,* 55–70.

33. Leopold von Sacher-Masoch, *Liebesgeschichten aus verschiedenen Jahrhunderten* (Leipzig: Ernst Julius Günther, 1874), 83–120.

34. The Mapu story can be found in *Kol Kitve Avraham Mapu* (Tel Aviv: Dvir, 1939), 453–73. There is a curious passage in the story that reminds one of Sacher-Masoch where the

female demon Lillith proclaims that, following Shabbtai Zvi, the females will dominate the males (473).

35. The various versions of these stories are discussed by Gershom Scholem in *Sabbatai Sevi*, trans. R. J. Zwi Werblowsky (Princeton, NJ: Princeton University Press, 1973), 192n238.

36. Sacher-Masoch, *Liebesgeschichten*, 116.

37. Leopold von Sacher-Masoch, Prologue: "L'Errant," in *Le legs de Cain* (Paris: C. Levy, 1884). See also Deleuze, "De Sacher-Masoch au masochisme," 7–8, and Cleugh, *Marquis and the Chevalier*, 230–31.

38. Sacher-Masoch, *Contes juifs*, 105–16.

39. Sacher-Masoch, *Liebesgeschichten*, 123–54.

40. Some of his dates are wrong. He claims that King Michael Wisnowiezki died in 1675, while he really died in 1673. Johann Sobieski became king in 1674 (not 1675). The siege of Bialopol that he describes may be based on the battle of Trembowla, which took place in the antumn of 1675. See *The Cambridge History of Poland*, ed. W. F. Reddaway et al. (Cambridge: Cambridge University Press, 1950), 1:532–42. On Jewish self-defense in Poland, see Bernard Weinryb, *Jews of Poland* (Philadelphia: Jewish Publication Society, 1972), 191–92.

41. See the bibliographical essay on masochism in *American Handbook of Psychiatry*, 2nd ed., ed. Silvano Arieti (New York: Basic Books, 1974), 3:318–33.

Chapter 8

1. Gal. 5:20.

2. Peter Berger, *The Heretical Imperative: Contemporary Possibilities of Religious Affirmation* (Garden City, NY: Anchor Books, 1979), 28.

3. b. Sanhedrin 43a.

4. b. Hagigah 15a.

5. See Gershom Scholem, *Jewish Gnosticism, Merkabah Mysticism and Talmudic Tradition* (New York: Jewish Theological Seminary of America, 1960), 14–19, Yehuda Liebes, *Hata'o shel Elisha* (Jerusalem: Akadamon, 1990), and Alon Goshen-Gottstein, *The Sinner and the Amnesiac: The Rabbinic Invention of Elisha ben Abuya and Eleazar ben Arach* (Stanford, CA: Stanford University Press, 2000).

6. Shaye J. D. Cohen, "The Significance of Yavneh: Pharisees, Rabbis and the End of Jewish Sectarianism," *Hebrew Union College Annual* 55 (1984): 51. Daniel Boyarin has suggested that the Council at Yavneh may have even been invented in response to Nicaea. See his "A Tale of Two Synods: Nicaea, Yavneh, and the Making of Orthodox Judaism," *Exemplaria* 12, no. 1 (Spring 2000): 21–62.

7. Berger, *Heretical Imperative*, 12.

8. When I speak of "modern Jewish culture" or "modern Jewish thought," I am excluding writers who would define themselves as traditionalists (or Orthodox). Naturally, the very use of these kinds of categories already begs the question.

9. David Biale, *Gershom Scholem: Kabbalah and Counter-history* (Cambridge, MA: Harvard University Press, 1979).

10. On Arnold, see Erich Seeberg, *Gottfried Arnold* (Darmstadt: Wissenschaftliche Buchgesellschaft, 1964).

11. Daniel Schwartz, *The First Modern Jew: Spinoza and the History of an Image* (Princeton, NJ: Princeton University Press, 2012). See also Jonathan Skolnik, "Kaddish for Spinoza: Memory and Modernity in Celan and Heine," *New German Critique* 77 (Spring-Summer 1999): 169–86.

12. See, as a prime example, Berthold Auerbach, *Spinoza: Ein historische Roman* (Stuttgart: J. Scheible, 1837).

13. Heinrich Graetz, *History of the Jews,* trans. Bella Lowy (London: Myers, 1904), 5:125.

14. It is this sort of interpretation of Spinoza and other Marrano heretics as protomodern Jews that informs Yirmiyahu Yovel's stimulating *Spinoza and Other Heretics* (Princeton, NJ: Princeton University Press, 1989). For an excellent recent biography that puts Spinoza in his Sephardic and Dutch context, see Steven Nadler, *Spinoza: A Life* (Cambridge: Cambridge University Press, 1999).

15. This is what Amos Funkenstein argued in *Perceptions of Jewish History* (Berkeley: University of California Press, 1993), 36–49 (for his whole discussion of counterhistory).

16. See Jacob Katz, *Exclusiveness and Tolerance: Studies in Jewish-Gentile Relations in Medieval and Modern Times* (New York: Schocken Books, 1961), 167, 174, 177, 187.

17. Emden's statement comes from a letter he wrote to the Council of the Four Lands that appeared as an appendix to his *Seder Olam Rabbah ve-Zuta* and also in his *Sefer Shimush*. This translation is taken from Harvey Falk, "Rabbi Jacob Emden's Views on Christianity," *Journal of Ecumenical Studies* 19, no. 1 (Winter 1982): 107.

18. Moses Mendelssohn, *Jerusalem,* trans. Allan Arkush (Hanover, NH: Brandeis University Press, 1983), 134.

19. For a discussion of some nineteenth-century Jewish attitudes toward Jesus, see Walter Jacob, *Christianity through Jewish Eyes: The Quest for Common Ground* (Cincinnati, OH: Hebrew Union College Press, 1974), and, most importantly, Matthew Hoffman, *From Rebel to Rabbi: Reclaiming Jesus and the Making of Modern Jewish Culture* (Stanford, CA: Stanford University Press, 2007).

20. Susannah Heschel, *Abraham Geiger and the Jewish Jesus* (Chicago: University of Chicago Press, 1998).

21. Abraham Geiger, *Judaism and Its History,* trans. Maurice Mayer (London: M. Thalmessinger, 1866), 215.

22. In addition to the books of Jacobs and Hoffman mentioned above, some other synoptic works include Thomas Walker, *Jewish Views of Jesus* (New York: Arno, 1973), Shalom Ben-Chorin, "The Image of Jesus in Modern Judaism," *Journal of Ecumenical Studies* 11 (1974): 401–30, and for America specifically, George Berlin, *Defending the Faith: Nineteenth-Century American Jewish Writings on Christianity and Jesus* (Albany: State University of New York Press, 1989).

23. Joseph Klausner, *Jesus of Nazareth: His Life, Times, and Teaching,* trans. Herbert Danby (New York: Macmillan, 1925), 391–93.

24. See *Dos Naye Lebn* 1, no. 7 (June 1909), for the debate between Chaim Zhitlovsky and S. A. Ansky over whether Jesus ought to be adopted as a Jewish social revolutionary. This debate is analyzed by Hoffman in *From Rebel to Rabbi*.

25. Lamed Shapiro, "The Cross," in *The Jewish Government and Other Stories*, ed. and trans. Curt Leviant (New York: Twayne, 1971). See Avraham Nowersztern, "The Pogrom Theme in the Work of Lamed Shapiro" [in Yiddish], *Di Goldene Keyt* 106 (1981), and David Roskies's chapter "Jews on the Cross," in his *Against the Apocalypse: Responses to Catastrophe in Modern Jewish Culture* (Cambridge, MA: Harvard University Press, 1984). This material is reviewed and analyzed anew by Hoffman in *From Rebel to Rabbi*, and I thank him again for many of these references.

26. Roskies, *Against the Apocalypse*.

27. See Zivia Amishai-Maisels, "The Jewish Jesus," *Journal of Jewish Art* 9 (1983): 84–104.

28. Rashi on Isaiah 53.

29. Shalom Spiegel, *The Last Trial: On the Legends and Lore of the Command to Abraham to Offer Isaac as a Sacrifice; the Akedah* (New York: Schocken Books, 1967). The debate over the relationship between Judaism and Christianity that these chronicles contain was reawakened in 1993 by Israel Yuval with his essay "Vengeance and Damnation, Blood and Defamation: From Jewish Martyrdom to Blood Libel Accusations" [in Hebrew], *Zion* 55, no. 1 (1993): 33–90. See further the double issue of *Zion* 59, nos. 2–3 (1994), devoted to responses to Yuval and, more recently, Israel Yuval, *Two Nations in Your Womb: Perceptions of Jews and Christians in Late Antiquity and the Middle Ages* (Berkeley: University of California Press, 2006).

30. See the excellent translation of the chronicles in Robert Chazan, *European Jewry and the First Crusade* (Berkeley: University of California Press, 1987).

31. Translation from Dan Ben-Amos and Jerome Mintz, eds. and trans., *In Praise of the Baal Shem Tov* (Bloomington: Indiana University Press, 1979), 86–87.

32. The various sources on Elisha are discussed in Liebes, *Hata'o shel Elisha*.

33. Richard Rubenstein, *After Auschwitz* (Indianapolis, IN: Bobbs-Merrill, 1966), 68.

34. See M. D. Hoffman, *Toledot Elisha ben Avuyah* (1880), and S. Back, *Elisha ben Abuya—Acher* (1891).

35. See Michael Brenner, "Gnosis and History: Polemics of German-Jewish Identity," *New German Critique* 77 (Spring-Summer 1999): 47–50 (for Graetz).

36. Heinrich Graetz, *Gnosticismus und Judenthum* (Krotoschin: B. L. Monasch, 1846), 63.

37. Graetz, *Gnosticismus und Judenthum*, 70–71.

38. The book continues to be used: my daughter read it in the eighth grade of her Jewish day school.

39. See Milton Steinberg, *A Partisan Guide to the Jewish Problem* (Indianapolis, IN: Bobbs-Merrill, 1945), esp. 174–82.

40. I thank Jeffrey Gurock for drawing my attention to this little-known fact. See his *A Modern Heretic and a Traditional Community: Mordecai M. Kaplan, Orthodoxy and American Judaism* (New York: Columbia University Press, 1997).

41. Milton Steinberg, *Basic Judaism* (New York: Harcourt Brace Jovanovich, 1947), 11.

42. Steinberg, *Basic Judaism*, 43. As the end of this quotation suggests, Steinberg turns out to be something of a closet socialist!

43. Steinberg, *Basic Judaism*, 42.

44. Steinberg, *Partisan Guide*, 193.

45. Needless to say, more recent scholarly work on rabbinic sources has increasingly thrown doubt on the historicity of many of the sources that Steinberg uses. See especially the work of Jacob Neusner and Daniel Boyarin.

46. Milton Steinberg, *As a Driven Leaf* (New York: Bobbs-Merrill, 1939), 355.

47. JT Hagigah 2:1.

48. Midrash on Proverbs 31:10.

49. This, of course, was not true of Spinoza, who was quite well connected with intellectuals of his day, and the myth of the solitary lens grinder does not stand up. More interesting is that Steinberg's Elisha loses his wife but does not have the daughter who is attested in rabbinic sources.

50. Steinberg, *As a Driven Leaf*, 472.

51. Steinberg, *As a Driven Leaf*, 472.

Chapter 9

1. Gershom Scholem, *Tagebücher*, August 17, 1914 (Frankfurt: Jüdischer Verlag, 1995), 1:31–32.

2. Scholem, *Tagebücher*, May 22, 1915, 1:119–21. See further Michael Brenner, "From Self-Declared Messiah to Scholar of Messianism: The Recently Published Diaries of Young Gerhard Scholem in a New Light," *Jewish Social Studies*, n.s., 3, no. 1 (Fall 1996): 177–82. Brenner failed to notice the earlier reference to Shabbtai Zvi.

3. Gershom Scholem, *From Berlin to Jerusalem*, trans. Harry Zohn (New York: Schocken Books, 1980), 36–37.

4. Gershom Scholem, "Redemption through Sin," trans. Hillel Halkin, in Gershom Scholem's *The Messianic Idea in Judaism* (New York: Schocken Books, 1971), 78.

5. Shmuel Werses, *Haskalah ve-Shabta'ut* (Jerusalem: Merkaz Shazar, 1988).

6. Edward W. Said, *Orientalism* (New York: Pantheon, 1978), 203.

7. Said, *Orientalism*, 12.

8. An important contribution is John Efron's *German Jewry and the Allure of the Sephardic* (Princeton, NJ: Princeton University Press, 2016). Efron focuses primarily on German Jews' views of medieval Spain and not on the Orient generally. For some other observations with a focus on German Jews, see Paul Mendes-Flohr, "*Fin-de-Siècle* Orientalism, the *Ostjuden* and the Aesthetics of Jewish Self-Affirmation," *Studies in Contemporary Jewry* 1 (1984): 96–139. Further on German Jewish literature and the Orient, see Nina Berman, *Orientalismus, Kolonialismus und Moderne: Zum Bild des Orients in der deutschsprachigen Kultur um 1900* (Stuttgart: Mezler and Poeschel, 1997). For some general observations focused on literary history, see Ammiel Alcalay, "Exploding Identities: Notes on Ethnicity and Literary

History," *Jewish Social Studies*, n.s., 1, no. 2 (Winter 1995): 15–27. For some French Jewish attitudes, see Michel Abitol, "The Encounter between French Jewry and the Jews of North Africa: Analysis of a Discourse," in *The Jews in Modern France*, ed. Frances Malino and Bernard Wasserstein (Hanover, NH: University Press of New England, 1985). See also Daniel J. Schroeter, "Orientalism and the Jews of the Mediterranean," *Journal of Mediterranean Studies* 4, no. 2 (1994): 183–96. Finally, Gil Anidjar has suggested how the category of Jewish Orientalism might fruitfully be applied to a critical analysis of the historiography of the Kabbalah. See his "Jewish Mysticism Alterable and Unalterable: On Orienting Kabbalah Studies and the 'Zohar of Christian Spain,'" *Jewish Social Studies* 3, no. 1 (Fall 1996): 89–157.

9. Martin Buber, "The Spirit of the Orient and Judaism," in *On Judaism*, trans. Eva Jospe (New York: Schocken Books, 1967), 56–78.

10. Mendes-Flohr, "*Fin-de-Siècle* Orientalism."

11. See Michael Brenner, *The Renaissance of Jewish Culture in Weimar Germany* (New Haven, CT: Yale University Press, 1996), 135–42. Brenner focuses primarily on the positive identification of the Oriental Jew, while I believe that the relationship was more complex.

12. For a very useful recent survey of the relationship of Zionists to the Orient, see Amnon Rubenstein, *Me-Herzl ad-Rabin ve-Halah* (Jerusalem: Schocken Books, 1997), 71–103.

13. Aron Rodrigue, *French Jews, Turkish Jews: The Alliance Israelite Universelle and the Politics of Jewish Schooling in Turkey, 1860–1925* (Bloomington: Indiana University Press, 1990).

14. Steven Aschheim, *Brothers and Strangers: The East European Jew in German and German Jewish Consciousness, 1800–1923* (Madison: University of Wisconsin Press, 1982).

15. Ismar Schorsch, "The Myth of Sephardic Supremacy," *Leo Baeck Institute Year Book* 34 (1989): 47–66; Efron, *German Jewry*.

16. Esriel Carlebach, *Exotische Juden* (Berlin: Heine-Bund, 1932).

17. Josef Kastein, *Shabbtai Zewi: Der Messias von Ismir* (Berlin: Rowohlt, 1930), 155, and *The Messiah of Ismir: Shabbtai Zevi*, trans. Huntley Paterson (New York: Viking Press, 1931), 133. The translation here is substantially mine.

18. Kastein, *Shabbtai Zewi*, 220.

19. Kastein, *Shabbtai Zewi*, 228. Emphasis added.

20. Kastein, *Shabbtai Zewi*, 230.

21. Heinrich Graetz, *History of the Jews*, trans. Bella Lowy (London: Myers, 1904), 5:125.

22. Hannah Arendt suggested such a political interpretation of Sabbatianism in a few pregnant sentences in an essay in 1946 in "The Jewish State: Fifty Years After," reprinted in *The Jew as Pariah*, ed. Ron Feldman (New York: Grove Press, 1978), 166–68.

23. Kastein, *Shabbtai Zewi*, 163.

24. Kastein, *Shabbtai Zewi*, 16.

25. Kastein, *Shabbtai Zewi*, 376. For Kastein's general view of Jewish history, see his *History and Destiny of the Jews*, trans. Huntley Paterson (Garden City, NY: Garden City Publishing, 1936)

26. Kastein, *Shabbtai Zewi*, 371.

27. Shai Ish-Hurwitz, "Ha-Hasidut ve-ha-Haskalah," *He-Atid* 2 (1909), 96, and *Me-Ayin u-Le'ayin* (Berlin: Ahisefer, 1914), 259ff. On Ish-Hurwitz, see Stanley Nash, *In Search of Hebraism—Shai Hurvitz and His Polemics in the Hebrew Press* (Leiden: Brill, 1980), and Werses, *Haskalah*, 9, 253, 259–60.

28. Theodor Herzl, *Yoman*, Kitve Herzl (Tel Aviv: Nyuman, 1960), 2:371. For Herzl's other statements on Sabbatianism, see Werses, *Haskalah*, 254–58.

29. Theodor Herzl, *Altneuland*, trans. Paula Arnold (Haifa, Israel: Haifa Publishing, 1961), 82.

30. Herzl, *Yoman*, 1:89. The importance of technology in Herzl's conception of Zionism is also evident in *Der Judenstaat* (Osnabruck, Germany: Ozeller, 1968).

31. See Herzl, *Altneuland*, 151, where Herzl refers to emissaries sent to eastern Europe, America, and Algeria.

32. I am indebted to Michael Gluzman's brilliant work on *Altneuland* in which he contrasts the homoerotic relationship between Friedrich and Kingscourt and the heterosexual frame of the novel. Gluzman is the first to notice how central sexual identity and desire are to Herzl's narrative. See his *Ha-guf ha-tsiyoni: Le'umiyut, migdar, u-miniyut ba-sifrut ha-yisraelit ha-hadasha* (Tel Aviv: Ha-Kibutz ha-Me'uhad, 2007).

33. Said, *Orientalism*, 186–90.

34. Kastein, *Shabbtai Zewi*, 132.

35. Kastein, *Shabbtai Zewi*, 136.

36. Kastein, *Shabbtai Zewi*, 183–85.

37. See Ada Rapoport-Albert, *Women and the Messianic Heresy of Sabbatai Zevi* (Oxford: Littman Library of Jewish Civilization, 2011).

38. Israel Zangwill, *Dreamers of the Ghetto* (London: William Heinnemann, 1924), 113.

39. Zangwill, *Dreamers of the Ghetto*, 131.

40. Zangwill, *Dreamers of the Ghetto*, 132.

41. Zangwill, *Dreamers of the Ghetto*, 159–60.

42. Zangwill, *Dreamers of the Ghetto*, 160.

43. See my interpretation of the play, "The Melting Pot and Beyond: Jews and the Politics of American Identity," in *Insider/Outsider: American Jews and Multiculturalism*, ed. David Biale, Susannah Heschel, and Michael Galchinsky (Berkeley: University of California Press, 1998), 17–33.

44. See Joseph H. Udelson, *Dreamer of the Ghetto: The Life and Works of Israel Zangwill* (Tuscaloosa: University of Alabama Press, 1990). The theme of intermarriage among early Zionists deserves investigation. Max Nordau was another Zionist leader who married a Christian.

45. S. Ash, *Dramatishe Shriften* (Vilna, Lithuania: B. Kletzkin, 1922), 1:82. Translation based on Sholom Ash, *Shabbtai Zevi* (Philadelphia: Jewish Publication Society, 1930), 28. The translation, by Florence Whyte and George Rapall Noyes, is said to be "from the Rus-

sian version." On the whole, this translation is filled with either deliberate or accidental errors.

46. Ash, *Dramatishe Shriften*, 1:114 and 116. For an earlier statement that Shabbtai Zvi considered himself a "God-Man," see S. Meschelssohn, *Sabbathey Zvy* (Galgau, Poland: S. Meschelssohn, 1856), 38.

47. Ash, *Dramatishe Shriften*, 118.

48. Ash, *Dramatishe Shriften*, 126.

49. For the older view, see Solomon Liptzin, *Germany's Stepchildren* (Cleveland, OH: Meridian, 1961), 173–84. Michael Brenner argues that Wassermann was, in fact, searching for a positive Jewish identity. See his *Jewish Renaissance*, 133–36.

50. Brenner, *Jewish Renaissance*, 135, quoting an essay Wassermann wrote for the almanac of the Prague Zionist student organization, reprinted in Jacob Wassermann, *Deutscher und Jude: Reden und Schriften* (Heidelberg: Lambert Schneider, 1984), 23.

51. Brenner, *Jewish Renaissance*, 136, quoting Wassermann's letter to the *Jüdische Rundschau* 94 (November 27, 1928): 660.

52. Jacob Wassermann, *The Dark Pilgrimage*, trans. Cyrus Brooks (New York: Liveright, 1933), 24.

53. Wassermann, *Dark Pilgrimage*, 67.

54. Wassermann, *Dark Pilgrimage*, 79–80.

55. Jacob Wassermann, *My Life as German and Jew*, trans. S. N. Brainin (New York: Coward-McMan, 1933), 127.

56. Wassermann, *My Life*, 37.

57. Scholem, *Tagebücher*, 1:135–36.

58. See my *Gershom Scholem: Kabbalah and Counter-history* (Cambridge, MA: Harvard University Press, 1979), chap. 3.

59. Scholem, *Tagebücher*, 1:198–99. Emphasis in original.

60. The same might be said for his neglect of the erotic theology of Sabbatianism (as opposed to Frankism), discussed in detail by Avraham Elqayam, "To Know Messiah: The Dialectics of Sexual Discourse in the Messianic Thought of Nathan of Gaza," *Tarbiz* 65, no. 4 (July-September 1996): 637–70.

61. I distinguish here between the role of women and the role of female symbolism, especially the *shekhinah*, to which, of course, Scholem devoted considerable attention.

62. Gershom Scholem, *Major Trends in Jewish Mysticism*, 3rd ed. (New York: Schocken Books, 1961), 37.

63. Anidjar, "Jewish Mysticism." I am very much in debt to this fine essay for suggesting the ways in which the twentieth-century study of Kabbalah may be filled with Orientalist assumptions.

64. Scholem, "Redemption through Sin," 126.

65. See my *Gershom Scholem*, chap. 8, and "The Threat of Messianism: An Interview with Gershom Scholem," *New York Review of Books*, August 14, 1980 (see chapter 13 below).

66. Gershom Scholem, "The Messianic Idea in Judaism," in *Messianic Idea in Judaism*, 35–36.

Chapter 10

1. Leo Strauss, *Persecution and the Art of Writing* (Glencoe, IL: Free Press, 1952), 21.
2. Karl Mannheim, *Ideology and Utopia*, trans. Louis Wirth and Edward Shils (New York: Oxford University Press, 1971).
3. Strauss, *Persecution*, 19–21.
4. See, for instance, Leo Strauss, "How to Study Spinoza's *Theologico-Political Treatise*," in *Persecution*, 143, and, further, Werner Dannhauser, "Leo Strauss: Becoming Naive Again," *American Scholar* 44 (1974–75): 638. It should be noted that Strauss distinguishes his method from Spinoza's despite a basic similarity between them. See Strauss, *Persecution*, 147. For an analysis of Strauss's relation to his subjects, see Allan Bloom, "Leo Strauss: September 20, 1899–October 18, 1973," *Political Theory* 2 (1974): 381–87. For a critique of Strauss's hermeneutics, see M. F. Burnyeat, review of *Studies in Platonic Political Philosophy*, by Leo Strauss, *New York Review of Books*, May 30, 1985, 30–36.
5. Leo Strauss, *Spinoza's Critique of Religion*, trans. E. M. Sinclair (New York: Schocken Books, 1965), 1. For an analysis of Strauss as a Jewish thinker, I am indebted to an unpublished essay by Michael Morgan (Dept. of Philosophy, Indiana University), "The Curse of Historicity: The Role of History in Leo Strauss' Jewish Thought."
6. On Weimar culture in general, see Peter Gay, *Weimar Culture: The Outsider as Insider* (New York: Harper and Row, 1968). On Weimar Jews, see Donald Niewyk, *Jews in Weimar Germany* (Baton Rouge: Louisiana State University Press, 1980). For Weimar intellectuals (especially Jews) as heretics and antinomians, see Benjamin Lazier, *God Interrupted: Heresy and the European Imagination between the World Wars* (Princeton, NJ: Princeton University Press, 2008).
7. See Martin Jay, *The Dialectical Imagination* (Boston: Little, Brown, 1973).
8. For Schoeps's political position, see his *Wir deutschen Juden* (Berlin: Vortrupp, 1934). On Schoeps, see George Mosse, "The Influence of the Volkish Idea on German Jewry," in his *Germans and Jews* (New York: Fertig, 1970).
9. See Scholem's autobiography, *From Berlin to Jerusalem* (New York: Schocken Books, 1980).
10. In his *Stern der Erlösung* (Frankfurt: J. Kauffmann, 1921), Rosenzweig argues against rooting Judaism in the soil of a state; the "eternal people" must be divorced from the politics of this world. But in constructing this argument, Rosenzweig defined Judaism not as a system of beliefs but as a "blood community." Unlike other *Blut und Boden* writers of the time, Rosenzweig's brand of nationalism divorced the *Blut* from the *Boden*.
11. Buber and Arendt were among the leaders of the Ichud group, which opposed political Zionism in the 1940s and sought the establishment of a "binational" state in Palestine.
12. Strauss, *Spinoza's Critique of Religion*, 5.

13. Strauss, *Spinoza's Critique of Religion*, 6.

14. For Scholem's stance on Jewish messianism, see my *Gershom Scholem: Kabbalah and Counter-history* (Cambridge, MA: Harvard University Press, 1979), chap. 7.

15. Strauss, *Spinoza's Critique of Religion*, 6.

16. Strauss wrote the introductory essay to the English translation of Hermann Cohen's *Religion of Reason Out of the Sources of Judaism*, trans. Simon Kaplan (New York: F. Ungar, 1972); he states there, no doubt autobiographically: "I grew up in an environment in which Cohen was the center of attraction for philosophically minded Jews who were devoted to Judaism; he was the master whom they revered" (xxiii).

17. Strauss, introduction to Cohen, *Religion of Reason*, chap. 13.

18. Hannah Arendt, *The Origins of Totalitarianism* (New York: Harcourt, Brace, 1951), 74, 240. See further 301. On these themes in Arendt, see chapter 11 below.

19. Leo Strauss, introduction to *Persecution*, 16–17. See further Leo Strauss, *The City and Man* (Chicago: Rand, McNally, 1964), Strauss's posthumously published *Studies in Platonic Political Philosophy* (Chicago: University of Chicago Press, 1983), and, finally, Burnyeat's critique of this reading of Plato in his review of *Studies*.

20. *Louis Ginzberg: Jubilee Volume on the Occasion of His Seventieth Birthday* (New York: American Academy of Jewish Research, 1945), 357–93.

21. See Ernst Bloch, *Atheism in Christianity*, trans. J. T. Swann (New York: Herder and Herder, 1972); Gershom Scholem, *Major Trends in Jewish Mysticism*, 3rd ed. (New York: Schocken Books, 1961); Hans Joachim Schoeps, *Das Judenchristentum* (Bern, Switzerland: Franke, 1964); Hans Jonas, *Gnosis und spätantiker Geist* (Göttingen, Germany: Vandehoek and Ruprecht, 1934).

22. See my *Gershom Scholem*, introduction and chap. 9.

23. See Walter Benjamin, "Theses on the Philosophy of History," in *Illuminations*, trans. Harry Zohn (New York: Schocken Books, 1969), 253–64.

24. See Bloom, "Leo Strauss," 390. Bloom does not provide a source for this quotation from Strauss.

25. Strauss, *Persecution*, 38–94.

26. Scholem understood the connection between his own method and that of Strauss, as he wrote in his *On the Kabbalah and Its Symbolism*, trans. R. Mannheim (New York: Schocken Books, 1969), 51n1. Scholem knew Strauss in the years before he moved to Palestine in 1923. See his *Walter Benjamin—Die Geschichte einer Freundschaft* (Frankfurt: Suhrkamp, 1975), 126.

27. Strauss, *Persecution*, 31–32.

28. A logician might easily find severe problems of self-reference in the methods of all these thinkers, a circularity in deriving one's method from one's sources. Yet from the point of view of the sociology of philosophy, it stands to reason that the desire to appropriate an alien tradition in opposition to conventional wisdom would give rise to such paradoxes. I might add parenthetically that my own use of Strauss's categories to understand Strauss falls

into the same logical sticky wicket. I have considered some of the consequences of this problem in my *Gershom Scholem*, chap. 9.

29. I refer to Burnyeat's review of Strauss, *Studies*.

Chapter 11

1. The controversy even provoked a whole book against her. See Jacob Robinson, *And the Crooked Shall Be Made Straight* (New York: Macmillan, 1965). Robinson is the only author who deals with the legal issues raised by Arendt, but he becomes entangled in the technicalities and misses the real innovation Arendt proposes. For other important articles attacking Arendt, see particularly Norman Podhoretz, "Hannah Arendt on Eichmann," *Commentary*, September 1963, 201–8, and Benjamin Schwartz, "The Religion of Politics," *Dissent* 17 (1970): 144–61. Schwartz is the only author who has tried to understand Arendt's position on the Eichmann case in the light of her other writings. Yet Schwartz consistently misinterprets Arendt to the point where he gives a caricature of her position. For instance, he asserts that she holds that being a citizen is of higher value to her than being merely human, when the opposite is the case (see below).

2. For a careful and comprehensive discussion of the legal aspects of the case, see Peter Papadatos, *The Eichmann Trial* (New York: Praeger, 1964). There is more recently a large literature on the trial and Arendt's interpretation of it. See Ruggero D'Alessandro, *The Thinker and the Specialist: Hannah Arendt and the Eichmann Trial* (Milan: Mimesis International, 2015); Richard Golsan and Sarah Misemer, eds., *The Trial That Never Ends: Hannah Arendt's Eichmann in Jerusalem in Retrospect* (Toronto: University of Toronto Press, 2017); Deborah E. Lipstadt, *The Eichmann Trial* (New York: Schocken Books, 2011). On Eichmann himself, see David Cesarani, *Becoming Eichmann: Rethinking the Life, Crimes and Trial of Adolf Eichmann* (Cambridge, MA: Da Capo Press, 2004), and Bettina Stangneth, *Eichmann before Jerusalem: The Unexamined Life of a Mass Murderer* (New York: Knopf, 2014).

3. Hannah Arendt, *Eichmann in Jerusalem: A Report on the Banality of Evil* (New York: Penguin Books, 2006), 259.

4. Arendt, *Eichmann in Jerusalem*, 262–63.

5. Hannah Arendt, "Herzl and Lazare" (July 1942), "Zionism Reconsidered" (October 1945), and "The Jewish State: Fifty Years After" (May 1946), all reprinted in *The Jew as Pariah*, ed. Ron H. Feldman (New York: Grove Press, 1978), 125–30, 131–63, and 164–77 respectively. For an expanded edition of Arendt's Jewish writings, see Hannah Arendt, *The Jewish Writings*, ed. Jerome Kohn and Ron H. Feldman (New York: Schocken Books, 2007). While chief editor of Schocken Books, she edited and published Lazare's *Job's Dungheap* (New York: Schocken Books, 1948).

6. Arendt, "Herzl and Lazare," 128.

7. Arendt, *Eichmann in Jerusalem*, 278–79.

8. Arendt, *Eichmann in Jerusalem*, 125.

9. Arendt, *Eichmann in Jerusalem*, 277. See Yosal Rogat, *The Eichmann Trial and the Rule of Law* (Santa Barbara, CA: Center for the Study of Democratic Institutions, 1961).

10. Arendt, *Eichmann in Jerusalem*, 294–95.

11. See Leo Strauss, *Natural Right and History* (Chicago: University of Chicago Press, 1953). Arendt differs from Strauss in that she tends to glorify the polis and criticize Plato on most issues, while he is more squarely a Platonist. For a general history of the concept of natural law, see Otto Gierke's classic study, *Natural Law and the Theory of Society* (Cambridge: Cambridge University Pres, 1934).

12. Arendt, *Eichmann in Jerusalem*, 268–69.

13. The two best analyses of the Nuremberg Charter, the trial, and subsequent trials (including Eichmann) are Robert Woetzel, *The Nuremberg Trials in International Law* (New York: Praeger, 1962), and Lawrence Douglas, *Memory and Justice: Making Law and History in the Trials of the Holocaust* (New Haven, CT: Yale University Press, 2001).

14. Hannah Arendt, *The Origins of Totalitarianism* (New York: Meridian Press, 1958), 290–302.

15. Arendt, *Origins of Totalitarianism*, 300, 299.

16. Arendt, *Origins of Totalitarianism*, 299.

17. Arendt, *Origins of Totalitarianism*, 301.

18. See particularly Part II, "The Public and Private Realm," in Hannah Arendt, *The Human Condition* (Chicago: University of Chicago Press, 1958), 23–71.

19. Arendt, *Human Condition*, 173–76.

20. See her essay "Karl Jaspers: Citizen of the World?," in *Men in Dark Times* (New York: Harcourt, Brace, 1968), 71–80.

21. Arendt, *Origins of Totalitarianism*, 74, 240.

22. See especially Arendt, "Zionism Reconsidered."

23. Arendt, *Origins of Totalitarianism*, 74.

24. Hannah Arendt, "We Refugees," in *Jew as Pariah*, 65–66; originally published in *Menorah Journal*, January 1943, 69–77.

25. Hannah Arendt, "We Refugees," 66.

26. The exchange with Scholem was first published in *Encounter* 22, no. 124 (1964): 51–53, and was reprinted in Arendt, *Jew as Pariah*, 240–51.

27. Arendt, exchange with Scholem, 246.

Chapter 12

1. In *Geist und Werk aus der Werkstatt unserer Autoren. Festschrift zum 75. Geburtstag von Dr. Daniel Brody* (Zurich: Rhein-Verlag, 1958), 209–15.

2. Gershom Scholem, *Judaica III: Studien zur jüdischen Mystik* (Frankfurt: Suhrkamp, 1973), 264–71. The tenth aphorism was expanded in this version.

3. Two writers in other languages who treat Scholem's aphoristic writings are Ernst Simon, "Das dunkle Licht, Gershom Scholems Judaica III," *Mitteilungsblatt des Irgun*

Olej Markaz Europa, April 5, 1974 5–6, and Jürgen Habermas, "Die verkleidete Tora. Rede zum 80. Geburtstag von Gershom Scholem," *Merkur*, January 1978, 96–104. See also Ernst Simon, "Uber einige theologische Sätze von Gershom Scholem," *Mitteilungsblatt*, December 8, 1972, 3ff., and December 15, 1972, 4ff.

4. See my *Gershom Scholem: Kabbalah and Counter-history* (Cambridge, MA: Harvard University Press, 1979), esp. chap. 4.

5. An excellent treatment of this theme is by Leon Goldstein, *Historical Knowing* (Austin: University of Texas Press, 1976). Goldstein argues against the view that historians know the past in the same way as natural scientists claim to know nature. Since the past can never be recovered perceptually, historical knowing must be an act of reconstruction based on interpretation of sources. Goldstein therefore gives a modern philosophical expression to the "crisis of historicism" of the early twentieth century.

6. I have chosen to translate *Sätze* as "aphorisms" rather than "sentences" (the literal translation) or "theses." Although, as I argue below, Scholem clearly wrote these aphorisms with Benjamin's "Theses on the Philosophy of History," he avoided using that word.

7. First published in *Neue Rundschau* 61, no. 3 (1950), and translated into English in Walter Benjamin, *Illuminations*, trans. Harry Zohn (New York: Schocken Books, 1969), 253–64.

8. First published in German by Schocken Verlag in 1935 and available in a bilingual edition, *Parables and Paradoxes* (New York: Schocken Books, 1958). On Scholem's and Benjamin's interpretations of Kafka, see Robert Alter, *Necessary Angels: Modernity in Kafka, Benjamin and Scholem* (Cambridge, MA: Harvard University Press, 1991), and my *Gershom Scholem: Master of the Kabbalah* (New Haven, CT: Yale University Press, 2018), 110–11, 118–19, 124.

9. See Moses Nachmanides, introduction to his *Commentary on the Torah*.

10. Zohar, I, 15a.

11. Gershom Scholem, *Die Geheimnisse der Schöpfung* (Berlin: Schocken Verlag, 1935), 45.

12. For Buber's view in relation to Jewish texts, see his *Geschichten des Rabbi Nachman* (Frankfurt: Ruetten und Loening, 1906).

13. Bacharach's name was actually Naphtali ben Jacob Elchanan Bacharach. He lived in the first half of the seventeenth century, and his *Emek Ha-Melek*, which was based largely on the writings of Israel Sarug, brought together some of the variant interpretations of Lurianic Kabbalah. It was one of the most widely distributed of the post-Lurianic texts and drew considerable criticism from those who regarded its interpretation of Luria as faulty. See Scholem's article on Bacharach in the *Encyclopedia Judaica* (Jerusalem: Keter, 1972) and in his *Sabbatai Sevi* (Princeton, NJ: Princeton University Press, 1973), 68–73.

14. Nahman of Bratslav, *Likute ha-Moharan* (Jerusalem: Rabbi Israel Odesser Foundation, 2008), sec. 64.

15. Interestingly, Scholem derives this notion of the necessity of the oral law to make the written law "usable" not from a Jewish source but from the nineteenth-century Christian Kabbalist Franz Josef Molitor. See his *Philosophie der Geschichte oder über die Tradition*

(Frankfurt: Verlag des Hermannschen Buchhandlung, 1827–57), 1:4. Scholem quotes Molitor to this effect in *The Messianic Idea in Judaism and Other Essays on Jewish Spirituality* (New York: Schocken Books, 1971), 285.

16. See Isaiah Tishby, *Torat ha-Ra' ve-ha-Klippah be-Kabbalat ha-Ari* (Jerusalem: Magnes Press, 1984).

17. Nathan's ideas can be found in his penitential devotions and in his *Derush ha-Taninim* ("Treatise on the Dragons"). See Tishby's analysis of the devotions in *Tarbiz* 15 (1944): 161–80 and Scholem, *Sabbatai Sevi*, 300–311.

18. Scholem has treated this issue in a number of places. Perhaps his most philosophical presentation is his "Schöpfung aus Nichts und die Selbstverschränkung Gottes," in *Über einige Grundbegriffe des Judentums* (Frankfurt: Suhrkamp, 1970), 53–90. On the various treatments of the relationship of *ain-sof* and *ayin*, see Isaiah Tishby, *Mishnat ha-Zohar* (Jerusalem: Mosad Bialik, 1971), 1:107–11.

19. See my *Gershom Scholem: Kabbalah and Counter-History*, chaps. 3 and 4.

20. See particularly Gershom Scholem, *Major Trends in Jewish Mysticism*, 3rd ed. (New York: Schocken Books, 1961), chap. 1. This conclusion has been vigorously contested by Moshe Idel in *Kabbalah: New Perspectives* (New Haven, CT: Yale University Press, 1989), 59–73 and elsewhere.

21. For Scholem's theory of the influence of Lurianic Kabbalah, see his *Sabbatai Sevi*, 22–93; for his views on the impact of Sabbatianism, see his *Major Trends*, chap. 8, and "Redemption through Sin," in *Messianic Idea*, 78–141. Against Scholem, see Idel, *Kabbalah*, 256–60.

22. Scholem, *Messianic Idea*, 21.

23. See in particular Gershom Scholem, "Das Ringen zwischen dem biblischen Gott und dem Gott Plotinus in der alten Kabbala," in *Über einige Grundbegriffe*, 9–52.

24. For Scholem's treatment of this question in the Kabbalah, see Gershom Scholem, "The Name of God and the Linguistic Theory of the Kabbala," *Diogenes* 79 (1972): 59–80, and 80 (1972): 164–94.

25. Moses Cordovero (1522–70). Cordovero attempted a systematic summary of the Kabbalah in his *Pardes Rimonim* (1592; repr. Jerusalem: n.p., 1962). For a comprehensive treatment of Cordovero's theology and particularly the question of pantheism in his system, see Joseph Ben Shlomo, *Torat he-Elohut shel Rabbi Moshe Cordovero* (Jerusalem: Mosad Bialik, 1965).

26. The quotation attributed to one of the "greatest Kabbalists" may refer to Abraham Abulafia, whose mysticism of names was theurgic or magical. See Moshe Idel, *The Mystical Experience in Abraham Abulafia* (Albany: SUNY Press, 1988).

27. Gershom Scholem, "Offener Brief an den Verfasser der Schrift 'Jüdischer Glaube in dieser Zeit,'" *Bayerische Israelitische Gemeindezeitung*, August 15, 1932, 241–44. The essay is perhaps the best statement of Scholem's own theological position. See my *Gershom Scholem: Kabbalah and Counter-History*, 94–100.

28. Jonas Wehle (1752–1823) was the leader of the Frankist circle in Prague. See Gershom Scholem, "Jacob Frank and the Frankists," in *Encyclopedia Judaica*.

29. I published this letter for the first time in my *Gershom Scholem: Kabbalah and Counter-History*, 74–76 (in German, 215–16). It has since received numerous interpretations.

30. See Scholem, "Redemption through Sin."

31. The Benjamin essay "Franz Kafka: On the Tenth Anniversary of His Death" appears in translation in *Illuminations*, 111–40. The letters between Scholem and Benjamin on Kafka appear in Walter Benjamin and Gershom Scholem, *Briefwechsel* (Frankfurt: Suhrkamp, 1980), starting on May 6, 1934, and continuing through the summer of that year. They have been translated to English as *The Correspondence of Walter Benjamin and Gershom Scholem, 1932–1940*, trans. Gary Smith and Andre Lefevere (Cambridge, MA: Harvard University Press, 1992).

32. Scholem to Benjamin, July 17, 1934, in Benjamin and Scholem, *Briefwechsel*, 157–58.

33. Letter to Scholem of June 12, 1938. Published in English translation in Benjamin, *Illuminations*, 141–45 (quotation from 144).

34. Biale, *Gershom Scholem: Kabbalah and Counter-history*, 76.

Chapter 14

1. Some of the early writings of Zvi Yehudah Kook have been collected in *Le-Netivot Yisrael*, 2nd ed. (Jerusalem: Amutat Hoshen Lev, 1997).

2. Biographical information on Rav Kook is available in the *Encyclopedia Judaica*, cols. 1182–87. See also I. Epstein, *Abraham Yitzhak Hacohen Kook: His Life and Times* (London: Bahad, 1951). A recent and up-to-date biography is by Yehudah Mirsky, *Rav Kook: Mystic in a Time of Revolution* (New Haven, CT: Yale University Press, 2014).

3. A "liberal" view of Rav Kook is in Zvi Yaron, *Mishnato shel ha-Rav Kook* (Jerusalem: Ha-Histadrut ha-Zionit ha-Olamit, 1974). For similar views of Rav Kook, see J. B. Agus, *High Priest of Rebirth: The Life, Times and Thought of Abraham Isaac Kuk*, 2nd ed. (New York: Bloch, 1972), and Mirsky, *Rav Kook*.

4. *Shdemot* 56 (Winter 1975): 142–45.

5. Kook, *Orot ha-Kodesh*, 3 vols. (Jerusalem: Mosad ha-Rav Kook, 1963–64), 1:145–46, and *Hazon ha-Geulah* (Jerusalem: n.p., 1941), 140–41.

6. Kook, *Hazon ha-Geulah*, 140–41.

7. See Ber Borochov, *Nationalism and Class Struggle* (New York: Young Poale Zion, 1937).

8. On "realistic" or "political" messianism, see Amos Funkenstein, *Perceptions of Jewish History* (Berkeley: University of California Press, 1993), 131–54.

9. Kook, *Orot ha-Kodesh*, 1:152.

10. The metaphor appears in *Lehishat Saraf* (1726), fol. 2. See Gershom Scholem, *The Messianic Idea in Judaism* (New York: Schocken Books, 1971), 116 and 349n34.

11. Kook, *Ha-mahshavah ha-Yisraelit* (Jerusalem: Mosad ha-Rav Kook, 1967) *responsum* from 1923.

12. Kook, *Perakim be-mishnato ha-iyunit shel ha-Rav Kook* (Jerusalem: Amanah, 1961), 15–16.

13. Kook, *Shevet ha-Aretz* (Jerusalem: Amanah, 1965), 7.

14. Kook, *Hazon ha-Geulah*, 315.

15. This theme recurs frequently in the pronouncements of the leaders of Gush Emunim. See, for example, the statement in Moshe Kohn, *Who's Afraid of Gush Emunim* (Jerusalem: Jerusalem Post Press, 1975), 17: "I think that we have to close the options by massive settlement in the areas. When the other side sees this happening, and loses hope of our buckling under to international pressure, they'll start talking to us." Such pragmatic analyses derive from the less political notions expressed by Rav Kook.

Epilogue

1. We have recounted this story in our jointly written memoir, *Aerograms across the Ocean: A Love Story in Letters, 1970–1972* (Berkeley, CA: Wildcat Books, 2021).

STANFORD STUDIES IN JEWISH HISTORY AND CULTURE

David Biale and Sarah Abrevaya Stein, Editors

This series features novel approaches to examining the Jewish past in the form of innovative work that brings the field into productive dialogue with the newest scholarly concepts and methods. Open to a range of disciplinary and interdisciplinary approaches, from history to cultural studies, this series publishes exceptional scholarship balanced by an accessible tone, illustrating histories of difference and addressing issues of current urgency. Books in this list push the boundaries of Jewish Studies and speak compellingly to a wide audience of scholars and students.

Alan Verskin, *Diary of a Black Jewish Messiah: The Sixteenth-Century Journey of David Reubeni through Africa, the Middle East, and Europe*
2023

Aomar Boum, Illustrated by Nadjib Berber, *Undesirables: A Holocaust Journey to North Africa*
2022

Dina Porat, *Nakam: The Holocaust Survivors Who Sought Full-Scale Revenge*
2022

Christian Bailey, *German Jews in Love: A History*
2022

Matthias B. Lehmann, *The Baron: Maurice de Hirsch and the Jewish Nineteenth Century*
2022

Liora R. Halperin, *The Oldest Guard: Forging the Zionist Settler Past*
2021

Samuel J. Spinner, *Jewish Primitivism*
2021

Sonia Gollance, *It Could Lead to Dancing: Mixed-Sex Dancing and Jewish Modernity*
2021

Julia Elsky, *Writing Occupation: Jewish Émigré Voices in Wartime France*
2020

Alma Rachel Heckman, *The Sultan's Communists: Moroccan Jews and the Politics of Belonging*
2020

Golan Y. Moskowitz, *Queer Jewish Sendak: A Wild Visionary in Context*
2020

Devi Mays, *Forging Ties, Forging Passports: Migration and the Modern Sephardi Diaspora*
2020

Clémence Boulouque, *Another Modernity: Elia Benamozegh's Jewish Universalism*
2020

Dalia Kandiyoti, *The Converso's Return: Conversion and Sephardi History in Contemporary Literature and Culture*
2020

Natan M. Meir, *Stepchildren of the Shtetl: The Destitute, Disabled, and Mad of Jewish Eastern Europe, 1800-1939*
2020

Marc Volovici, *German as a Jewish Problem: The Language Politics of Jewish Nationalism*
2020

Dina Danon, *The Jews of Ottoman Izmir: A Modern History*
2019

Omri Asscher, *Reading Israel, Reading America: The Politics of Translation Between Jews*
2019

Yael Zerubavel, *Desert in the Promised Land*
2018

Sunny S. Yudkoff, *Tubercular Capital: Illness and the Conditions of Modern Jewish Writing*
2018

Sarah Wobick-Segev, *Homes Away from Home: Jewish Belonging in Twentieth-Century Paris, Berlin, and St. Petersburg*
2018

Eddy Portnoy, *Bad Rabbi: And Other Strange but True Stories from the Yiddish Press*
2017

Jeffrey Shandler, *Holocaust Memory in the Digital Age: Survivors' Stories and New Media Practices*
2017

For a complete listing of titles in this series, visit the
Stanford University Press website, www.sup.org.

The authorized representative in the EU for product safety and compliance is:
Mare Nostrum Group
B.V Doelen 72
4831 GR Breda
The Netherlands